The 80/20 Principle

'The 80/20 Princ … d
living.
Tim Ferriss, …

'Time managemeni is not about organising your daily tasks, it is about organising your essential daily tasks, and dumping the rest. Koch has made millions from this – a bestseller based on just one idea – proving that it works.'
GQ's 25 Best Business Books

'Congratulations! *The 80/20 Principle* is terrific.'
Al Ries, bestselling author of Focus *and* Positioning

'There are ideas in here that could change your life.'
The Good Book Guide

'Koch is a passionate 80/20er. Read this and you will be too.'
Andrew Campbell, Ashridge Strategic Management Centre

'Both astute and entertaining, this is an intriguing book to help people concentrate on not wasting their lives.'
Professor Theodore Zeldin, St Antony's College, Oxford

'We give this Dali-esque masterwork 5 stars… a beautiful collage of well-written prose… the book is worth many times its price.'
The Weston Review, Tampa Bay, Florida

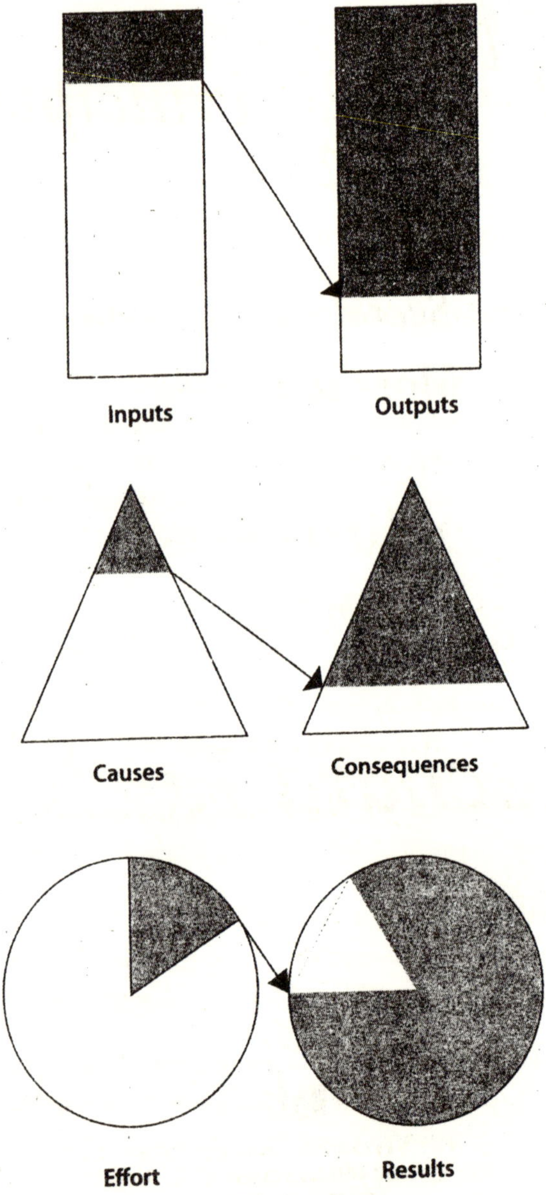
Inputs
Outputs
Causes
Consequences
Effort
Results

The 80/20 Principle

The Secret of Achieving More with Less

UPDATED 20TH ANNIVERSARY EDITION

Richard Koch

NICHOLAS BREALEY PUBLISHING
London • Boston

This updated 20th anniversary edition first published in 2017
by Nicholas Brealey Publishing
An imprint of John Murray Press
An Hachette UK company

2

First published in 1997

A CIP catalogue record for this title is available from the British Library.

ISBN 978-1-47365-687-1
eBook ISBN 978-1-85788-909-3

Typeset in Bembo 12.5/15.75pt by Palimpsest Book Production Limited, Falkirk, Stirlingshire

Printed and bound in India by Manipal Technologies Limited, Manipal

John Murray Press policy is to use papers that are natural, renewable and recyclable products and made from wood grown in sustainable forests. The logging and manufacturing processes are expected to conform to the environmental regulations of the country of origin.

Although the author expresses a view on the likely future performance of certain investment instruments, this should not be taken as an incitement to deal in any of them, nor is it to be regarded as investment advice. Each individual should consider their investment position in relation to their own circumstances with the benefit of professional advice. No responsibility can be assumed by either the author or the publisher for investment or any other decisions taken on the basis of views expressed in this book.

Nicholas Brealey Publishing
John Murray Press
Carmelite House
50 Victoria Embankment
London, EC4Y 0DZ, UK
Tel: 020 3122 6000

Nicholas Brealey Publishing
Hachette Book Group
Market Place Center, 53 State Street
Boston,
MA 02109, USA
Tel: (617) 523 3801

www.nicholasbrealey.com
www.richardkoch.net

For a very long time, the Pareto law [the 80/20 Principle] has lumbered the economic scene like an erratic block on the landscape: an empirical law which nobody can explain.

Josef Steindl

God plays dice with the Universe. But they're loaded dice. And the main objective is to find out by what rules they were loaded and how we can use them for our own ends.

Joseph Ford

We cannot be certain to what height the human species may aspire… We may therefore safely acquiesce in the pleasing conclusion that every age of the world has increased, and still increases, the real wealth, the happiness, the knowledge, and perhaps the virtue, of the human race.

Edward Gibbon

Contents

Part Three: Work Less, Earn and Enjoy More

Part Four: The 80/20 Future

Part Five: The Principle Revisited

Preface to the Updated 20th Anniversary Edition

The 80/20 Principle is marching on – not just this book, but the principle itself. In the past ten to twenty years, there have been incredibly significant changes in business, society, our personal lives, and in our understanding of how and why the 80/20 Principle operates. This has required a major addition to the book.

The principle has never been as ubiquitous or important as it is now. In the past, the principle gave those who used it a serious advantage. In the future it will be an *essential* tool – and probably *the* essential tool – for anyone who wants to succeed or be happy.

So what has happened in the past few years? Briefly, three things:

1 Top-down and large organizations are giving way – at least in the ability to generate high growth, profits

and cash – to networks, and to network ventures such as Apple, Google, Facebook, Uber, Amazon, eBay, and Betfair. These kinds of networks and network organizations are coming to dominate society and this is why 80/20 is becoming more prevalent.

All networks exhibit positive feedback loops – the big get bigger, the rich get richer, the famous get more famous, and networks benefiting the world (such as network businesses and the philanthropic organizations they often spawn) and those not benefiting the world (such as drug gangs and ISIS) become wealthier and more powerful.

The new Chapter 17 says what networks and network businesses are, and why nobody in their right mind – if they are ambitious – would work for anything but a network or a network business.

2 The 80/20 pattern that we have come to recognize for over a century – and which has been remarkably consistent, varying mainly between say 70/30 and 90/10 – is rapidly increasing to 90/10 and 99/1.

The new Chapter 18 describes how the lopsided distribution of causes and results is becoming more acute, as improbable events and rapid transformation of fortunes become more possible and influential.

3 There are a few rules of thumb that make all the difference between success and failure, between personal fulfilment and personal angst, and between happiness and misery. The new Chapter 19 describes five mega-rules to live by.

There is one more thing that I have discovered. The greatest manifestation of 80/20 was not included in the early editions of this book. A new Chapter 16 describes 'Your Hidden Friend' which can exert a super-potent and amazingly favourable influence on your life. The hidden friend operates at extraordinary speed and impact for no conscious effort at all. And properly trained, your hidden friend can transform your life. This requires a little effort – the trick is to know how to do the training, the coding, of your hidden friend. Chapter 16 describes how.

So there we have it. Four great new chapters. Go forth and shout the good news about the principle from the rooftops.

The 80/20 Principle has already sold more than a million copies in thirty-six languages. I dare to hope and expect that this new edition – which I think is more valuable – will multiply that record.

For what has already been achieved, I am profoundly grateful to you, the readers – the beneficiaries, perhaps, but also the evangelists. I know from your messages and emails how mind-blowing so many of you are finding the principle. Long may it continue, and thank you all so much. I may have touched your lives, but you have certainly touched mine, and I am most grateful.

Richard Koch
richardkoch8020@gmail.com
Gibraltar, March 2017

The 80/20 Rap

Did you know that there is an excellent 80/20 rap song, courtesy of the incomparable Wyatt Mo 'Gee Jackson? You can listen to it on the web if you like at www.richardkoch.net – it lasts three minutes, like a pop song should. Here are the lyrics, which are interspersed with me summing up the message of this book (in italic):

Richard Koch is a businessman,
He discovered a truth, yes a master plan.
Write a book about it, became a hit,
It's not only cool, it's also legit.

The 80/20 Principle is the title,
The lessons it teaches you are vital,
Sit back and listen to this soundbite,
By the time that you're finished you'll see the light.

The 80/20 principle, the key to success,
The 80/20 principle, achieve more or less,
The 80/20 principle, the key to success,
The 80/20 principle, achieve more.

So what is the 80/20 principle? The 80/20 principle asserts that a minority, a small number, of causes, inputs or effort usually leads to a majority of the results, outputs or rewards, so most of the outputs result from a very small part of the causes or inputs.

The 80/20 principle, the key to success,
The 80/20 principle, achieve more with less,
The 80/20 principle, the key to success,
The 80/20 principle, achieve more.

Taken literally, this means that, for example, 80 per cent of what we achieve in our job comes from 20 per cent of the time we spend. Thus for all practical purposes, four-fifths of our effort, pretty much all of it really, is largely irrelevant, and this is contrary, of course, to what we normally expect.

The 80/20 principle, the key to success,
The 80/20 principle, achieve more with less,
The 80/20 principle, the key to success,
The 80/20 principle, achieve more.

So the 80/20 principle states that there is an inbuilt imbalance between causes and results, inputs and outputs, efforts and rewards. A good benchmark for this imbalance is provided by the 80/20 relationship. A typical pattern will show that 80 per cent of outputs result from 20 per cent of inputs. 80 per cent of consequences flow from 20 per cent of causes. Or 80 per cent of results come from 20 per cent of effort. In business, many examples of the 80/20 principle have been validated: 20 per cent of products usually account for about 80 per cent of dollar sales; so do 20 per cent of customers. And 20 per cent of products or customers also usually account for 80 per cent of an organization's profits.

The 80/20 principle, the key to success,
The 80/20 principle, achieve more with less,
The 80/20 principle, the key to success,
The 80/20 principle, achieve more.

Part One

Overture

The universe is wonky!

What is the 80/20 Principle? The 80/20 Principle tells us that in any population, some things are likely to be much more important than others. A good benchmark or hypothesis is that 80 per cent of results or outputs flow from 20 per cent of causes, and sometimes from a much smaller proportion of powerful forces.

Everyday language is a good illustration. Sir Isaac Pitman, who invented shorthand, discovered that just 700 common words make up two-thirds of our conversation. Including the derivatives of these words, Pitman found that these words account for 80 per cent of common speech. In this case, fewer than 1 per cent of words (the New Shorter Oxford English Dictionary *lists over half a million words) are used 80 per cent of the time. We could call this an 80/1 principle. Similarly, over 99 per cent of talk uses fewer than 20 per cent of words: we could call this a 99/20 relationship.*

The movies illustrate the 80/20 Principle. A recent study shows that 1.3 per cent of movies earn 80 per cent of box office revenues, producing virtually an 80/1 rule (see pages 21–22).

The 80/20 Principle is not a magic formula. Sometimes the relationship between results and causes is closer to 70/30 than to 80/20 or 80/1. But it is very rarely true that 50 per cent of causes lead to 50 per cent of results. The universe is predictably unbalanced. Few things really matter.

Truly effective people and organizations batten on to the few powerful forces at work in their worlds and turn them to their advantage.

Read on to find out how you can do the same …

1 Welcome to the 80/20 Principle

For a very long time, the Pareto law [the 80/20 Principle] has lumbered the economic scene like an erratic block on the landscape; an empirical law which nobody can explain.

Josef Steindl[1]

The 80/20 Principle can and should be used by every intelligent person in their daily life, by every organization, and by every social grouping and form of society. It can help individuals and groups achieve much more, with much less effort. The 80/20 Principle can raise personal effectiveness and happiness. It can multiply the profitability of corporations and the effectiveness of any organization. It even holds the key to raising the quality and quantity of public services while cutting their cost. This book, the first ever on the 80/20 Principle,[2] is written from a burning conviction, validated in personal and business experience, that this principle is one of the best ways of dealing with and transcending the pressures of modern life.

What is the *80/20 Principle*?

The 80/20 Principle asserts that a minority of causes, inputs or effort usually lead to a majority of the results, outputs or rewards. Taken literally, this means that, for example, 80 per cent of what you achieve in your job comes from 20 per cent of the time spent. Thus for all practical purposes, four-fifths of the effort – a dominant part of it – is largely irrelevant. This is contrary to what people normally expect.

So the 80/20 Principle states that there is an inbuilt imbalance between causes and results, inputs and outputs, and effort and reward. A good benchmark for this imbalance is provided by the 80/20 relationship: a typical pattern will show that 80 per cent of outputs result from 20 per cent of inputs; that 80 per cent of consequences flow from 20 per cent of causes; or that 80 per cent of results come from 20 per cent of effort. Figure 1 shows these typical patterns.

In business, many examples of the 80/20 Principle have been validated. 20 per cent of products usually account for about 80 per cent of dollar sales value; so do 20 per cent of customers. 20 per cent of products or customers usually also account for about 80 per cent of an organization's profits.

In society, 20 per cent of criminals account for 80 per cent of the value of all crime. 20 per cent of motorists cause 80 per cent of accidents. 20 per cent of those who marry comprise 80 per cent of the divorce statistics (those who consistently remarry and redivorce distort the statistics and give a lopsidedly pessimistic impression of the extent of marital fidelity). 20 per cent of children attain 80 per cent of educational qualifications available.

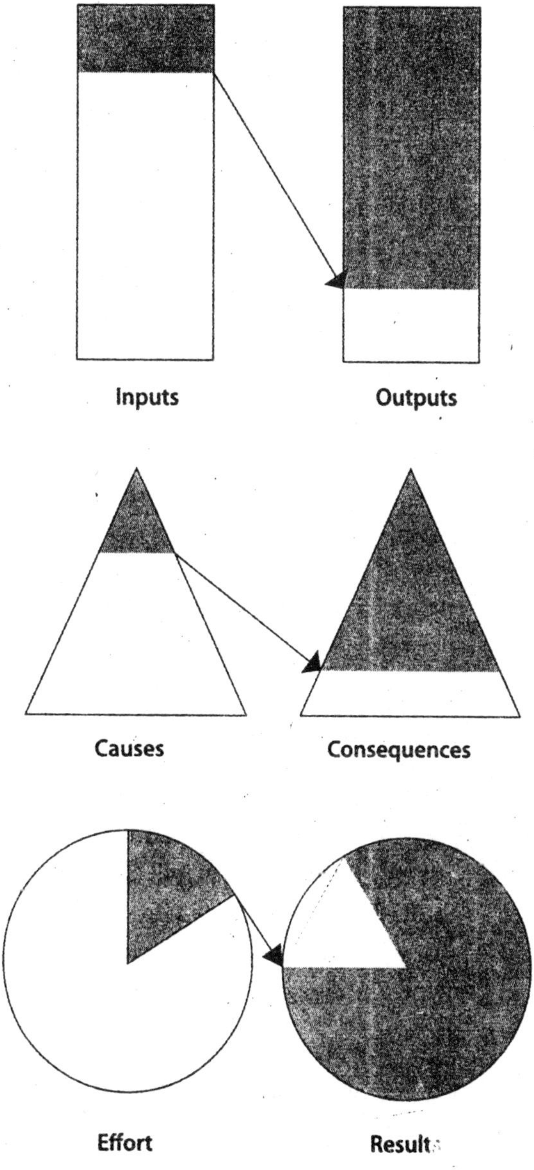

Figure 1 The 80/20 Principle

In the home, 20 per cent of your carpets are likely to get 80 per cent of the wear. 20 per cent of your clothes will be worn 80 per cent of the time. And if you have an intruder alarm, 80 per cent of the false alarms will be set off by 20 per cent of the possible causes.

The internal combustion engine is a great tribute to the 80/20 Principle. 80 per cent of the energy is wasted in combustion and only 20 per cent gets to the wheels; this 20 per cent of the input generates 100 per cent of the output![3]

Pareto's discovery: systematic and predictable lack of balance

The pattern underlying the 80/20 Principle was discovered in 1897 by Italian economist Vilfredo Pareto (1848–1923). His discovery has since been called many names, including the Pareto Principle, the Pareto Law, the 80/20 Rule, the Principle of Least Effort and the Principle of Imbalance; throughout this book we will call it the 80/20 Principle. By a subterranean process of influence on many important achievers, especially business people, computer enthusiasts and quality engineers, the 80/20 Principle has helped to shape the modern world. Yet it has remained one of the great secrets of our time – and even the select band of cognoscenti who know and use the 80/20 Principle only exploit a tiny proportion of its power.

So what did Vilfredo Pareto discover? He happened to be looking at patterns of wealth and income in nineteenth-century England. He found that most income and wealth went to a minority of the people in his samples. Perhaps there was nothing very surprising in this. But he also discovered two other facts that he thought highly significant. One was that there was a consistent mathematical relationship between the proportion of people (as a percentage of the total relevant population) and the amount of income or wealth that this group enjoyed.[4] To simplify, if 20 per cent of the population enjoyed 80 per cent of the wealth,[5] then you could reliably predict that 10 per cent would have, say, 65 per cent of the wealth, and 5 per cent would have 50 per cent. The key point is not the percentages, but the fact that the distribution of wealth across the population was *predictably unbalanced*.

Pareto's other finding, one that really excited him, was that this pattern of imbalance was repeated consistently whenever he looked at data referring to different time periods or different countries. Whether he looked at England in earlier times, or whatever data were available from other countries in his own time or earlier, he found the same pattern repeating itself, over and over again, with mathematical precision.

Was this a freak coincidence, or something that had great importance for economics and society? Would it work if applied to sets of data relating to things other than wealth or income? Pareto was a terrific innovator, because before him no one had looked at two related sets of data – in this case, the distribution of incomes or wealth, compared to the number of income earners or property owners – and compared percentages between the two sets of data. (Nowadays this method is commonplace, and has led to major breakthroughs in business and economics.)

Sadly, although Pareto realized the importance and wide range of his discovery, he was very bad at explaining it. He moved on to a series of fascinating but rambling sociological theories, centring on the role of élites, which were hijacked at the end of his life by Mussolini's fascists. The significance of the 80/20 Principle lay dormant for a generation. While a few economists, especially in the US,[6] realized its importance, it was not until after the Second World War that two parallel yet completely different pioneers began to make waves with the 80/20 Principle.

1949: Zipf's Principle of Least Effort

One of these pioneers was the Harvard professor of philology, George K Zipf. In 1949 Zipf discovered the 'Principle of Least Effort', which was actually a rediscovery and elaboration of Pareto's principle. Zipf's principle said that resources (people, goods, time, skills or anything else that is productive) tended to arrange themselves so as to minimize work, so that approximately 20–30 per cent of any resource accounted for 70–80 per cent of the activity related to that resource.[7]

Professor Zipf used population statistics, books, philology and industrial behaviour to show the consistent recurrence of this unbalanced pattern. For example, he analysed all the Philadelphia marriage licences granted in 1931 in a 20-block area, demonstrating that 70 per cent of the marriages occurred between people who lived within 30 per cent of the distance.

Incidentally, Zipf also provided a scientific justification for the messy desk by justifying clutter with another law: frequency of use draws near to us things that are frequently used. Intelligent secretaries have long known that files in frequent use should not be filed!

1951: Juran's Rule of the Vital Few and the rise of Japan

The other pioneer of the 80/20 Principle was the great quality guru, Romanian-born US engineer Joseph Moses Juran (1904–2008), the man behind the Quality Revolution of 1950–90. He made what he alternately called the 'Pareto Principle' and the 'Rule of the Vital Few' virtually synonymous with the search for high product quality.

In 1924, Juran joined Western Electric, the manufacturing division of Bell Telephone System, starting as a corporate industrial engineer and later setting up as one of the world's first quality consultants.

His great idea was to use the 80/20 Principle, together with other statistical methods, to root out quality faults and improve the reliability and value of industrial and consumer goods. Juran's path-breaking *Quality Control Handbook* was first published in 1951 and extolled the 80/20 Principle in very broad terms:

> *The economist Pareto found that wealth was non-uniformly distributed in the same way [as Juran's observations about quality losses]. Many other instances can be found – the distribution of crime amongst criminals, the distribution of accidents among hazardous processes, etc. Pareto's principle of unequal distribution applied to distribution of wealth and to distribution of quality losses.*[8]

No major US industrialist was interested in Juran's theories. In 1953 he was invited to Japan to lecture, and met a receptive audience. He stayed on to work with several Japanese corporations, transforming the value and quality of their consumer goods. It was only once the Japanese threat to US industry had become apparent, after 1970, that Juran was taken seriously in the West. He moved back to do for US industry what he had done for the Japanese. The 80/20 Principle was at the heart of this global quality revolution.

From the 1960s to the 1990s: progress from using the 80/20 Principle

IBM was one of the earliest and most successful corporations to spot and use the 80/20 Principle, which helps to explain why most computer systems specialists trained in the 1960s and 1970s are familiar with the idea.

In 1963, IBM discovered that about 80 per cent of a computer's time is spent executing about 20 per cent of the operating code. The company immediately rewrote its operating software to make the most used 20 per cent very accessible and user friendly, thus making IBM computers more efficient and faster than competitors' machines for the majority of applications.

Those who developed the personal computer and its software in the next generation, such as Apple, Lotus and Microsoft, applied the 80/20 Principle with even more gusto to make their machines cheaper and easier to use for a new tranche of customers, including the now celebrated 'dummies' who would previously have given computers a very wide berth.

Winner take all

A century after Pareto, the implications of the 80/20 Principle have surfaced in a recent controversy over the astronomic and ever-rising incomes going to superstars and those very few people at the top of a growing number of professions. Film director Steven Spielberg earned $165 million in 1994. Joseph Jamial, the most highly paid trial lawyer, was paid $90 million. Merely competent film directors or lawyers, of course, earn a tiny fraction of these sums.

The twentieth century saw massive efforts to level incomes, but inequality, removed in one sphere, kept popping up in another. In the USA from 1973 to 1995, average real incomes rose by 36 per cent, yet the comparable figure for non-supervisory workers fell by 14 per cent. During the 1980s, all of the gains went to the top 20 per cent of earners, and a mind-boggling 64 per cent of the total increase went to the top 1 per cent! The ownership of shares in the US is also heavily concentrated within a small minority of households: 5 per cent of US households own about 75 per cent of the household sector's equity. A similar effect may be seen in the role of the dollar: almost 50 per cent of world trade is invoiced in dollars, far above America's 13 per cent share of world exports. And, while the dollar's share of foreign exchange reserves is 64 per cent, the ratio of American GDP to global output is just over 20 per cent. The 80/20 Principle will always reassert itself, unless conscious, consistent and massive efforts are made and sustained to overcome it.

Why the 80/20 Principle is so important

The reason that the 80/20 Principle is so valuable is that it is counter-intuitive. We tend to expect that all causes will have roughly the same significance. That all customers are equally valuable. That every bit of business, every product and every dollar of sales revenue is as good as any other. That all employees in a particular category have roughly equivalent value. That each day or week or year we spend has the same significance. That all our friends have roughly equal value to us. That all enquiries or phone calls should be treated in the same way. That one university is as good as another. That all problems have a large number of causes, so that it is not worth isolating a few key causes. That all opportunities are of roughly equal value, so that we treat them all equally.

We tend to assume that 50 per cent of causes or inputs will account for 50 per cent of results or outputs. There seems to be a natural, almost democratic, expectation that causes and results are generally equally balanced. And, of course, sometimes they are. But this '50/50 fallacy' is one of the most inaccurate and harmful, as well as the most deeply rooted, of our mental maps. The 80/20 Principle asserts that when two sets of data, relating to causes and results, can be examined and analysed, the most likely result is that there will be a pattern of imbalance. The imbalance may be 65/35, 70/30, 75/25, 80/20, 95/5, or 99.9/0.1, or any set of numbers in between. However, the two numbers in the comparison don't have to add up to 100 (see page 29).

The 80/20 Principle also asserts that when we know the true relationship, we are likely to be surprised at how unbalanced it is. Whatever the actual level of imbalance, it is likely to exceed our prior estimate. Executives may suspect that some customers and some products are more profitable than others, but when the extent of the difference is proved, they are likely to be surprised and sometimes dumbfounded. Teachers may know that the majority of their disciplinary troubles or most truancy arises from a minority of pupils, but if records are analysed the extent of the imbalance will probably be larger than expected. We may feel that some of our time is more valuable than the rest, but if we measure inputs and outputs the disparity can still stun us.

Why should you care about the 80/20 Principle? Whether you realize it or not, the principle applies to your life, to your social world and to the place where you work. Understanding the 80/20 Principle gives you great insight into what is really happening in the world around you.

The overriding message of this book is that our daily lives can be greatly improved by using the 80/20 Principle. Each individual can be more effective and happier. Each profit-seeking corporation can become very much more profitable. Each non-profit organization can also deliver much more useful outputs. Every government can ensure that its citizens benefit much more from its existence. For everyone and every institution, it is possible to obtain much more that is of value, and avoid what has negative value, with much less input of effort, expense or investment.

At the heart of this progress is a process of substitution. Resources that have weak effects in any particular use are not used, or are used sparingly. Resources that have powerful effects are used as much as possible. Every resource is ideally used where it has the greatest value. Wherever possible, weak resources are developed so that they can mimic the behaviour of the stronger resources.

Business and markets have used this process, to great effect, for hundreds of years. The French economist J-B Say coined the word 'entrepreneur' around 1800, saying that 'the entrepreneur shifts economic resources out of an area of lower productivity into an area of higher productivity and yield'. But one fascinating implication of the 80/20 Principle is how far businesses and markets still are from producing optimal solutions. For example, the 80/20 Principle asserts that 20 per cent of products, or customers or employees, are really responsible for about 80 per cent of profits. If this is true – and detailed investigations usually confirm that some such very unbalanced pattern exists – the state of affairs implied is very far from being efficient or optimal. The implication is that 80 per cent of products, or customers or employees, are only contributing 20 per cent of profits. That there is great waste. That the most powerful resources of the company are being held back by a majority of much less effective resources. That profits could be multiplied if more of the best sort of products could be sold, employees hired or customers attracted (or convinced to buy more from the firm).

In this kind of situation one might well ask: why continue to make the 80 per cent of products that only generate 20 per cent of profits? Companies rarely ask these questions, perhaps because to answer them would mean very radical action: to stop doing four-fifths of what you are doing is not a trivial change.

What J-B Say called the work of entrepreneurs, modern financiers call arbitrage. International financial markets are very quick to correct anomalies in valuation, for example between exchange rates. But business organizations and individuals are generally very poor at this sort of entrepreneurship or arbitrage, at shifting resources from where they have weak results to where they have powerful results, or at cutting off low-value resources and buying more high-value resources. Most of the time, we do not realize the extent to which some resources, but only a small minority, are super-productive – what Joseph Juran called the 'vital few' – while the majority – the 'trivial many' – exhibit little productivity or else actually have negative value. If we did realize the difference between the vital few and the trivial many in all aspects of our lives, and if we did something about it, we could multiply anything that we valued.

The 80/20 Principle and chaos theory

Probability theory tells us that it is virtually impossible for all the applications of the 80/20 Principle to occur randomly, as a freak of chance. We can only explain the principle by positing some deeper meaning or cause that lurks behind it.

Pareto himself grappled with this issue, trying to apply a consistent methodology to the study of society. He searched for 'theories that picture facts of experience and observation', for regular patterns, social laws or 'uniformities' that explain the behaviour of individuals and society.

Pareto's sociology failed to find a persuasive key. He died long before the emergence of chaos theory, which has great parallels with the 80/20 Principle and helps to explain it.

The last third of the twentieth century saw a revolution in the way that scientists think about the universe, overturning the prevailing wisdom for the past 350 years. That prevailing wisdom was a machine-based and rational view, which itself was a great advance on the mystical and random view of the world which was held in the Middle Ages. The machine-based view converted God from being an irrational and unpredictable force into a more user-friendly clockmaker-engineer.

The view of the world held from the seventeenth century and still prevalent today, except in advanced scientific circles, was immensely comforting and useful. All phenomena were reduced to regular, predictable, *linear* relationships. For example, *a* causes *b*, *b* causes *c*, and *a* + *c* cause *d*. This world view enabled any individual part of the universe – the operation of the human heart, for example, or of any individual market – to be analysed separately, because the whole was the sum of the parts and vice versa.

But in the twenty-first century it seems much more accurate to view the world as an evolving organism where the whole system is more than the sum of its parts, and where relationships between the parts are non-linear. Causes are difficult to pin down, there are complex interdependencies between causes, and causes and effects are blurred. The snag with linear thinking is that it doesn't always work, it is an oversimplification of reality. Equilibrium is illusory or fleeting. The universe is wonky.

Yet chaos theory, despite its name, does not say that everything is a hopeless and incomprehensible mess. Rather, there is a self-organizing logic lurking behind the disorder, a *predictable non-linearity* – something which economist Paul Krugman has called 'spooky', 'eerie' and 'terrifyingly exact'.[9] The logic is more difficult to describe than to detect, and is not totally dissimilar to the recurrence of a theme in a piece of music.

Certain characteristic patterns recur, but with infinite and unpredictable variety.

Chaos theory and the 80/20 Principle illuminate each other

What have chaos theory and related scientific concepts got to do with the 80/20 Principle? Although no one else appears to have made the link, I think the answer is: a great deal.

➤ The principle of imbalance

The common thread between chaos theory and the 80/20 Principle is the issue of *balance* – or, more precisely, *imbalance*. Both chaos theory and the 80/20 Principle assert (with a great deal of empirical backing) that the universe is unbalanced. They both say that the world is not linear; cause and effect are rarely linked in an equal way. Both also place great store by self-organization: some forces are always more forceful than others and will try to grab more than their fair share of resources. Chaos theory helps to explain why and how this imbalance happens by tracing a number of developments over time.

➤ The universe is not a straight line

The 80/20 Principle, like chaos theory, is based around the idea of non-linearity. A great deal of what happens is unimportant and can be disregarded. Yet there are always a few forces that have an influence way beyond their numbers. These are the forces that must be identified and watched. If they are forces for good, we should multiply them. If they are forces we don't like, we need to think very carefully about how to neutralize them. The 80/20 Principle supplies a very powerful empirical test of non-linearity in any system: we can ask, do 20 per cent of causes lead to 80 per cent of results? Is 80 per cent of any phenomenon associated with only 20 per cent of a related phenomenon? This is a useful method to flush out non-linearity, but it is even more useful because it directs us to identifying the unusually powerful forces at work.

➤ Feedback loops distort and disturb balance

The 80/20 Principle is also consistent with, and can be explained by reference to, the feedback loops identified by chaos theory, whereby small initial influences can become greatly multiplied and produce highly unexpected results, which nevertheless can be explained in retrospect. In the absence of feedback loops, the natural distribution of phenomena would be 50/50 – inputs of a given frequency would lead to commensurate results. It is only because of positive and negative feedback loops that causes do not have equal results. Yet it also seems to be true that powerful positive feedback loops only affect a small minority of the inputs. This helps to explain why those small minority of inputs can exert so much influence.

We can see positive feedback loops operating in many areas, explaining how it is that we typically end up with 80/20 rather than 50/50 relationships between populations. For example, the rich get richer, not just (or mainly) because of superior abilities, but because riches beget riches. A similar phenomenon exists with goldfish in a pond. Even if you start with goldfish almost exactly the same size, those that are slightly bigger become very much bigger, because, even with only slight initial advantages in stronger propulsion and larger mouths, they are able to capture and gobble up disproportionate amounts of food.

➤ The tipping point

Related to the idea of feedback loops is the concept of the tipping point. Up to a certain point, a new force – whether it is a new product, a disease, a new rock group or a new social habit such as jogging or rollerblading – finds it difficult to make headway. A great deal of effort generates little by way of results. At this point many pioneers give up. But if the new force persists and can cross a certain invisible line, a small amount of additional effort can reap huge returns. This invisible line is the tipping point.

The concept comes from the principles of epidemic theory. The tipping point is 'the point at which an ordinary and stable phenomenon – a low-level flu outbreak – can turn into a public-health crisis',[10] because of the number of people who are infected and can therefore infect others. And since the behaviour of epidemics is non-linear and they don't behave in the way we expect, 'small changes – like bringing new infections down to thirty thousand from forty thousand – can have huge effects... It all depends when and how the changes are made.'[11]

➤ First come, best served

Chaos theory advocates 'sensitive dependence on initial conditions'[12] – what happens first, even something ostensibly trivial, can have a disproportionate effect. This resonates with, and helps to explain, the 80/20 Principle. The latter states that a minority of causes exert a majority of effects. One limitation of the 80/20 Principle, taken in isolation, is that it always represents a snapshot of what is true now (or, more precisely, in the very recent past when the snapshot was taken). This is where chaos theory's doctrine of sensitive dependence on initial conditions is helpful. A small lead early on can turn into a larger lead or a dominant position later on, until equilibrium is disturbed and another small force then exerts a disproportionate influence.

A firm that, in the early stages of a market, provides a product that is 10 per cent better than its rivals may end up with 100 or 200 per cent greater market share, even if the rivals later provide a better product. In the early days of motoring, if 51 per cent of drivers or countries decide to drive on the right rather than the left of the road, this will tend to become the norm for nearly 100 per cent of road users. In the early days of using a circular clock, if 51 per cent of clocks go what we now call 'clockwise' rather than 'counter-clockwise', this convention will become dominant, although clocks could just as logically have moved to the left. In fact, the clock over Florence cathedral moves counter-clockwise and shows 24 hours.[13] Soon after 1442 when the cathedral was built, the authorities and clockmakers standardized on a 12-hour, 'clockwise' clock, because the majority of clocks had those features. Yet if 51 per cent of clocks had ever been like the clock over Florence cathedral, we would now be reading a 24-hour clock backwards.

These observations regarding sensitive dependence on initial conditions do not exactly illustrate the 80/20 Principle. The examples given involve *change over time*, whereas the

80/20 Principle involves a *static* breakdown of causes *at any one time*. Yet there is an important link between the two. Both phenomena help to show how the universe abhors balance. In the former case, we see a natural flight away from a 50/50 split of competing phenomena. A 51/49 split is inherently unstable and tends to gravitate towards a 95/5, 99/1 or even 100/0 split. Equality ends in dominance: that is one of the messages of chaos theory. The 80/20 Principle's message is different yet complementary. It tells us that, at any one point, a majority of any phenomenon will be explained or caused by a minority of the actors participating in the phenomenon. 80 per cent of the results come from 20 per cent of the causes. A few things are important; most are not.

The 80/20 Principle sorts good movies from bad

One of the most dramatic examples of the 80/20 Principle at work is with movies. Two economists[14] made a study of the revenues and lifespans of 300 movies released over an 18-month period. They found that four movies – just 1.3 per cent of the total – earned 80 per cent of box office revenues; the other 296 movies or 98.7 per cent earned only 20 per cent of the gross. So movies, which are a good example of unrestricted markets at work, produce virtually an 80/1 rule, a very clear demonstration of the principle of imbalance.

Even more intriguing is why. It transpires that movie goers behave just like gas particles in random motion. As identified by chaos theory, gas particles, pingpong balls or movie goers all behave at random, but produce a predictably unbalanced result. Word of mouth, from reviews and the first audiences, determines whether the second set of audiences will be large or small, which determines the next set and so on. Movies like *Independence Day* or *Mission Impossible* continue to play to packed houses, while other star-studded and expensive movies, like *Waterworld* or *Daylight*, very quickly play to smaller and smaller houses, and then none at all. This is the 80/20 Principle working with a vengeance.

A guide to this guidebook

Chapter 2 explains how you can put the 80/20 Principle into practice and explores the distinction between 80/20 Analysis and 80/20 Thinking, both of which are useful methods derived from the 80/20 Principle. 80/20 Analysis is a systematic, quantitative method of comparing causes and effects. 80/20 Thinking is a broader, less precise and more intuitive procedure, comprising the mental models and habits that enable us to hypothesize what are the important causes of anything important in our lives, to identify these causes, and to make sharp improvements in our position by redeploying our resources accordingly.

Part Two, Corporate Success Needn't be a Mystery, summarizes the most powerful business uses of the 80/20 Principle. These uses have been tried and tested and found to be of immense value, yet remain curiously unexploited by most of the business community. There is little in my summary that is original, but anyone seeking major profit improvement, whether for a small or large business, should find this a very useful primer and the first ever to appear in a book.

Part Three, Work Less, Earn and Enjoy More, shows how

the 80/20 Principle can be used to raise the level at which you are operating in both your work and personal life. This is a pioneering attempt to apply the 80/20 Principle on a novel canvas; and the attempt, although I am sure it is imperfect and incomplete in many ways, does lead to some surprising insights. For example, 80 per cent of the typical person's happiness or achievement in life occurs in a small proportion of that life. The peaks of great personal value can usually be greatly expanded. The common view is that we are short of time. My application of the 80/20 Principle suggests the reverse: that we are actually awash with time and profligate in its abuse.

Part Four, the 80/20 Future, which is new in this edition, discusses how networks have become increasingly prevalent, causing the principle also to become more influential, and also more extreme – so that the norm is tending towards 90/10 or 99/1 rather than 80/20. Part Four also highlights how you can react, to become much more successful as a result of the new trend towards the supremacy of networks and the principle.

Part Five, The Principle Revisited, considers feedback I have received and how my thinking on the 80/20 Principle has developed since the first edition of this book.

Why the 80/20 Principle brings good news

I want to end this introduction on a personal rather than a procedural note. I believe that the 80/20 Principle is enormously hopeful. Certainly, the principle brings home what may be evident anyway: that there is a tragic amount of waste everywhere, in the way that nature operates, in business, in society and in our own lives. If the typical pattern is for 80 per cent of results to come from 20 per cent of inputs, it is necessarily typical too that 80 per cent, the great majority, of inputs are having only a marginal – 20 per cent – impact.

The paradox is that such waste can be wonderful news, if we can use the 80/20 Principle creatively, not just to identify and castigate low productivity but to do something positive about it. There is enormous scope for improvement, by rearranging and redirecting both nature and our own lives. Improving on nature, refusing to accept the status quo, is the route of all progress: evolutionary, scientific, social and personal. George Bernard Shaw put it well: 'The reasonable man adapts himself to the world. The unreasonable one persists in trying to adapt the world to himself. Therefore all progress depends on the unreasonable man.'[15]

The implication of the 80/20 Principle is that output can be not just increased but multiplied, if we can make the low-productivity inputs nearly as productive as the high-productivity inputs. Successful experiments with the 80/20 Principle in the business arena suggest that, with creativity and determination, this leap in value can usually be made.

There are two routes to achieving this. One is to reallocate the resources from unproductive to productive uses, the secret of all entrepreneurs down the ages. Find a round hole for a round peg, a square hole for a square peg, and a perfect fit for any shape in between. Experience suggests that every resource has its ideal arena, where the resource can be tens or hundreds of times more effective than in most other arenas.

The other route to progress – the method of scientists,

doctors, preachers, computer systems designers, educationalists and trainers – is to find ways to make the unproductive resources more effective, even in their existing applications; to make the weak resources behave as though they were their more productive cousins; to mimic, if necessary by intricate rote-learning procedures, the highly productive resources.

The few things that work fantastically well should be identified, cultivated, nurtured and multiplied. At the same time, the waste – the majority of things that will always prove to be of low value to man and beast – should be abandoned or severely cut back.

As I have been writing this book and observed thousands of examples of the 80/20 Principle, I have had my faith reinforced: faith in progress, in great leaps forward, and in mankind's ability, individually and collectively, to improve the hand that nature has dealt. Joseph Ford comments: 'God plays dice with the universe. But they're loaded dice. And the main objective is to find out by what rules they were loaded and how we can use them for our own ends.'[16]

The 80/20 Principle can help us achieve precisely that.

2 *How to Think 80/20*

Chapter 1 explained the concept behind the 80/20 Principle; this chapter will discuss how the 80/20 Principle works in practice and what it can do for you. Two applications of the principle, 80/20 Analysis and 80/20 Thinking, provide a practical philosophy which will help you understand and improve your life.

Definition of the 80/20 Principle

The 80/20 Principle states that there is an inbuilt imbalance between causes and results, inputs and outputs, and effort and reward. Typically, causes, inputs or effort divide into two categories:

- the majority, that have little impact
- a small minority, that have a major, dominant impact.

Typically also, results, outputs or rewards are derived from a small proportion of the causes, inputs or effort aimed at producing the results, outputs or rewards.

The relationship between causes, inputs or efforts on the one hand, and results, outputs or rewards on the other, is therefore typically unbalanced.

When this imbalance can be measured arithmetically, a good benchmark for the imbalance is the 80/20 relationship – 80 per cent of results, outputs or rewards are derived from only 20 per cent of the causes, inputs or effort. About 80 per cent of the world's energy is consumed by 15 per cent of the world's population, for example.[1] 80 per cent of the world's wealth is possessed by 25 per cent of the world's people.[2] In health care, '20 percent of your population base and/or 20 percent of its disease elements will consume 80 percent of your resources'.[3]

Figures 2 and 3 show this 80/20 pattern. Let us imagine that a company has 100 products and has found out that the most profitable 20 products account for 80 per cent of all profits. In Figure 2, the bar on the left comprises the 100 products, each occupying an equal hundredth of the space.

In the bar on the right are the total profits of the company from the 100 products. Imagine that the profits from the one most profitable product are filled in from the top of the right-hand bar downwards. Let us say that the most profitable product makes 20 per cent of total profits. Figure 2 therefore shows that one product, or 1 per cent of the products, occupying one hundredth of the space on the left, makes 20 per cent of the profits. The shaded areas represent this relationship.

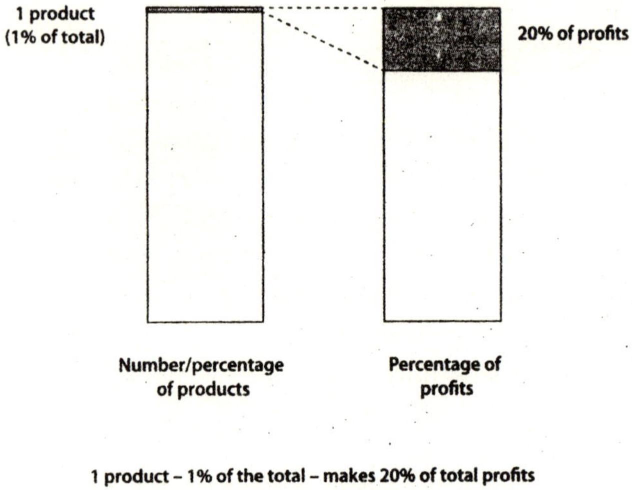

Figure 2

If we continue counting the next most profitable product and so on down the bar, until we have the profits from the top 20 products, we can then shade in the right-hand bar according to how much of the total profit these top 20 products make. We show this in Figure 3, where we see (in our fictitious example) that these 20 products, 20 per cent of the number of products, comprise 80 per cent of the total profits (in the shaded area). Conversely, in the white area, we can see the flip side of this relationship: 80 per cent of the products only make, in total, 20 per cent of the profits.

The 80/20 numbers are only a benchmark, and the real relationship may be more or less unbalanced than 80/20. The 80/20 Principle asserts, however, that in most cases the relationship is much more likely to be closer to 80/20 than to 50/50. If all of the products in our example made the same profit, then the relationship would be as shown in Figure 4.

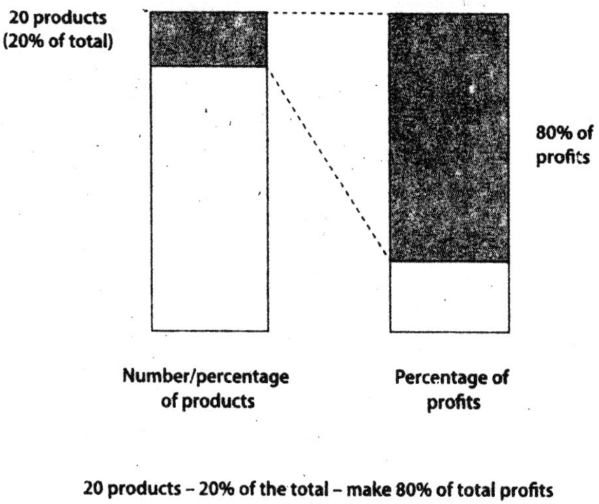

Figure 3 A typical 80/20 pattern

The curious but crucial point is that, when such investigations are conducted, Figure 3 turns out to be a much more typical pattern than Figure 4. Nearly always, a small proportion of total products produces a large proportion of profits.

Of course, the exact relationship may not be 80/20. 80/20 is both a convenient metaphor and a useful hypothesis, but it is not the only pattern. Sometimes, 80 per cent of the profits come from 30 per cent of the products; sometimes 80 per cent of the profits come from 15 per cent or even 10 per cent of the products. The numbers compared do not have to add up to 100, but the picture usually looks unbalanced, much more like Figure 3 than Figure 4.

It is perhaps unfortunate that the numbers 80 and 20 add up to 100. This makes the result look elegant (as, indeed, would a result of 50/50, 70/30, 99/1 or many other combinations) and it is certainly memorable, but it makes many

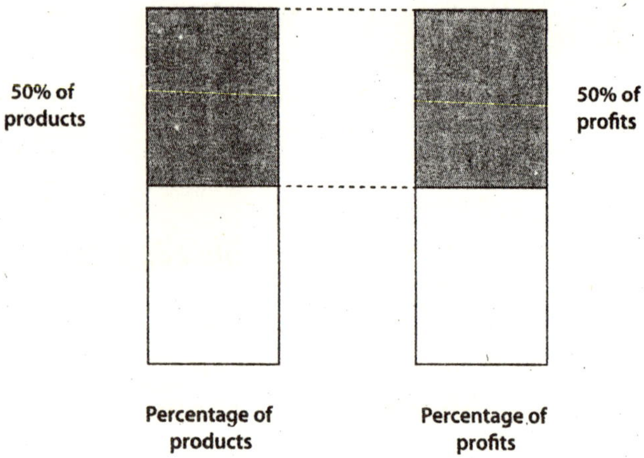

Figure 4 An unusual 50/50 pattern

people think that we are dealing with just one set of data, one 100 per cent. This is not so. If 80 per cent of people are right-handed and 20 per cent are left-handed, this is not an 80/20 observation. To apply the 80/20 Principle you have to have two sets of data, both adding up to 100 per cent, and one measuring a variable quantity owned, exhibited or caused by the people or things making up the other 100 per cent.

What the 80/20 Principle can do for you

Every person I have known who has taken the 80/20 Principle seriously has emerged with useful, and in some cases life-changing, insights. You have to work out your own uses for the principle: they will be there if you look creatively. Part Three (Chapters 9 to 16) will guide you on your odyssey, but I can illustrate with some examples from my own life.

How the 80/20 Principle has helped me

When I was a raw student at Oxford, my tutor told me never to go to lectures. 'Books can be read far faster,' he explained. 'But never read a book from cover to cover, except for pleasure. When you are working, find out what the book is saying much faster than you would by reading it through. Read the conclusion, then the introduction, then the conclusion again, then dip lightly into any interesting bits.' What he was really saying was that 80 per cent of the value of a book can be found in 20 per cent or fewer of its pages, and absorbed in 20 per cent of the time most people would take to read it through.

I took to this study method and extended it. At Oxford there is no system of continuous assessment and the class of degree earned depends entirely on Finals, the examinations taken at the end of the course. I discovered from the 'form book', that is by analysing past examination papers, that at least 80 per cent (sometimes 100 per cent) of an examination could be well answered with knowledge from 20 per cent or fewer of the subjects that the exam was meant to cover. The examiners could therefore be much better impressed by a student who knew an awful lot about relatively little, rather than a fair amount about a great deal. This insight enabled me to study very efficiently. Somehow, without working very hard, I ended up with a congratulatory First Class degree. I used to think this proved that Oxford dons were gullible. I now prefer to think, perhaps improbably, that they were teaching us how the world worked.

I went to work for Shell, serving my time at a dreadful oil refinery. This may have been good for my soul, but I rapidly realized that the best-paying jobs for young and inexperienced people such as I lay in management consultancy. So I went to Philadelphia, and picked up an effortless MBA from Wharton (scorning the boot-camp style so-called learning experience from Harvard). I joined a leading US consultancy that on day one paid me four times what Shell had paid me when I left. No doubt 80 per cent of the money to be had by people of my tender age was concentrated in 20 per cent of the jobs.

Since there were too many colleagues in the consultancy who were smarter than me, I moved to another US strategy 'boutique'. I identified it because it was growing faster than the firm I had joined, yet had a much smaller proportion of really smart people.

Who you work for is more important than what you do

Here I stumbled across many paradoxes of the 80/20 Principle. 80 per cent of the growth in the strategy consultancy industry – then, as now, growing like gangbusters – was being appropriated by firms that then had, in total, fewer than 20 per cent of the industry's professional staff. 80 per cent of rapid promotions were also available in just a handful of firms. Believe me, talent had very little to do with it. When I left the first strategy firm and joined the second, I raised the average level of intelligence in both.

Yet the puzzling thing was that my new colleagues were more effective than my old ones. Why? They didn't work any harder. But they followed the 80/20 Principle in two key ways. First, they realized that for most firms, 80 per cent of profits come from 20 per cent of clients. In the consulting industry that means two things: large clients and long-term clients. Large clients give large assignments, which means you can use a higher proportion of lower-cost, younger consultants. Long-term client relationships create trust and raise the cost to the client of switching to another consulting firm. Long-term clients tend not to be price sensitive.

In most consulting firms, the real excitement comes from winning new clients. In my new firm, the real heroes were those who worked on the largest existing clients for the longest possible time. They did this by cultivating the top bosses of those client corporations.

The second key insight the consulting firm had was that in any client, 80 per cent of the results available would flow from concentrating on the 20 per cent of most important issues. These were not necessarily the most interesting ones from a curious consultant's viewpoint. But, whereas our competitors would look superficially at a whole range of issues and then leave them for the client to act (or not) on the recommendations, we kept plugging away at the most important issues until we had bludgeoned the client into successful action. The clients' profits often soared as a result, as did our consulting budgets.

Are you working to make others rich or is it the reverse?

I soon became convinced that, for both consultants and their clients, effort and reward were at best only loosely linked. It was better to be in the right place than to be smart and work hard. It was best to be cunning and focus on results rather than inputs. Acting on a few key insights produced the goods. Being intelligent and hard working did not. Sadly, for many years, guilt and conformity to peer-group pressure kept me from fully acting on this lesson; I worked far too hard.

By this time, the consulting firm had several hundred professional staff and about 30 people, including myself, who were called partners. But 80 per cent of the profits went to one man, the founder, even though numerically he constituted less than 4 per cent of the partnership and a fraction of 1 per cent of the consulting force.

Instead of continuing to enrich the founder, two other junior partners and I spun off to set up our own firm doing exactly the same thing. We in turn grew to have hundreds of consultants. Before long, although the three of us, on any measure, did less than 20 per cent of the firm's valuable work, we enjoyed over 80 per cent of the profits. This, too, caused me guilt. After six years I quit, selling my shares to the other partners. At this time, we had doubled our revenues and profits every year and I was able to secure a good price for my shares. Shortly after, the recession of 1990 hit the consulting industry. Although I will counsel you later to give up guilt, I was lucky with my guilt. Even those who follow the 80/20 Principle need a bit of luck, and I have always enjoyed far more than my share.

Wealth from investment can dwarf wealth from working

With 20 per cent of the money received, I made a large investment in the shares of one corporation, Filofax. Investment advisers were horrified. At the time I owned about 20 shares in quoted public companies, but this one stock, 5 per cent of the number of shares I owned, accounted for about 80 per cent of my portfolio. Fortunately, the proportion proceeded to grow still further, as over the next three years Filofax shares multiplied several times in value. When I sold some shares, in 1995, it was at nearly 18 times the price I had paid for my first stake.

I made two other large investments, one in a start-up restaurant called Belgo and the other in MSI, a hotel company that at the time owned no hotels. Together, these three investments at cost comprised about 20 per cent of my net worth. But they have accounted for more than 80 per cent of my subsequent investment gains, and now comprise over 80 per cent of a much larger net worth.

As Chapter 14 will show, 80 per cent of the increase in wealth from most long-term portfolios comes from fewer than 20 per cent of the investments. It is crucial to pick this 20 per cent well and then concentrate as much investment as possible into it. Conventional wisdom is not to put all your eggs in one basket. 80/20 wisdom is to choose a basket carefully, load all your eggs into it, and then watch it like a hawk.

How to use the 80/20 Principle

There are two ways to use the 80/20 Principle, as shown in Figure 5.

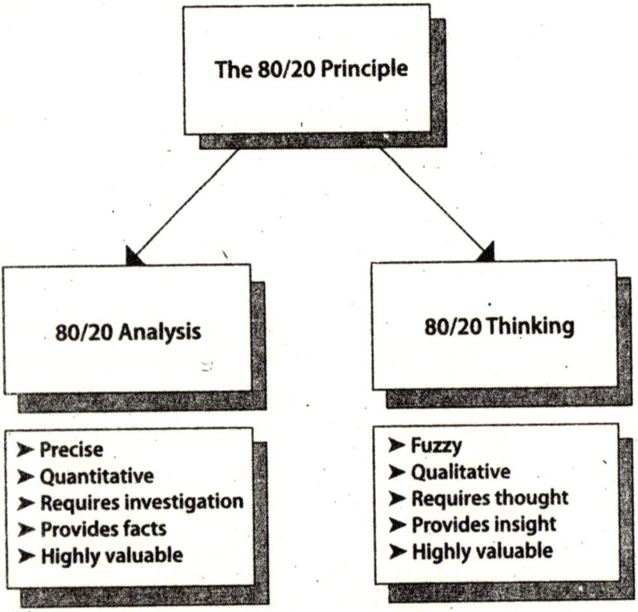

Figure 5 Two ways to use the 80/20 Principle

Traditionally, the 80/20 Principle has required 80/20 Analysis, a quantitative method to establish the precise relationship between causes/input/effort and results/outputs/rewards. This method uses the possible existence of the 80/20 relationship as a hypothesis and then gathers the facts so that the true relationship is revealed. This is an empirical procedure which may lead to any result ranging from 50/50 to 99.9/0.1. If the result does demonstrate a marked imbalance between inputs and outputs (say a 65/35 relationship or an even more unbalanced one), then normally action is taken as a result (see below).

A new and complementary way to use the 80/20 Principle is what I call 80/20 Thinking. This requires deep thought about any issue that is important to you, and asks you to make a judgement on whether the 80/20 Principle is working in that area. You can then act on the insight. 80/20 Thinking does not require you to collect data or actually test the hypothesis. Consequently, 80/20 Thinking may on occasion mislead you – it is dangerous to assume, for example, that you already know what the 20 per cent is if you identify a relationship – but I will argue that 80/20 Thinking is much less likely to mislead you than is conventional thinking. 80/20 Thinking is much more accessible and faster than 80/20 Analysis, although the latter may be preferred when the issue is extremely important and you find it difficult to be confident about an estimate.

We look first at 80/20 Analysis, and then at 80/20 Thinking.

80/20 Analysis

80/20 Analysis examines the relationship between two sets of comparable data. One set of data is always a universe of people or objects, usually a large number of 100 or more, that can be turned into a percentage. The other set of data relates to some interesting characteristic of the people or objects that can be measured and also turned into a percentage.

For example, we might decide to look at a group of 100 friends, all of whom are at least occasional beer drinkers, and compare how much beer they drank last week.

So far, this method of analysis is common to many statistical techniques. What makes 80/20 Analysis unique is that the measurement ranks the second set of data in descending order of importance, and makes comparisons between percentages in the two sets of data.

In our example, then, we will ask all our 100 friends how many glasses of beer they drank last week and array the answers in a table in descending order. Figure 6 shows the top 20 and bottom 20 from the table.

80/20 Analysis can compare percentages from the two sets of data (the friends and the amount of beer drunk). In this case, we can say that 70 per cent of the beer was drunk by just 20 per cent of the friends. This would therefore give us a 70/20 relationship. Figure 7 introduces an 80/20 frequency distribution chart (or 80/20 Chart for short) to summarize the data visually.

Why is this called 80/20 Analysis?

When comparing these relationships, the most frequent observation, made long ago (probably in the 1950s), was that 80 per cent of the quantity being measured came from 20 per cent of the people or objects. 80/20 has become shorthand for this type of unbalanced relationship, whether or not the precise result is 80/20 (statistically, an exact 80/20 relationship is unlikely). It is the convention of 80/20 that it is the *top* 20 per cent of causes that is cited, not the bottom. 80/20 Analysis is my name for the way that the 80/20 Principle has generally been used to date, that is in a quantitative and empirical way, to measure possible relationships between inputs and outputs.

We could equally well observe from the data on our beer-drinking friends that the bottom 20 per cent of people

Rank	Name	Glasses drunk	Cumulative
	Our top 20 beer drinkers		
1	Charles H	45	45
2	Richard J	43	88
3=	George K	42	130
3=	Fred P	42	172
5	Arthur M	41	213
6	Steve B	40	253
7	Peter T	39	292
8	Reg C	37	329
9=	George B	36	365
9=	Bomber J	36	401
9=	Fatty M	36	437
12	Marian C	33	470
13	Stewart M	32	502
14	Cheryl W	31	533
15=	Kevin C	30	563
15=	Nick B	30	593
15=	Ricky M	30	623
15=	Nigel H	30	653
19	Greg H	26	679
20	Carol K	21	700
	Our bottom 20 beer drinkers		
81=	Rupert E	3	973
81=	Patrick W	3	976
81=	Anne B	3	979
81=	Jamie R	3	982
85=	Stephanie F	2	984
85=	Carli S	2	986
87=	Roberta F	1	987
87=	Pat B	1	988
87=	James P	1	989
87=	Charles W	1	990
87=	Jon T	1	991
87=	Edward W	1	992
87=	Margo L	1	993
87=	Rosabeth M	1	994
87=	Shirley W	1	995
87=	Greg P	1	996
87=	Gilly C	1	997
87=	Francis H	1	998
87=	David C	1	999
87=	Darleen B	1	1000

Figure 6

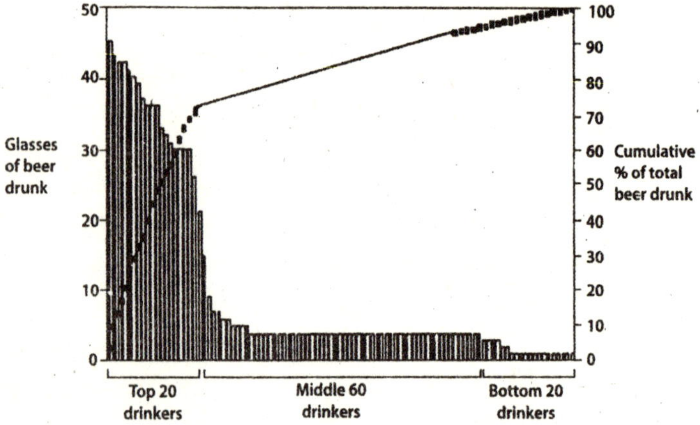

Figure 7 80/20 frequency distribution chart of beer drinkers

only consumed 30 glasses, or 3 per cent of the total. It would also be perfectly legitimate to call this a 3/20 relationship, although this is rarely done. The emphasis is nearly always on the heavy users or causes. If a brewery was conducting a promotion, or wanted to find out what beer drinkers thought about their range of beers, it would be most useful to go to the top 20.

We might also want to know what percentage of our friends combined to account for 80 per cent of total beer consumption. In this case, inspection of the part of the table not displayed (the middle part) would show that Mike G, the 28th biggest drinker with 10 glasses, took the cumulative total to 800 glasses. We could express this relationship, therefore, as 80/28: 80 per cent of total beer was drunk by just 28 per cent of our friends.

It should be clear from this example that 80/20 Analysis may result in any set of findings. Clearly, individual findings are more interesting and potentially more useful where there is an imbalance. If, for example, we had found that all of our friends had drunk exactly eight glasses each, the brewery would not have been very interested in using our group for a promotion or research. In this case, we would have had a 20/20 relationship (20 per cent of beer was drunk by the 'top' 20 per cent of friends) or an 80/80 relationship (80 per cent of beer was drunk by 80 per cent of friends).

Bar charts show 80/20 relationships best

An 80/20 Analysis is best displayed pictorially, by looking at two bars – as is particularly appropriate for our example! (Figures 2–4 above were bar charts.) The first bar in Figure 8 contains our 100 beer-drinking friends, each filling 1 per cent of the space, starting with the biggest beer drinker at the top and ending with the smallest beer drinkers at the

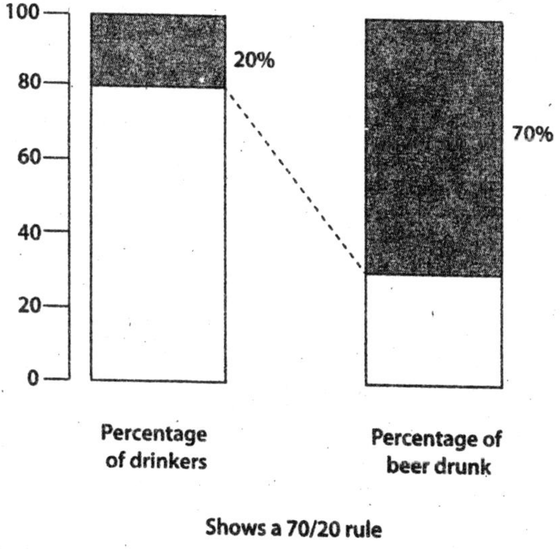

Figure 8

bottom. The second bar contains the total amount of beer drunk by each (and all) of our friends. At any point, we can see for a given percentage of our friends how much beer they accounted for.

Figure 8 shows what we discovered from the table (and could also see from Figure 7): that the top 20 per cent of beer drinkers accounted for 70 per cent of the beer drunk. The simple bars in Figure 8 take the data from Figure 7 and display them from top to bottom instead of from left to right. It doesn't matter which display you prefer.

If we wanted to illustrate what percentage of our friends drank 80 per cent of the beer, we would draw the bar charts slightly differently, as in Figure 9, to show the 80/28 relationship: 28 per cent of our friends drank 80 per cent of the beer.

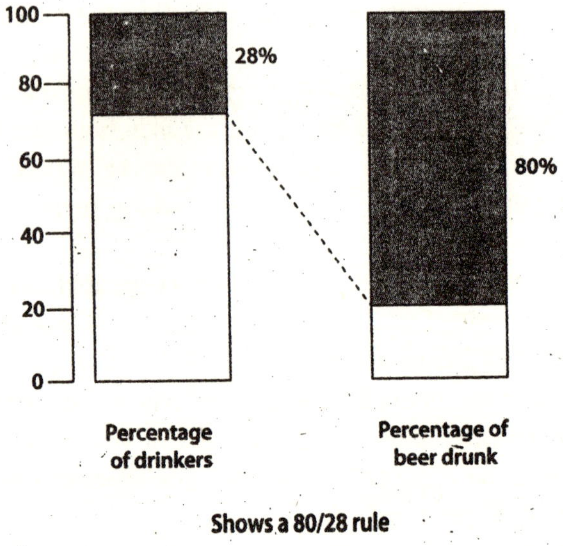

Figure 9

What is 80/20 Analysis used for?

Generally, to change the relationship it describes, or to make better use of it!

One use is to concentrate on the key causes of the relationship, the 20 per cent of inputs that lead to 80 per cent (or whatever the precise number is) of the outputs. If the top 20 per cent of beer drinkers account for 70 per cent of beer consumed, this is the group that a brewery should concentrate on reaching, in order to attract as high a share as possible of the business from the 20 per cent, and possibly also to increase their beer consumption still further. For all practical purposes, the brewery may decide to ignore the 80 per cent of beer drinkers who only consume 30 per cent of the beer; this simplifies the task immensely.

Similarly, a firm that finds that 80 per cent of its profits come from 20 per cent of its customers should use this information to concentrate on keeping that 20 per cent happy and increasing the business carried out with them. This is much easier, as well as more rewarding, than paying equal attention to the whole customer group. Or, if the firm finds that 80 per cent of its profits come from 20 per cent of its products, it should put most of its efforts behind selling more of those products.

The same idea applies to non-business applications of 80/20 Analysis. If you analysed the enjoyment you derived from all your leisure activities and found that 80 per cent of the enjoyment derived from 20 per cent of the activities, which currently took only 20 per cent of your leisure time, it would make sense to increase the time allocation from 20 to at least 80 per cent.

Take transport as another example. 80 per cent of traffic

jams occur on 20 per cent of roads. If you drive on the same route to work each day, you will know that roughly 80 per cent of delays usually occur at 20 per cent of the intersections. A sensible reaction would be for traffic authorities to pay particular attention to traffic phasing on those 20 per cent of jam-creating intersections. While the expense of such phasing might be too much for 100 per cent of junctions 100 per cent of the time, it would be money well spent in the key 20 per cent of locations for 20 per cent of the day.

The second main use of 80/20 Analysis is to do something about the 'underperforming' 80 per cent of inputs that contribute only 20 per cent of the output. Perhaps the occasional beer drinkers can be persuaded to drink more, for example by providing a blander product. Perhaps you could work out ways to get greater enjoyment out of the 'underperforming' leisure activities. In education, interactive teaching systems now replicate the technique used by college professors where questions are addressed randomly to any student, in order to combat the 80/20 rule, where 80 percent of classroom participation comes from 20 percent of the trainees. In US shopping malls it has been found that women (some 50 per cent of the population) account for 70 per cent of the dollar value of all purchases.[4] One way to increase the 30 per cent of sales to men might be to build stores specifically designed for them. Although this second application of 80/20 Analysis is sometimes very useful, and has been put to great effect in industry in improving the productivity of underperforming factories, it is generally harder work and less rewarding than the first use.

Don't apply 80/20 Analysis in a linear way

In discussing the uses of 80/20 Analysis, we must also briefly address its potential abuses. Like any simple and effective tool, 80/20 Analysis can also be misunderstood, misapplied and, instead of being the means to an unusual insight, serve as the justification for conventional thuggery. 80/20 Analysis, applied inappropriately and in a linear way, can also lead the innocent astray – you need constantly to be vigilant against false logic.

Let me illustrate this with an example from the book trade. It is easy to demonstrate that, in most times and places, about 20 per cent of book titles comprise about 80 per cent of books sold. For those who are steeped in the 80/20 Principle, this is not surprising. It might seem a short hop to the conclusion that bookshops should cut the range of books they stock or, indeed, that they should concentrate largely or exclusively on 'bestsellers'. Yet what is interesting is that in most cases, instead of sending profits up, restricting range has sent profits down.

This does not invalidate the 80/20 Principle, for two reasons. The key consideration is not the distribution of books sold, but what customers want. If customers go to the trouble of visiting a bookstore they want to find a reasonable range of books (as opposed to a kiosk or supermarket, where they don't expect range). Bookstores should concentrate on the 20 per cent of customers who account for 80 per cent of their profits and find out what those 20 per cent of customers want.

The other reason is that what matters even when considering books (as opposed to customers) is not the distribution of sales – the 20 per cent of books that represent 80 per cent of sales – but the distribution of profits – the 20 per cent of titles that generate 80 per cent of profits. Very often, these are not the so-called bestsellers, books written by well-known authors. In fact, a study in the US revealed that 'best sellers represent about 5% of total sales'.[5] The true bestsellers are often those books that never make it into the charts but sell a reliable quantity year in and year out, often at high margins. As the same US research comments, 'Core inventory represents those books that sell season-in and season-out. They are the "80" in the 80/20 rule, often accounting for the lion's share of sales in a particular subject.'

This illustration is salutary. It does not invalidate 80/20 Analysis at all, since the key questions should always be which customers and products generate 80 per cent of profits. But it does show the danger of not thinking clearly enough about how the analysis is applied. When using the 80/20 Principle, be selective and be contrarian. Don't be seduced into thinking that the variable that everyone else is looking at – in this case, the books on the latest bestseller list – is what really matters. This is linear thinking. The most valuable insight from 80/20 Analysis will always come from examining non-linear relationships that others are neglecting. In addition, because 80/20 Analysis is based on a freezeframe of the situation at a particular point rather than incorporating changes over time, you must be aware that if you inadvertently freeze the wrong or an incomplete picture, you will get an inaccurate view.

80/20 Thinking and why it is necessary

80/20 Analysis is extremely useful. But most people are not natural analysts, and even analysts cannot stop to investigate the data every time they have to make a decision – it would bring life to a shuddering halt. Most important decisions have never been made by analysis and never will be, however clever our computers become. Therefore, if we want the 80/20 Principle to be a guide in our daily lives, we need something less analytical and more instantly available than 80/20 Analysis. We need *80/20 Thinking.*

80/20 Thinking is my phrase for the application of the 80/20 Principle to daily life, for non-quantitative applications of the principle. As with 80/20 Analysis, we start with a hypothesis about a possible imbalance between inputs and outputs but, instead of collecting data and analysing them, we estimate them. 80/20 Thinking requires, and with practice enables, us to spot the few really important things that are happening and ignore the mass of unimportant things. It teaches us to see the wood for the trees.

80/20 Thinking is too valuable to be confined to causes where data and analysis are perfect. For every ounce of insight generated quantitatively, there must be many pounds of insight arrived at intuitively and impressionistically. This is why 80/20 Thinking, although helped by data, must not be constrained by it.

To engage in 80/20 Thinking, we must constantly ask ourselves: what is the 20 per cent that is leading to 80 per cent? We must never assume that we automatically know what the answer is, but take some time to think creatively about it. What are the vital few inputs or causes, as opposed to the trivial many? Where is the haunting melody being drowned by the background noise?

80/20 Thinking is then used in the same way as the results from 80/20 Analysis: to change behaviour and, normally, to concentrate on the most important 20 per cent. You know that 80/20 Thinking is working when it multiplies effectiveness. Action resulting from 80/20 Thinking should lead us to get much more from much less.

When we are using the 80/20 Principle we do not *assume* that its results are good or bad or that the powerful forces we observe are necessarily good. We *decide* whether they are good (from our own perspective), and either determine to give the minority of powerful forces a further shove in the right direction, or work out how to frustrate their operation.

The 80/20 Principle turns conventional wisdom upside down

Application of the 80/20 Principle implies that we should do the following:

- ➤ celebrate exceptional productivity, rather than raise average efforts
- ➤ look for the short cut, rather than run the full course
- ➤ exercise control over our lives with the least possible effort
- ➤ be selective, not exhaustive

- strive for excellence in few things, rather than good performance in many
- delegate or outsource as much as possible in our daily lives and be encouraged rather than penalized by tax systems to do this (use gardeners, car mechanics, decorators and other specialists to the maximum, instead of doing the work ourselves)
- choose our careers and employers with extraordinary care, and if possible employ others rather than being employed ourselves
- *only* do the thing we are best at doing and enjoy most
- look beneath the normal texture of life to uncover ironies and oddities
- in every important sphere, work out where 20 per cent of effort can lead to 80 per cent of returns
- calm down, work less and target a limited number of very valuable goals where the 80/20 Principle will work for us, rather than pursuing every available opportunity
- make the most of those few 'lucky streaks' in our life where we are at our creative peak and the stars line up to guarantee success.

There are no boundaries to the 80/20 Principle

No sphere of activity is immune from the influence of the 80/20 Principle. Like the six wise, blind Indian men who tried to discern the shape of an elephant, most users of the 80/20 Principle only know a fraction of its scope and power. Becoming an 80/20 thinker requires active participation and creativity on your part. If you want to benefit from 80/20 Thinking, *you* have to do it!

Now is a good time to start. If you want to begin with applications for your organization, go straight on to Part Two, which documents most of the important business applications of the 80/20 Principle. If you are more immediately interested in using the principle to make major improvements in your life, skip to Part Three, a novel attempt to relate the 80/20 Principle to the fabric of our daily lives.

Part Two

Corporate Success Needn't Be a Mystery

3 The Underground Cult

Now we see in a mirror dimly, but then we shall see face to face. Now I know in part; then I shall understand fully.

1 Corinthians 13:12

It is difficult to gauge the extent to which the 80/20 Principle is already known in business. This is almost certainly the first book on the subject, yet in my research I was easily able to find several hundred articles referring to the use of 80/20 in all kinds of businesses, all over the world. Many successful firms and individuals swear by the use of the 80/20 Principle, and most holders of MBAs have heard of it.

Yet considering that the 80/20 Principle has affected the lives of hundreds of millions of people even though they may be unaware of it, it remains strangely uncelebrated. It is time to put this right.

The first 80/20 wave: the quality revolution

The quality revolution that took place between 1950 and 1990 transformed the quality and value of branded consumer goods and other manufactures. The quality movement has been a crusade to obtain consistently higher quality at lower cost, by the application of statistical and behavioural techniques. The objective, now almost reached with many products, is to obtain a zero rate of product defects. It is possible to argue that the quality movement has been the most significant driver of higher living standards throughout the world since 1950.

The movement has an intriguing history. Its two great messiahs, Joseph Juran (1904–2008) and W Edwards Deming (1900–1993), were both Americans (although Juran was born in Romania). Respectively an electrical engineer and a statistician, they developed their ideas in parallel after the Second World War, but found it impossible to interest any major US corporation in the quest for extraordinary quality. Juran published the first edition of his *Quality Control Handbook*, the bible of the quality movement, in 1951, but it received a very flat reception. The only serious interest came from Japan and both Juran and Deming moved there in the early 1950s. Their pioneering work took an economy known at the time for shoddy imitations and transformed it into a powerhouse of high quality and productivity.

It was only when Japanese goods, such as motorcycles and photocopiers, began to invade the US market that most American (and other western) corporations started to take the quality movement seriously. From 1970, and especially after 1980, Juran, Deming and their disciples undertook an equally successful transformation of western quality standards, leading to huge improvements in the level and consistency of quality, dramatic reductions in fault rates, and large falls in manufacturing costs.

The 80/20 Principle was one of the key building blocks of the quality movement. Joseph Juran was the most enthusiastic messiah of the principle, although he called it 'the Pareto Principle' or 'the Rule of the Vital Few'. In the first edition of the *Quality Control Handbook*, Juran commented that 'losses' (that is, manufactured goods that have to be rejected because of poor quality) do not arise from a large number of causes:

> *Rather, the losses are always maldistributed in such a way that a small percentage of the quality characteristics always contributes a high percentage of the quality loss.* *

The footnote commented that:

> **The economist Pareto found that wealth was non-uniformly distributed in the same way. Many other instances can be found – the distribution of crime amongst criminals, the distribution of accidents among hazardous processes, etc. Pareto's principle of unequal distribution applied to distribution of wealth and to distribution of quality losses.*[1]

Juran applied the 80/20 Principle to statistical quality control. The approach is to identify the problems causing lack of quality and to rank them from the most important – the 20 per cent of defects causing 80 per cent of quality problems – to the least important. Both Juran and Deming came to use the phrase 80/20 increasingly, encouraging diagnosis of the few defects causing most of the problems.

Once the 'vital few' sources of off-quality product have been identified, effort is focused on dealing with these issues, rather than trying to tackle all the problems at once.

As the quality movement has progressed from an emphasis on quality 'control' through to the view that quality must be built into products in the first place, by all operators, and to total quality management and increasingly sophisticated use of software, the emphasis on 80/20 techniques has grown, so that today almost all quality practitioners are familiar with 80/20. Some recent references illustrate the ways in which the 80/20 Principle is now being used.

In a recent article in the *National Productivity Review*, Ronald J Recardo asks:

> *Which gaps adversely affect your most strategic consumers? As with many other quality problems, Pareto's Law prevails here too: if you remedy the most critical 20 percent of your quality gaps, you will realize 80 percent of the benefits. This first 80 percent typically includes your breakthrough improvements.*[2]

Another writer, focusing on corporate turnarounds, comments:

> *For every step in your business process, ask yourself if it adds value or provides essential support. If it does neither, it's waste. Cut it. [This is] the 80/20 rule, revisited: You can eliminate 80 percent of the waste by spending only 20 percent of what it would cost you to get rid of 100 percent of the waste. Go for the quick gain now.*[3]

The 80/20 Principle was also used by Ford Electronics Manufacturing Corporation in a quality programme that won the Shingo prize:

> *Just-in-time programs have been applied using the 80/20 rule (80 percent of the value is spread over 20 percent of the volume) and top-dollar usages are analyzed constantly. Labor and overhead performance were replaced by Manufacturing Cycle Time analysis by product line, reducing product cycle time by 95 percent.*[4]

New software incorporating the 80/20 Principle is being used to raise quality:

> *[With the ABC DataAnalyzer] the data is entered or imported into the spreadsheet area, where you highlight it and click on your choice of six graph types: histograms, control charts, run charts, scatter diagrams, pie charts and Pareto charts.*
>
> *The Pareto chart incorporates the 80 to 20 rule, which might show, for instance, that out of 1,000 customer complaints roughly 800 can be eliminated by correcting only 20 per cent of the causes.*[5]

The 80/20 Principle is also increasingly being applied to product design and development. For example, a review of the use that the Pentagon has made of total quality management explains that:

> *Decisions made early in the development process fix the majority of life cycle costs. The 80/20 rule describes this outcome, since 80 percent of the life-cycle costs are usually locked in after only 20 percent of the development time.*[6]

The impact of the quality revolution on customer satisfaction and value, and on the competitive positions of individual firms and indeed of whole nations, has been little noted but is truly massive. The 80/20 Principle was clearly one of the 'vital few' inputs to the quality revolution. But the underground influence of the 80/20 Principle did not stop there. It also played a key role in a second revolution that combined with the first to create today's global consumer society.

The second 80/20 wave: the information revolution

The information revolution that began in the 1960s has already transformed work habits and the efficiency of large tracts of business. It is just beginning to do more than this: to help change the nature of the organizations that are today's dominant force in society. The 80/20 Principle was, is and will be a key accessory of the information revolution, helping to direct its force intelligently.

Perhaps because they were close to the quality movement, the computing and software professionals behind the information revolution were generally familiar with the 80/20 Principle and used it extensively. To judge by the number of computing and software articles that refer to the 80/20 Principle, most hardware and software developers understand and use it in their daily work.

The information revolution has been most effective when using the 80/20 Principle's concepts of selectivity and simplicity. As two separate project directors testify:

> *Think small. Don't plan to the nth degree on the first day. The return on investment usually follows the 80/20 rule: 80*

> *percent of the benefits will be found in the simplest 20 percent of the system, and the final 20 percent of the benefits will come from the most complex 80 percent of the system.*[7]

Apple used the 80/20 Principle in developing the Apple Newton Message Pad, an electronic personal organizer:

> *The Newton engineers took advantage of a slightly modified version [of 80/20]. They found that .01 percent of a person's vocabulary was sufficient to do 50 percent of the things you want to do with a small handheld computer.*[8]

Increasingly, software is substituting for hardware, using the 80/20 Principle. An example is the RISC software invented in 1994:

> *RISC is based on a variation of the 80/20 rule. This rule assumes that most software spends 80 percent of its time executing only 20 percent of the available instructions. RISC processors ... optimize the performance of that 20 percent, and keep chip size and cost down by eliminating the other 80 percent. RISC does in software what CISC [the previously dominant system] does in silicon.*[9]

Those who apply software know that, even though it is incredibly efficient, usage follows 80/20 patterns. As one developer states:

> *The business world has long abided by the 80/20 rule. It's especially true for software, where 80 percent of a product's uses take advantage of only 20 percent of its capabilities. That means that most of us pay for what we don't want or need.*

> *Software developers finally seem to understand this, and many are betting that modular applications will solve the problem.*[10]

Design of software is crucial, so that the most used functions are the easiest to use. The same approach has been used for new database services:

> *How do ... software developers [do] it? First, they identify what customers want most of the time and how they want to do it – the old 80/20 rule (people use 20 percent of a program's functions 80 percent of the time). Good software developers make high-use functions as simple and automatic and inevitable as possible.*
>
> *Translating such an approach to today's database services would mean looking at key customer use all the time... How many times do customers call search service support desks to ask which file to pick or where a file can be found? Good design could eliminate such calls.*[11]

Wherever one turns, effective innovations in information – in data storage, retrieval and processing – focus heavily on the up to 20 per cent of key needs.

The information revolution has a long way to run

The information revolution is the most subversive force business has ever known. Already the phenomenon of 'information power to the people' has given knowledge and authority to front-line workers and technicians, destroying the power and often the jobs of middle management who were previously protected by proprietary knowledge. The information revolution has also decentralized corporations physically: the phone, the PC, broadband and the increasing miniaturization and mobility of these technologies have already begun to destroy the power of corporate palaces and those who sit, or used to sit, in them. Ultimately, the information revolution will help to destroy the profession of management itself, thus enabling much greater direct value creation by 'doers' in corporations for their key customers.[12] The value of automated information is increasing exponentially, much faster than we can use it. The key to using this power effectively, now and in the future, lies in selectivity: in applying the 80/20 Principle.

Peter Drucker points the way:

> *A database, no matter how copious, is not information. It is information's ore… The information a business most depends on is available, if at all, only in a primitive and disorganized form. For what a business needs the most for its decisions – especially its strategic ones – are data about what goes on outside of it. It is only outside the business where there are results, opportunities, and threats.*[13]

Drucker argues that we need new ways of measuring wealth creation. Ian Godden and I call these new tools 'automated performance measures'[14]; they are just beginning to be created by some corporations. But well over 80 per cent (probably around 99 per cent) of the information revolution's resources are still being applied to counting better what we used to count ('paving over the cowpats') rather than creating and simplifying measures of genuine corporate wealth creation. The tiny proportion of effort that uses the information revolution to create a different sort of corporation will have an explosive impact.

The 80/20 Principle is still the best-kept business secret

Considering the importance of the 80/20 Principle and the extent to which it is known by managers, it remains extremely discreet. Even the 80/20 term itself caught on very slowly and without any visible landmarks. Given the piecemeal use and gradual spread of the 80/20 Principle, it remains under-exploited, even by those who recognize the idea. It is extremely versatile. It can be profitably applied to any industry and any organization, any function within an organization and any individual job. The 80/20 Principle can help the chief executive, line managers, functional specialists and any knowledge worker, down to the lowest level or the newest trainee. And although its uses are manifold, there is an underlying, unifying logic that explains why the 80/20 Principle works and is so valuable.

Why the 80/20 Principle works in business

The 80/20 Principle applied to business has one key theme – to generate the most money with the least expenditure of assets and effort.

The classical economists of the nineteenth and early twentieth centuries developed a theory of economic equilibrium and of the firm that has dominated thinking ever since. The theory states that under perfect competition firms do not make excess returns, and profitability is either zero or the 'normal' cost of capital, the latter usually being defined by a modest interest charge. The theory is internally consistent and has the sole flaw that it cannot be applied to real economic activity of any kind, and especially not to the operations of any individual firm.

The 80/20 theory of the firm

In contrast to the theory of perfect competition, the 80/20 theory of the firm is both verifiable (and has, in fact, been verified many times) and helpful as a guide to action. The 80/20 theory of the firm goes like this:

➤ In any market, some suppliers will be much better than others at satisfying customer needs. These suppliers will obtain the highest price realizations and also the highest market shares.

➤ In any market, some suppliers will be much better than

others at minimizing expenditure relative to revenues. In other words, these suppliers' products will cost less than other suppliers, for equivalent output and revenue; or, alternatively, they will be able to generate equivalent output with lower expenditure.

➤ Some suppliers will generate much higher surpluses than others. (I use the phrase 'surpluses' rather than 'profits', because the latter normally implies the profit available for shareholders. The concept of surplus implies the level of funds available for profits or reinvestment, over and above what is needed normally to keep the wheels turning.) Higher surpluses will result in one or more of the following: (1) greater reinvestment in product and service, to produce greater superiority and appeal to customers; (2) investment in gaining market share through greater sales and marketing effort, and/or takeovers of other firms; (3) higher returns to employees, which will tend to have the effect of retaining and attracting the best people in the market; and/or (4) higher returns to shareholders, which will tend to raise share prices and lower the cost of capital, facilitating investment and/or takeovers.

➤ Over time, 80 per cent of the market will tend to be supplied by 20 per cent or fewer of the suppliers, who will normally also be more profitable.

At this point it is possible that the market structure may reach an equilibrium, although it will be a very different kind of equilibrium from that beloved of the economists' perfect competition model. In the 80/20 equilibrium, a few suppliers, the largest, will offer customers better value for money and have higher profits than smaller rivals. This is frequently observed in real life, despite being impossible according to the theory of perfect competition. We may term our more realistic theory the 80/20 law of competition.

But the real world does not generally rest long in a tranquil equilibrium. Sooner or later (usually sooner), there are always changes to market structure caused by competitors' innovations.

➤ Both existing suppliers and new suppliers will seek to innovate and obtain a high share of a small but defensible part of each market (a 'market segment'). Segmentation of this kind is possible by providing a more specialized product or service ideally suited to particular types of customer. Over time, markets will tend to comprise more market segments.

Within each of these segments, the 80/20 law of competition will operate. The leaders in each specialist segment may either be firms operating largely or exclusively in that segment or industry generalists, but their success will be dependent, in each segment, on obtaining the greatest revenue with the lowest expenditure of effort. In each segment, some firms will be much better than others at doing this, and will tend to accumulate segment market share as a result.

Any large firm will operate in a large number of segments, that is, in a large number of customer/product combinations where a different formula is required to maximize revenue relative to effort, and/or where different competitors are met. In some of these segments, the individual large firm will generate large surpluses, and in other segments much lower surpluses (or even deficits). It will tend to be true, therefore, that 80 per cent of surpluses or profits are generated by 20 per cent of segments, and by 20 per cent of customers and by 20 per cent of products. The most profitable segments will tend to (but will not always) be where the firm enjoys the highest market shares, and where the firm has the most loyal customers (loyalty being defined by being longstanding and least likely to defect to competitors).

➤ Within any firm, as with all entities dependent on nature and human endeavour, there is likely to be an inequality between inputs and outputs, an imbalance between effort and reward. Externally, this is reflected in the fact that some markets, products and customers are much more profitable than others. Internally, the same principle is reflected by the fact that some resources, be they people, factories, machines or permutations of these, will produce very much more value relative to their cost than will other resources. If we were able to measure it (as we can with some jobs, such as those of salespeople), we would find that some people generate a very large surplus (their attributable share of revenue is very much greater than their full cost), whereas many people generate a small surplus or a deficit. Firms that generate the largest surpluses also tend to have the highest average surplus per employee, but in all firms the true surplus generated by each employee tends to be very unequal: 80 per cent of the surplus is usually generated by 20 per cent of employees.

➤ At the lowest level of aggregation of resources within the firm, for example an individual employee, 80 per cent of the value created is likely to be generated in a small part, approximately 20 per cent, of the time when, through a combination of circumstances including personal characteristics and the exact nature of the task, the employee is operating at several times his or her normal level of effectiveness.

➤ The principles of unequal effort and return therefore operate at all levels of business: markets, market segments, products, customers, departments and employees. It is this lack of balance, rather than a notional equilibrium, that characterizes all economic activity. Apparently small differences create large consequences. A product has only to be

10 per cent better value than that of a competing product to generate a sales difference of 50 per cent and a profit difference of 100 per cent.

Three action implications

One implication of the 80/20 theory of firms is that successful firms operate in markets where it is possible for that firm to generate the highest revenues with the least effort. This will be true both absolutely, that is, relative to monetary profits; and relatively, that is, in relation to competition. A firm cannot be judged successful unless it has a high absolute surplus (in traditional terms, a high return on investment) and also a higher surplus than its competitors (higher margins).

A second practical implication for all firms is that it is always possible to raise the economic surplus, usually by a large degree, by focusing only on those market and customer segments where the largest surpluses are currently being generated. This will always imply redeployment of resources into the most surplus-generating segments, and will normally also imply a reduction in the total level of resource and expenditure (in plain words, fewer employees and other costs).

Firms rarely reach the highest level of surplus that they could attain, or anywhere near it, both because managers are often not aware of the potential for surplus and because they often prefer to run large firms rather than exceptionally profitable ones.

A third corollary is that it is possible for every corporation to raise the level of surplus by reducing the inequality of output and reward within the firm. This can be done by identifying the parts of the firm (people, factories, sales offices, overhead units, countries) that generate the highest surpluses and reinforcing these, giving them more power and resources; and, conversely, identifying the resources generating low or negative surpluses, facilitating dramatic improvements and, if these are not forthcoming, stopping the expenditure on these resources.

These principles constitute a useful 80/20 theory of the firm, but they must not be interpreted too rigidly or deterministically. The principles work because they are a reflection of relationships in nature, which are an intricate mixture of order and disorder, of regularity and irregularity.

Look for 'irregular' insights from the 80/20 Principle

It is important to try to grasp the fluidity and force driving 80/20 relationships. Unless you appreciate this, you will interpret the 80/20 Principle too rigidly and fail to exploit its full potential.

The world is full of small causes that, when combined, can have momentous consequences. Think of a saucepan of milk that, when heated above a certain temperature, suddenly changes form, swelling up and bubbling over. One moment you have a nice, orderly pan of hot milk; the next moment you can either have a wonderful cappuccino or, if you are a second too late, a mess on top of your stove. Things take a little more time in business, but one year you can have an excellent and very profitable IBM dominating the computer industry and, before long, a combination of small causes resulting in a blinded monolith staggering to avoid destruction.

Creative systems operate away from equilibrium. Cause and effect, input and output, operate in a non-linear way. You do not usually get back what you put in; you may sometimes get very much less and sometimes get very much more. Major alterations in a business system can flow from apparently insignificant causes. At any one time, people of equal intelligence, skill and dedication can produce quite unequal results, as a result of small structural differences. Events cannot be predicted, although predictable patterns tend to recur.

Identify lucky streaks

Control is therefore impossible. But it is possible to influence events and, perhaps even more important, it is possible to detect irregularities and benefit from them. The art of using the 80/20 Principle is to identify which way the grain of reality is currently running and to exploit that as much as possible.

Imagine you are in a crazy casino, full of unbalanced roulette wheels. All numbers pay odds of 35 to 1, but individual numbers come up more or less frequently at different tables. At one, number five comes up one time in twenty, at another table it only comes up one time in fifty. If you back the right number at the right table, you can make a fortune. If you stubbornly keep backing number five at a table where it comes up one time in fifty, your money will all disappear, regardless of how high your starting bank.

If you can identify where your firm is getting back more

than it is putting in, you can up the stakes and make a killing. Similarly, if you can work out where your firm is getting back much less than it is investing, you can cut your losses.

In this context, the 'where' can be anything. It can be a product, a market, a customer or type of customer, a technology, a channel of distribution, a department or division, a country, a type of transaction or an employee, type of employee or team. The game is to spot the few places where you are making great surpluses and to maximize them; and to identify the places where you are losing and get out.

We have been trained to think in terms of cause and effect, of regular relationships, of average levels of return, of perfect competition and of predictable outcomes. This is not the real world. The real world comprises a mass of influences, where cause and effect are blurred, and where complex feedback loops distort inputs; where equilibrium is fleeting and often illusory; where there are patterns of repeated but irregular performance; where firms never compete head to head and prosper by differentiation; and where a few favoured souls are able to corner the market for high returns.

Viewed in this light, large firms are incredibly complex and constantly changing coalitions of forces, some of which are going with the grain of nature and making a fortune, while others are going against the grain and stacking up huge losses. All this is obscured by our inability to disentangle reality and by the calming, averaging and highly distorting effects of accounting systems. The 80/20 Principle is rampant but largely unobserved. What we are generally allowed to see in business is the net effect of what happens, which is by no means the whole picture. Beneath the surface there are warring positive and negative inputs that combine to produce the effect we can observe above the surface. The 80/20 Principle is most useful when we can identify all the forces beneath the surface, so that we can stop the negative influences and give maximum power to the most productive forces.

How companies can use the 80/20 Principle to raise profits

Enough of history, philosophy and theory! We now switch gears to the intensely practical. Any individual business can gain immensely through practical application of the 80/20 Principle. It is time to show you how.

Chapters 4 to 7 cover the most important ways to raise profits via the 80/20 Principle. Chapter 8 closes Part Two with hints on how to embed 80/20 Thinking into your business life, so that you can gain an unfair advantage over colleagues and competitors alike.

We start in the next chapter with the most important use of the 80/20 Principle in any firm: to isolate where you are really making the profits and, just as important, where you are really losing money. Every business person thinks they know this already, and nearly all are wrong. If they had the right picture, their whole business would be transformed.

4 Why Your Strategy Is Wrong

Unless you have used the 80/20 Principle to redirect your strategy, you can be pretty sure that the strategy is badly flawed. Almost certainly, you don't have an accurate picture of where you make, and lose, the most money. It is almost inevitable that you are doing too many things for too many people.

Business strategy should not be a grand and sweeping overview. It should be more like an underview, a peek beneath the covers to look in great detail at what is going on. To arrive at a useful business strategy, you need to look carefully at the different chunks of your business, particularly at their profitability and cash generation.

Unless your firm is very small and simple, it is almost certainly true that *you make at least 80 per cent of your profits and cash in 20 per cent of your activity, and in 20 per cent of your revenues.* The trick is to work out *which* 20 per cent.

Where are you making the most money?

Identify which parts of the business are making very high returns, which are just about washing their faces and which are disasters. To do this we will conduct an 80/20 Analysis of profits by different categories of business:

- by product or product group/type
- by customer or customer group/type
- by any other split that appears to be relevant for your business for which you have data; for example by geographical area or distribution channel
- by competitive segment.

Start with *products*. Your business will almost certainly have information by product or product group. For each, look at the sales over the last period, month, quarter or year (decide which is most reliable) and work out the profitability after allocating all costs.

How easy or difficult this will be depends on the state of your management information. What you need may all be readily available, but if not you will have to build it up yourself. You are bound to have sales by product or product line and almost certainly the gross margin (sales less cost of sales). You will also know the total costs for the whole business (all the overhead costs). What you then have to do is to allocate all the overhead costs to each product group on some reasonable basis.

The crudest way is to allocate costs on a percentage of turnover. A moment's thought, however, should convince you that this will not be very accurate. Some products take a great deal of salespeople's time relative to their value, for example, and others take very little. Some are heavily advertised and others not at all. Some require a lot of fussing around in manufacturing whereas others are straightforward.

Take each category of overhead cost and allocate it to each product group. Do this for all the costs, then look at the results.

Typically some products, representing a minority of turnover, are very profitable; most products are modestly or marginally profitable; and some are really making large losses once you allocate all the costs.

Figure 10 shows the numbers for a recent study I conducted of an electronic instrumentation group. Figure 11 gives the same data visually; look at this if you prefer pictures to numbers.

Product	Sales	$000 Income	Return on sales (%)
Product group A	3,750	1,330	35.5
Product group B	17,000	5,110	30.1
Product group C	3,040	601	25.1
Product group D	12,070	1,880	15.6
Product group E	44,110	5,290	12.0
Product group F	30,370	2,990	9.8
Product group G	5,030	(820)	(15.5)
Product group H	4,000	(3,010)	(75.3)
Total	119,370	13,380	11.2

Figure 10 Electronic Instruments Inc, sales and profits table by product group

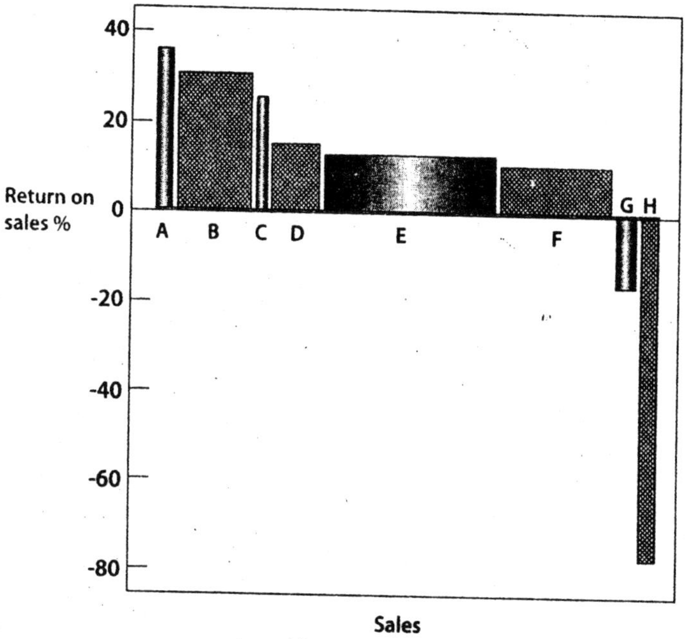

Figure 11 Electronic Instruments Inc, sales and profit chart by product group

We can see from the two figures that Product Group A accounts for only 3 per cent of sales, but for 10 per cent of profits. Product Groups A, B and C account for 20 per cent of sales, but for 53 per cent of profits. This becomes very clear if we compile an 80/20 Table or an 80/20 Chart, as in Figures 12 and 13 respectively.

We have not yet found the 20 per cent of sales that account for 80 per cent of profits, but we are on our way. If not 80/20, then 67/30: 30 per cent of product sales account for almost 67 per cent of profits. Already you may be thinking about what can be done to raise the sales of Product Groups

A, B and C. For example, you might want to reallocate all sales effort from the other 80 per cent of business, telling salespeople to concentrate on doubling the sales of Products A, B and C and not to worry about the rest. If they succeeded in doing this, sales would only go up by 20 per cent, but profits would rise more than 50 per cent.

You might also already be thinking about cutting costs, or raising prices, in Product Groups D, E and F; or about radical retrenchment or total exit from Product Groups G and H.

	Percentage of sales		Percentage of profits	
Product	Group	Cumulative	Group	Cumulative
Product group A	3.1	3.1	9.9	9.9
Product group B	14.2	17.3	38.2	48.1
Product group C	2.6	19.9	4.6	52.7
Product group D	10.1	30.0	14.1	66.8
Product group E	37.0	67.0	39.5	106.3
Product group F	25.4	92.4	22.4	128.7
Product group G	4.2	96.6	(6.1)	122.6
Product group H	3.4	100.0	(22.6)	100.0

Figure 12 Electronic Instruments Inc, 80/20 Table

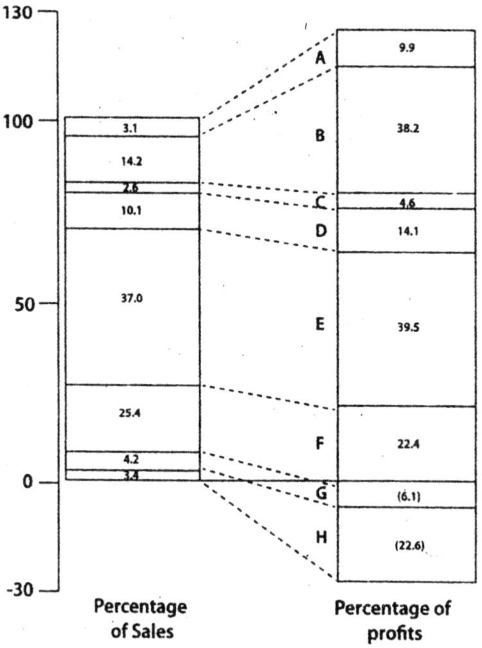

Figure 13 Electronic Instruments Inc, 80/20 Chart

What about customer profitability?

After products, go on to look at *customers*. Repeat the analysis, but look at total purchases by each customer or customer group. Some customers pay high prices but have a high cost to serve: these are often smaller customers. The very big customers may be easy to deal with and take large volumes of the same product, but screw you down on price. Sometimes these differences balance out, but often they do not. For the group we are calling Electronic Instruments Inc the results are shown in Figures 14 and 15.

Customer	Sales ($000)	Income ($000)	Return on sales (%)
Customer type A	18,350	7,865	42.9
Customer type B	11,450	3,916	34.2
Customer type C	43,100	3,969	9.2
Customer type D	46,470	(2,370)	(5.1)
Total	119,370	13,380	11.2

Figure 14 Electronic Instruments Inc, sales and profits table by customer group

A word of explanation about the customer groups. Type A customers are small, direct accounts paying very high prices and giving very fat gross margins. They are quite expensive to service but the margins more than compensate for this. Type B customers are distributors who tend to place large orders and have very low costs to serve, yet for one reason or another find it acceptable to pay fairly high prices, mainly because the electronic components bought are a tiny fraction of their total product costs. Type C customers are export accounts paying high prices. The snag with them, however, is that they are very expensive to service. Type D customers are large manufacturers who bargain very hard on price and also demand a great deal of technical support and many 'specials'.

Figures 16 and 17 show the 80/20 Table and 80/20 Chart respectively for the customer groups.

These figures reveal a 59/15 rule and an 88/25 rule: the most profitable customer category accounts for 15 per cent

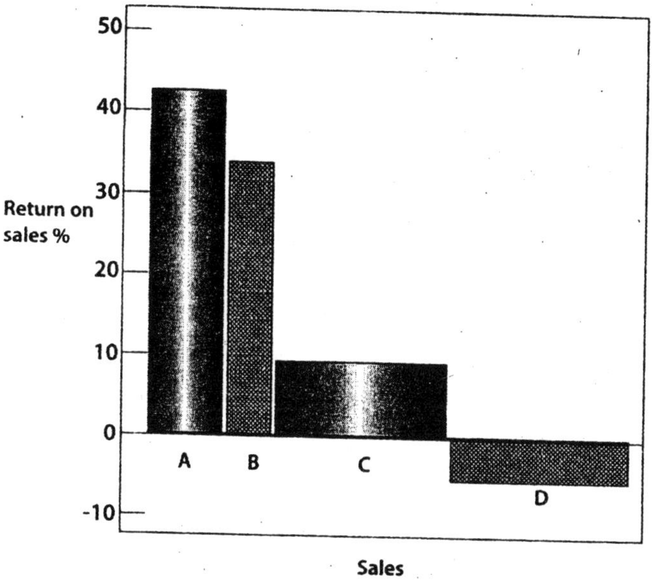

Figure 15 Electronic Instruments Inc, sales and profits chart by customer group

of revenues but 59 per cent of profits, and the most profitable 25 per cent of customers yields 88 per cent of profits. This is partly because the most profitable customers tend to take the most profitable products, but also because they pay more in relation to their cost to service.

The analysis led to a successful campaign to find more A and B customers: the small direct customers and the distributors. Even taking account of the cost of the campaign, the result was very profitable. Prices for C customers (the export accounts) were selectively raised and ways found to lower the cost of servicing some of them, particularly by greater use of telephone rather than face-to-face selling. The D customers (large manufacturers) were dealt with individually: nine of these accounted for 97 per cent of D sales. In some cases technical development services were charged for separately; in others prices were raised; and three accounts were tactically 'lost' to the company's most hated competitor after a bidding war. The managers really wanted the competitor to enjoy these losses!

	Percentage of sales		Percentage of profits	
Customer	Type	Cumulative	Type	Cumulative
Customer type A	15.4	15.4	58.9	58.9
Customer type B	9.6	25.0	29.3	88.2
Customer type C	36.1	61.1	29.6	117.8
Customer type D	38.9	100.0	(17.8)	100.0

Figure 16 Electronic Instruments Inc, 80/20 Table by customer type

80/20 Analysis applied to a consultancy firm

After products and customers, take any other split of business that appears especially relevant to your business. There was no special analysis in the case of the instrumentation company, but to illustrate the point consider the simple split of sales and profits for a strategy consultancy shown in Figures 18 and 19.

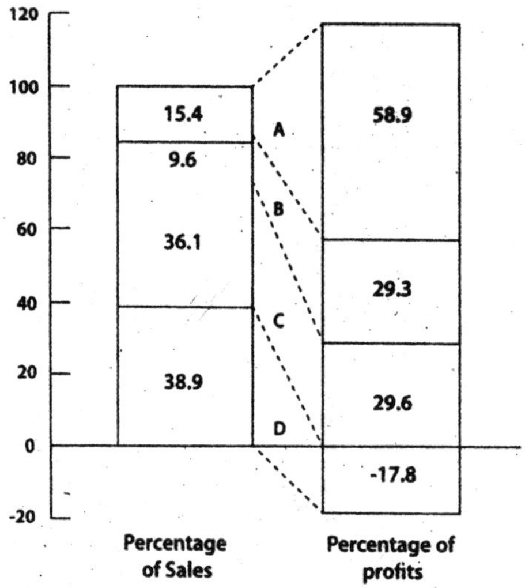

Figure 17 Electronic Instruments Inc, 80/20 Chart by customer type

These figures exhibit a 56/21 rule: large projects constitute only 21 per cent of turnover but give 56 per cent of profits.

Business split	$000 Sales	Profits	Return on sales (%)
Large projects	35,000	16,000	45.7
Small projects	135,000	12,825	9.5
Total	170,000	28,825	17.0

Figure 18 Strategy Consulting Inc, table of profitability of large versus small projects

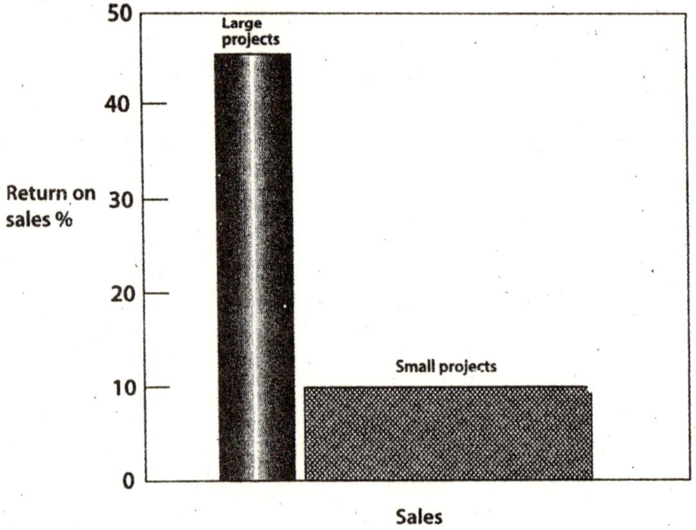

Figure 19 Strategy Consulting Inc, chart of profitability of large versus small clients

Another analysis, shown in Figures 20 and 21, splits the business into 'old' clients (more than three years old), 'new' clients (less than six months old) and those in between.

These figures tell us that 26 per cent of the business (old clients) made up 84 per cent of the profits: an 84/26 rule. The message here was to strive above all to keep and expand long-serving clients, who were the least price sensitive and who could be served most cheaply. New clients who do not turn into long-serving clients were recognized as being loss makers, leading to a much more selective approach to pitching for business: pitches were only made where it was believed the company concerned would turn into a long-term client.

Business split	$000 Sales	Profits	Return on sales (%)
Old clients	43,500	24,055	55.3
Intermediate clients	101,000	12,726	12.6
New clients	25,500	(7,956)	31.2
Total	170,000	28,825	17.0

Figure 20 Strategy Consulting Inc, table of profitability of old versus new clients

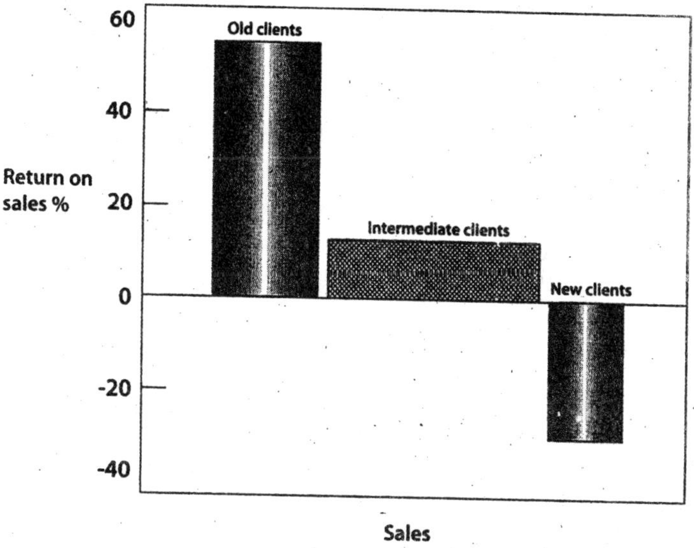

Figure 21 Strategy Consulting Inc, chart of profitability of old versus new clients

Business split	$000 Sales	Profits	Return on sales (%)
M&A	37,600	25,190	67.0
Strategic analysis	75,800	11,600	15.3
Operational projects	56,600	7,965	14.1
Total	170,000	28,825	17.0

Figure 22 Strategy Consulting Inc, table of profitability by project type

Figures 22 and 23 summarize a third analysis for the consultants, which divided projects into work on mergers and acquisitions (M&A), strategic analysis and operational projects.

This split demonstrated an 87/22 rule: the M&A work was wildly profitable, giving 87 per cent of profits for 22 per cent of revenues. Efforts were redoubled to sell more M&A work!

Operational projects for old clients, when analysed separately, turned out at about break-even, while large losses were made on operational projects for new clients. This led to a decision not to undertake the latter, while old clients were either charged much more for this kind of project or encouraged to farm them out to specialist operational consultancies.

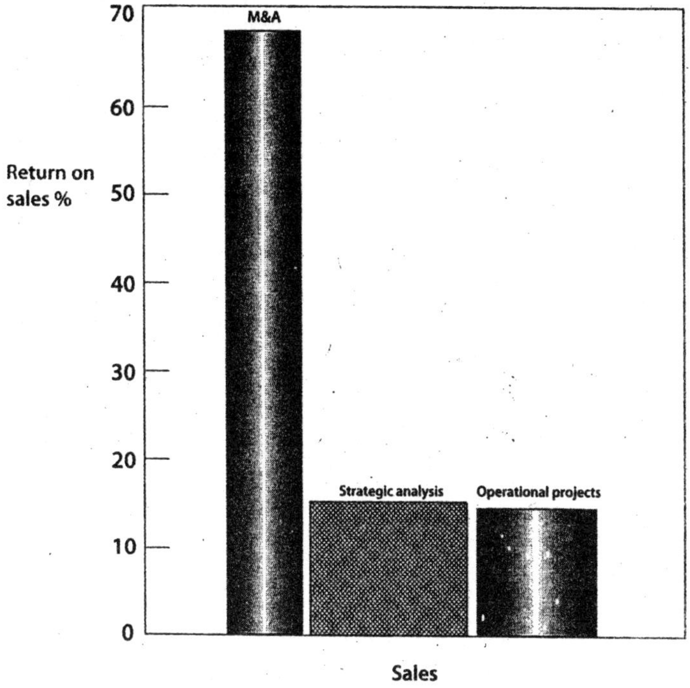

Figure 23 Strategy Consulting Inc, chart of profitability by project type

Segmentation is the key to understanding and driving up profitability

The best way to examine the profitability of your business is to break it down into *competitive segments*. While analyses by product, customer or any other relevant split are usually very valuable, the greatest insights come from a combination of customers and products into 'dollops' of business defined with reference to your most important competitors. Although this is not as difficult as it may sound, very few organizations break up their business in this way, so a short exposition is necessary.

What is a competitive segment?

A competitive segment is a part of your business where you face a different competitor or different competitive dynamics.

Take any part of your business that comes to mind: a product, a customer, a product line sold to a customer type, or any other split that may be important to you (for example, consultants may think of M&A work). Now ask yourself two simple questions:

➤ *Do you face a different main competitor in this part of your business compared to the rest of it?* If the answer is yes, then that part of the business is a separate competitive segment (or simply segment for short).

If you are up against a specialist competitor, your profitability will depend on the interaction of your product and service against theirs. Which do consumers prefer? And what is your total cost to deliver the product or service relative to your competitor's? Your profitability will be as much determined by your competitor as by anything else.

It is therefore sensible to think of this area of your business separately, to determine a strategy for it that will beat (or collude with) your competitor. It is certainly sensible to look at its profitability separately too: you may have a surprise.

But even if the part of your business you are looking at

has the same competitor as another part of your business (for example, your main competitor in Product A is the same as in Product B), then you need to ask another question.

➤ *Do you and your competitor have the same ratio of sales or market share in the two areas, or are they relatively stronger in one area and you relatively stronger in another?*

For example, if you have 20 per cent market share in Product A and the largest competitor has 40 per cent (they are twice as big as you), is it the same ratio in Product B: are they twice as big as you there? If you have 15 per cent market share in Product B but your competitor only has 10 per cent, then there is a different relative competitive position in the two products.

There will be real reasons for this. Consumers may prefer your brand in Product B but your competitor's in Product A. Possibly the competitor doesn't care much about what happens in Product B. Perhaps you are efficient and price competitive in Product B whereas the reverse is true in Product A. At this stage you don't need to know the reasons. All you need to do is observe that, although you face the same competitor, the balance of advantage is different in the two areas. They are therefore separate segments and will probably exhibit different profitability.

Thinking about competitors puts you straight on to the key business splits

Instead of starting with a conventional business definition, such as a product or the output from different parts of your organization, thinking about competitive segments lobs you straight at the most important way to split and think about your business.

At the instrumentation company referred to earlier, managers just could not agree among themselves how to analyse the business. Some thought that products were the key dimension. The view of others was that the most important split was whether the customers were in the pipeline business (broadly, oil companies) or in continuous process industries (such as food manufacturers). A third faction held that the US business was very different from the export business. Since they started from different assumptions, all of which were to some degree valid, it was very difficult to make progress either in organizing the business or in communicating with each other.

Dividing the business into competitive segments demolished these arguments. The rule is simple: if you don't face different competitors, or different relative competitive positions, it's not a separate segment. We quickly arrived at a rather inelegant, but very clear, set of segments that everyone could understand.

For a start, it was clear that the competitors were very different in most, but not all, products. Where the competitors were the same, with similar relative competitive positions, we lumped the products together. In most other cases we kept the products apart.

Then we asked whether the competitive positions were different for pipeline customers as distinct from process customers. In all but one product, the answer was no. But in that one product, liquid density machines, the largest competitors were different. We therefore settled for two segments here: liquid density pipeline and liquid density process.

	$000		
Segment	Sales	Profits	Return on sales (%)
1	2,250	1,030	45.8
2	3,020	1,310	43.4
3	5,370	2,298	42.8
4	2,000	798	39.9
5	1,750	532	30.4
6	17,000	5,110	30.1
7	3,040	610	25.1
8	7,845	1,334	17.0
9	4,224	546	12.9
10	13,000	1,300	10.0
11	21,900	1,927	8.8
12	18,100	779	4.3
13	10,841	(364)	(3.4)
14	5,030	(820)	(15.5)
15	4,000	(3,010)	(75.3)
Total	119,370	13,380	11.2

Figure 24 Electronic Instruments Inc, table of profitability by segment

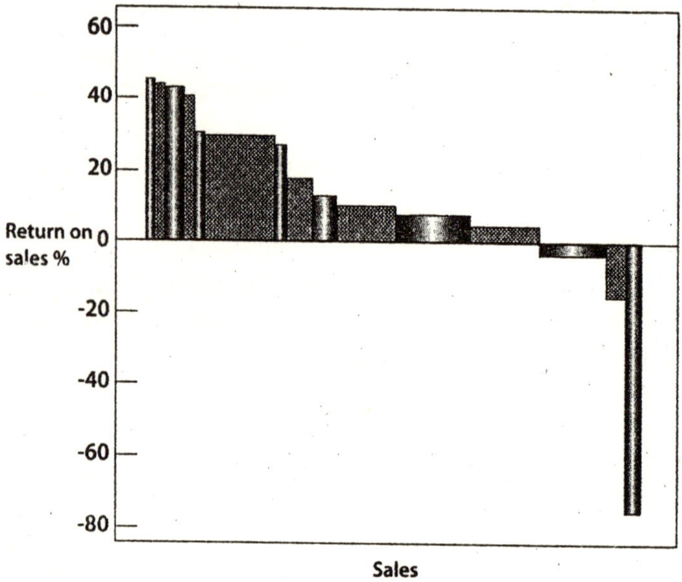

Figure 25 Electronic Instruments Inc, chart of profitability by segment

Finally, we asked whether the competitors or competitive positions were different in each segment in the US and in international business. In most cases the answer was yes. If the international business was significant enough, we asked the same question for different countries: was it the same competitor in the UK as in France or Asia? Where the competitors were different, we subdivided the business into separate segments.

We ended up with a patchwork quilt of 15 large segments (very small ones we reaggregated to avoid unnecessary work), usually defined by product and geographic region, but in one case by product and customer type (this was liquid density, where the segments were liquid density pipeline worldwide and liquid density process worldwide). Each segment had a different competitor or different competitive positions. We then analysed the split of sales and profits for each of the segments, and this is shown in Figures 24 and 25.

To highlight the imbalance between the split of revenues and profits, we can again construct either an 80/20 Table (Figure 26) or an 80/20 Chart (Figure 27).

We can see from these figures that the top six segments comprise only 26.3 per cent of total sales, but 82.9 per cent of profits: so here we have an 83/26 rule.

What did Electronic Instruments do to boost profits?

Figures 26 and 27 focused attention on three types of business.

The most profitable quarter of the business, segments 1–6, was classified initially as top priority A businesses, to be grown most aggressively. More than 80 per cent of profits came from these segments, yet they were receiving only an average amount of management time in line with their turnover. A decision was taken to raise the amount of time spent on these businesses to two-thirds of the total. The salesforce focused on trying to sell more of these products, both to existing customers and to new ones. It was realized that the group could afford to offer extra services or to cut prices slightly and still enjoy very good returns.

The second set of businesses comprised segments 7–12. In total these made up 57 per cent of total sales and 49 per cent of total profits; in other words, on average, slightly below-average

Segment	Percentage of sales Type	Percentage of sales Cumulative	Percentage of profits Type	Percentage of profits Cumulative
1	1.9	1.9	7.7	7.7
2	2.5	4.4	9.8	17.5
3	4.5	8.9	17.2	34.7
4	1.7	10.6	6.0	40.7
5	1.5	12.1	4.0	44.7
6	14.2	26.3	38.2	82.9
7	2.5	28.8	4.6	87.5
8	6.6	35.4	10.0	97.5
9	3.5	38.9	4.1	101.6
10	10.9	49.8	9.7	111.3
11	18.3	68.1	14.4	125.7
12	15.2	83.3	5.8	131.5
13	9.1	92.4	–2.7	128.8
14	4.2	96.6	–6.0	122.6
15	3.4	100.0	–22.6	100.0

Figure 26 Electronic Instruments Inc, 80/20 Table of sales and profits by segment

profitability. These segments were classified as B priority, although clearly some segments in this category (such as 7 and 8) were more interesting than others (such as 11 and 12). The priority to be accorded to these segments also depended on the answers to the two questions posed at the start of the chapter, that is, on whether each segment was a good market to be in and on how well the company was positioned in each segment. The answers to these questions are described in the final part of this chapter.

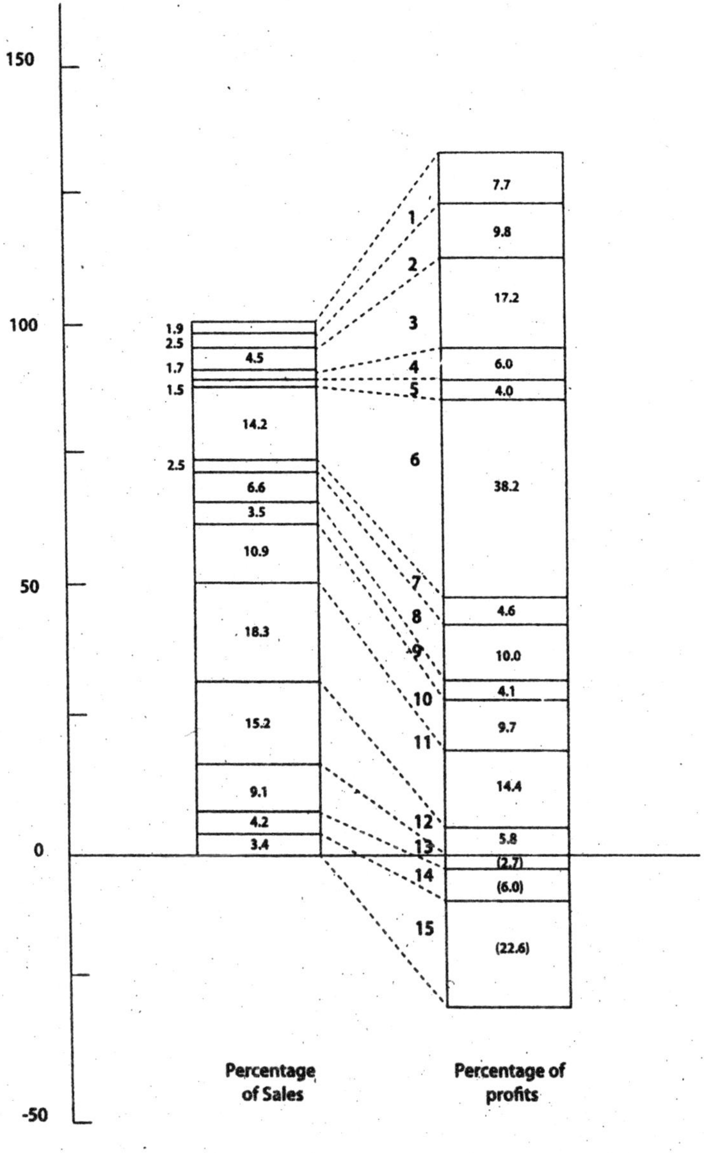

Figure 27 Electronic Instruments Inc, 80/20 Chart of profitability by segment

Priority	Segments	Percentage of sales	Percentage of profits	Actions
A	1–6	26.3	82.9	Raise sales effort Raise management time Flexibility on price
B	7–12	57.0	48.5	Lower management time Lower sales effort Raise some prices
X	13–15	16.7	(31.4)	Review viability
Total		100.0	100.0	

Figure 28 Electronic Instruments Inc, result of 80/20 Analysis

At this stage, a decision was taken to cut the amount of management time spent on the B segments from around 60 per cent to about half this level. Prices on some of the less profitable segments were also raised.

The third category, designated X priority, comprised the loss-making segments 13–15. A decision on what to do about these segments was deferred, as for the B category, until after analysis of market attractiveness and the strength of the company's position in each market.

Provisionally, however, it was possible to reset priorities as laid out in Figure 28.

Before reaching final decisions on any segment, however, the instrumentation group's top management examined the two other questions, besides profitability, that are key to strategy:

➤ Is the segment an attractive market to be in?
➤ How well is the firm positioned in each segment?

Figure 29 shows the final strategy conclusions for Electronic Instruments Inc.

Segment	Market attractive?	Firm well positioned?	Profitability
1	Yes	Yes	Very high
2	Yes	Yes	Very high
3	Yes	Yes	Very high
4	Yes	Yes	Very high
5	Yes	Yes	High
6	Yes	Yes	High
7	Yes	Moderately	High
8	Yes	Moderately	Fairly high
9	Yes	No	OK
10	Not very	Yes	OK
11	Not very	Yes	OK
12	No	Moderately	Poor
13	Yes	Improving	Loss making
14	No	Moderately	Loss making
15	No	No	Loss making

Figure 29 Electronic Instruments Inc, strategic diagnosis

What actions followed this diagnosis?

All of the A profit segments were also attractive markets – they were growing, had high barriers to entry for new competitors, had more demand than capacity, faced no threat from competing technologies and had high bargaining power *vis-à-vis* both customers and component suppliers. As a result, nearly all the competitors in these markets made good money.

My client was also well positioned in each segment, meaning that it had a high market share and was one of the top three suppliers. Its technology was above average and its cost position better than average (that is, lower cost) compared to its competitors.

Since these were also the most profitable segments, the analysis confirmed the implications of the 80/20 profit comparison. Segments 1–6 therefore remained A segments and effort was concentrated on keeping all existing business and gaining market share in these segments by increasing sales to current customers and converting new ones.

The strategy could now be refined for some of the other segments in the B category. Segment 9 was interesting. Profitability was moderate, but this was not because the market was unattractive: on the contrary, it was highly attractive, with most of the other players making very good profits. But my client had a low market share and a high cost position in this segment, largely because it was using old technology.

To update the technology would have taken a terrific effort and would have been very expensive. A decision was made, therefore, to 'harvest' the segment, which meant cutting the effort going to protect the business and raising prices. This was expected to lead to a loss in sales but, for a time, to higher profits. In fact, cutting the effort and raising prices did raise margins, but led to very little loss of sales in the short term. It turned out that the customers were mainly locked in to the old technology themselves and had little choice of alternative suppliers until they switched over to the new technology. For my client profitability rose from 12.9 per cent to over 20 per cent, although it was recognized that this might be a temporary fillip.

Segments 10 and 11 were ones where the instrumentation group had leading market shares, but they were structurally unattractive markets. Market size was declining, there was overcapacity and the customers held all the cards and could negotiate very keen prices. Despite the fact that it was a market leader, my client decided to deemphasize these segments and all new investment was cancelled.

Although for different reasons, the same decision applied to segment 12. The market was even more unattractive and the firm had only a moderate market share. All new marketing programmes, as well as investments, were sidelined.

What about the X category, the loss makers? Here it was found that two of the three segments, 14 and 15, were large but deeply unattractive markets in which the firm was in any case only a marginal player. A decision was made to leave both segments, in one case by selling part of a factory to a competitor. The price realized was very low, but at least there was some cash benefit and some jobs were preserved in addition to the losses being stopped. In the other case operations had to be closed altogether.

Segment 13, also in the X group, experienced a different fate. Although the group lost money in this business, it was a structurally attractive market: growing at 10 per cent per annum and with most competitors making high returns. In fact, although the group was making a loss after allocating all costs, the gross margin in the segment was quite high. Its problem was that it had only entered the market the previous year and was having to make heavy investments in technology and sales effort. But it was gaining market share and, if it kept up its rate of progress, could hope to become one of the largest suppliers within three years. At that stage, with higher sales to spread the costs, it could expect to make high returns. It decided to put even more effort into segment 13 so that the group could become a 'scale player' (that is, operate at the minimum size necessary to be profitable) as soon as possible.

Don't take 80/20 Analysis to simplistic conclusions

Segment 13 in the above example helps to illustrate the point that 80/20 Analysis of profits does not give us all the right answers. The analysis is bound to be a snapshot at a point in time and cannot (to start with) provide a picture of the trend or of forces that could change profitability. Profitability analysis of the 80/20 type is a necessary but not a sufficient condition of good strategy.

On the other hand, it is undoubtedly true that the best way to start making money is to stop losing money. Note that, with the exception of segment 13, the simple 80/20 profit analysis would have given more or less the right result in 14 out of the 15 segments, comprising over 90 per cent of revenues. This does not mean that strategic analysis should stop with 80/20 Analysis, but that it should start with it. For the full answer you must look at segment market attractiveness and at how well the firm is positioned in each segment. The actions taken by the instrumentation group are summarized in Figure 30.

Segments	Priority	Characteristics	Actions
1–6	A	Attractive markets Good market shares High profitability	Heavy management focus Sales effort raised Flexibility to gain sales
7–8	B	Attractive markets Moderate positions Good profitability	Hold position No special initiatives
9	C	Attractive market Poor technology and market share	Harvest (lower costs, raise prices)
10–11	C	Unattractive markets Good market shares Profitability OK	Less effort
12	C–	Unattractive market Moderate position Profitability poor	Much less effort
13	A	Attractive market Subscale but improving position Loss making	Gain share quickly
14–15	Z	Unattractive markets Moderate/poor positions Loss making	Sell/close

Figure 30 Electronic Instruments Inc, actions taken after all 80/20 Analyses

80/20 as a guide to the future – developing your firm into a different animal

This concludes our strategic review of existing business segments, where it is advisable to start with 80/20 profit analyses. As we have seen, these analyses are indispensable in arriving at segment strategy. But we have still not by any means exhausted the use of the 80/20 Principle in strategy. The principle is also of enormous value in identifying the next leaps forward for your business.

We tend to assume that our organizations, and our industries, are doing pretty much the best they can. We tend to think that our business world is highly competitive and has reached some sort of equilibrium or end-game. Nothing could be further from the truth!

It would be far better to start from the proposition that your industry is all screwed up and could be structured much more effectively to provide what customers want. And as far as your organization is concerned, your ambition could be to transform it within the next decade, so that in 10 years' time your people will look back, shake their heads ruefully and say to each other: 'I can't believe we used to do things that way. We must have been crazy!'

Innovation is the name of the game: it is absolutely crucial to future competitive advantage. We tend to think that innovation is difficult, but with creative use of the 80/20 Principle innovation can be both easy and fun! Consider, for example, the following ideas:

➤ 80 per cent of the profits made by all industries are made by 20 per cent of industries. Make a list of the most profitable industries that you are aware of – such as pharmaceuticals or consulting – and ask why your industry can't be more like these.

➤ 80 per cent of the profits made in any industry are made by 20 per cent of firms. If you aren't one of these, what are they doing right that you're not?

➤ 80 per cent of value perceived by customers relates to 20 per cent of what an organization does. What is that 20 per cent in your case? What is stopping you doing more of it? What is preventing you from 'making' an even more extreme version of that 20 per cent?

➤ 80 per cent of what an industry does yields no more than 20 per cent of the benefit to its customers. What is that 80 per cent? Why not abolish it? For instance, if you are a banker, why do you have branches? If you provide services, why not organize their provision via the telephone and the personal computer? Where might less be better, as with self-service? Could the customer be engaged in providing some of the services?

➤ 80 per cent of the benefit from any product or service can be provided at 20 per cent of the cost. Many consumers would buy a stripped-down, very cheap product. Is anyone providing it in your industry?

➤ 80 per cent of any industry's profits come from 20 per cent of its customers. Do you have a disproportionate share of these? If not, what would you need to do to get it?

Why do you need people?

Some examples of industry transformations may help. My grandmother used to run a corner grocery store. She received orders, would pick them out and then I (or some more reliable boy) would deliver them on a bike. Then a supermarket opened in the town. It engaged its customers in picking their own groceries and carting them back home. In return the supermarket offered a wider range, lower prices and a car park. Soon my grandmother's customers were flocking to the supermarket.

Some industries, such as petrol retailing, cottoned on to self-service quickly. Others, such as furniture retailing and banking, thought it was not for them. Every few years a new competitor, such as Ikea in furniture, proves that there is new life in the very old idea of self-service.

Discounting is also a perennial transformation strategy. Offer less choice, fewer frills, less service and much cheaper prices. 80 per cent of sales are concentrated in 20 per cent of products – just stock these. Another place I used to work, a wine merchant, stocked 30 different types of claret. Who needed that amount of choice? The firm was taken over by a discount chain and now a wine warehouse has opened up down the road.

Who would have thought 50 years ago that people would have wanted fast-food outlets? And today, who realizes that accessible mega-restaurants, the sort that offer a limited and predictable menu in glitzy surroundings at reasonable prices but insist that you give back the table after 90 minutes, constitute a death warrant for traditional owner-run restaurants?

Why do we insist on using people to do things that machines can do much more cheaply? When will airlines start to use robots to serve you? Most people prefer humans, but machines are more reliable and much cheaper. Machines may give 80 per cent of the benefit at 20 per cent of the cost. In some cases, as with cash machines (automatic teller machines, also known as holes in the wall), they provide a much better service, much faster and at a fraction of the cost. One day soon only old fogies like me will prefer to deal with humans and even I will have my doubts.

Are carpets obsolete?

I want to leave you to your own imagination. Just one final example, where use of the 80/20 Principle has transformed a company's fortunes and could conceivably change a whole industry.

Consider the Interface Corporation of Georgia, now an $800 million carpet supplier. It used to sell carpets; now it leases them, installing carpet tiles rather than whole carpets. Interface realized that 20 per cent of any carpet receives 80 per cent of the wear. Normally a carpet is replaced when most of it is still perfectly good. Under Interface's leasing scheme, carpets are regularly inspected and any worn or damaged carpet tile is replaced. This lowers costs for both Interface and the customer. A trivial 80/20 observation has transformed one company and could lead to widespread future changes in the industry.

Conclusion

The 80/20 Principle suggests that your strategy is wrong. If you make most of your money out of a small part of your activity, you should turn your company upside down and concentrate your efforts on multiplying this small part. Yet this is only part of the answer. Behind the need for focus lurks an even more powerful truth about business, and it is to this theme that we turn next.

5 Simple Is Beautiful

My effort is in the direction of simplicity. People in general have so little and it costs so much to buy even the barest necessities (let alone the luxuries to which I think everyone is entitled) because nearly everything we make is much more complex than it needs to be. Our clothing, our food, our household furnishings – all could be much simpler than they now are and at the same time be better-looking.

Henry Ford[1]

We saw in the previous chapter that nearly all businesses have within them chunks of business with widely varying profitability. The 80/20 Principle suggests something quite outrageous as a working hypothesis: that one-fifth of a typical company's revenues account for four-fifths of its profits and cash. Conversely, four-fifths of the average company's revenues account for only one-fifth of profits and cash. This is a bizarre hypothesis. If we assume that one such business has sales of £100 million and total profits of £5 million, for the

80/20 Principle to be correct £20 million of sales has to produce £4 million of profits – a return on sales of 20 per cent; while £80 million of sales has to produce just £1 million of profits, a return on sales of just 1.25 per cent. This means that the top fifth of business is *sixteen* times more profitable than the rest of the business.

What is extraordinary is that when it is tested, the hypothesis generally turns out to be correct, or not very far wide of the mark.

How can this be true? It is intuitively obvious that some business chunks may be considerably more profitable than others. But 16 times better? It almost beggars belief. And, routinely, executives who commission product-line profitability exercises often do refuse to believe the results when first presented with them. Even when they have checked the assumptions and verified them, they still end up baffled.

The next stage is often for managers to refuse to get rid of the 80 per cent of business that is unprofitable, on the apparently reasonable grounds that the 80 per cent makes a very large contribution to overheads. Removing the 80 per cent, they say, would clearly decrease profits, because you simply couldn't remove 80 per cent of your overhead in any sensible time frame.

When faced with these objections, corporate analysts or consultants generally give way to the managers. Only the most horribly unprofitable business is removed. And only minor efforts are made to increase the extremely profitable business.

Yet all this is a dreadful compromise, based on a misunderstanding. Few people stop to ask *why* the unprofitable business is so bad. Even fewer stop to think whether you could in practice, as well as in theory, have a business solely composed of the most profitable chunks and get rid of 80 per cent of the overhead.

The truth is that the unprofitable business is so unprofitable *because* it requires the overheads and because having so many different chunks of business makes the organization horrendously complicated. It is equally true that the very profitable business does not require the overheads, or only a very small portion of them. You *could* have a business solely composed of the profitable business and it *could* make the same absolute returns, provided that you organized things differently.

And why is this so? The reason is the same. It is that simple is beautiful. Business people seem to love complexity. No sooner is a simple business successful than its managers pour vast amounts of energy into making it very much more complicated. But business returns abhor complexity. As the business becomes more complex, its returns fall dramatically. This is not just because more marginal business is being taken. It is also because the act of making a business more complex depresses returns more effectively than any other means known to humanity.

It follows that the process can be reversed. A complex business can be made more simple and returns can soar. All it takes is an understanding of the costs of complexity (or the value of simplicity) and courage to remove at least four-fifths of lethal managerial overhead.

Simple is beautiful – complex is ugly

Those of us who believe in the 80/20 Principle will never succeed in transforming industry until we can demonstrate that simple is beautiful and why. Unless people understand this, they will never be willing to give up 80 per cent of their current business and overheads.

So we need to go back to basics and revise the common view of the roots of business success. To do so, we must get involved in a current controversy over whether size in business is a help or a hindrance. By resolving this dispute, we will also be able to show why simple is beautiful.

For something very interesting, and unprecedented, is happening to our industrial structure. Since the Industrial Revolution companies have become both bigger and more diversified. Until the end of the nineteenth century, nearly all companies were national or subnational, having the vast bulk of their revenues confined to their home country; and nearly all were in just one line of business. The twentieth century saw a series of transformations, changing the nature both of business and of our daily lives. First, thanks largely to Henry Ford's sensationally successful quest to 'democratize' the automobile, there was the burgeoning power of the assembly line, multiplying the revenues of the average firm, creating mass branded consumer goods for the first time in history, slashing the real cost of those goods and giving more and more power to the largest enterprises. Then there was the emergence of so-called multinational enterprises, that initially took the Americas and Europe, and later the whole world, as their canvas. Next came the conglomerates, a new breed of corporation that refused to confine itself to one line of business and rapidly spread its tentacles across many industrial sectors and a myriad of products. Then the invention and refinement of the hostile takeover, fuelled equally by management ambition and the financial lubrication of leverage, gave further impetus to size. Finally, in the last 30 years of the century, the determination of industrial leaders, mainly from Japan, to seize global leadership in their priority markets and as much market share as feasible provided the final reinforcement to the cult of corporate size.

For various reasons, therefore, the first 75 years of the twentieth century witnessed a progressive and apparently unstoppable expansion in the size of industrial enterprise and, until recently, in the proportion of business activity taken by the largest firms. But in the last two decades of that century, the latter trend suddenly, and dramatically, went into reverse. In 1979, the Fortune 500 largest US firms accounted for nearly 60 per cent of US gross national product, but by the early 1990s this had slumped to just 40 per cent.

Does this mean that small is beautiful?

No. This is definitely the wrong answer. There is absolutely nothing wrong with the belief long held by business leaders and strategists that scale and market share are valuable. Extra scale gives greater volume over which to spread fixed costs, especially the overhead costs that make up the lion's share of all costs (now that factories have been made so efficient). Market share, too, helps to raise prices. The most popular firm, that with the highest market share, the best reputation and brands and the most loyal customers, should command a price premium over lower-share competitors.

Yet why is it that larger firms are losing market share to smaller firms? And why does it happen that in practice, as opposed to theory, the advantages of scale and market share fail to translate into higher profitability? Why is it that firms often see their sales mushroom yet their returns on sales and capital actually fall, rather than rise as the theory would predict?

The cost of complexity

The most important answer is the *cost of complexity*. The problem is not extra scale, but extra complexity.

Additional scale, without additional complexity, will always give lower unit costs. To deliver to one customer more of one product or service, provided that it is exactly the same, will always raise returns.

Yet additional scale is rarely just more of the same. Even if the customer is the same, the extra volume usually comes from adapting an existing product, providing a new product and/or adding more service. This requires expensive overhead costs that are usually hidden, but always real. And if new customers are involved it is far worse. There are high initial costs in recruiting customers and they generally have different needs to existing customers, causing even greater complexity and cost.

Internal complexity has huge hidden costs

When new business is different to existing business, even if it is only slightly different, costs tend to go up, not just pro rata with the volume increase but well ahead of it. This is because complexity slows down simple systems and requires the intervention of managers to deal with the new requirements. The cost of stopping and starting again, of communication (and miscommunication) between extra people and above all the cost of the 'gaps' between people, when partially completed work is set down to await someone else's intervention and later picked up and passed on into another gap – all these costs are horrendous and all the more insidious because they are largely invisible. If the communication needs to straddle different divisions, buildings and countries, the result is even worse.

How this works is shown in Figure 31. Competitor B is larger than competitor A, yet has higher costs. This is not because the scale curve – additional volume equals lower costs – doesn't work. Rather, it is because B's extra volume has been bought at the cost of higher complexity. The effect of this is massive, and much greater than the additional cost that is visible relative to A. The scale curve operates, but its benefits are overturned by the extra complexity.

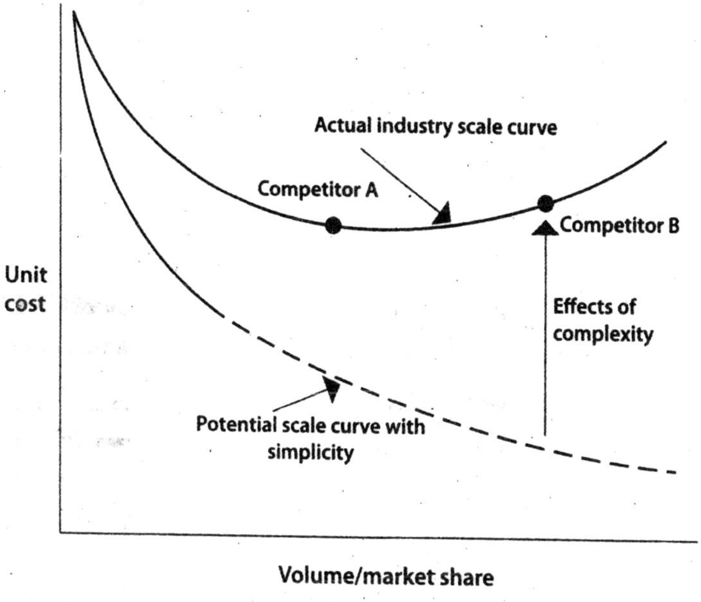

Figure 31 The cost of complexity

Simple is beautiful explains the 80/20 Principle

Understanding the cost of complexity allows us to take a major leap forward in the debate about corporate size. It is not that small is beautiful. All other things being equal, big is beautiful. But all other things are not equal. Big is only ugly and expensive because it is complex. Big can be beautiful. But it is simple that is *always* beautiful.

Even management scientists are belatedly realizing the value of simplicity. A study of 39 middle-sized German companies, led by Gunter Rommel,[2] found that only one characteristic differentiated the winners from the less successful firms: simplicity. The winners sold a narrower range of products to fewer customers and also had fewer suppliers. The study concludes that a simple organization was best at selling complicated products.

This mental breakthrough helps to explain why and how the seemingly outrageous claims of the 80/20 Principle, applied to corporate profits, can actually be true. A fifth of revenues can produce four-fifths of profits. The top 20 per cent of revenues can be 16 times more profitable than the bottom 20 per cent (or, where the bottom 20 per cent makes a loss, infinitely more profitable!). Simple is beautiful explains a large part of why the 80/20 Principle works:

➤ Simple and pure market share is much more valuable than has previously been recognized. The returns from pure scale have been obscured by the cost of complexity associated with impure scale. And different chunks of business have usually had different competitors and different relative strength *vis-à-vis* those competitors. Where a business is dominant in its narrowly defined niche, it is likely to make several times the returns earned in niches where one faces a dominant competitor (the mirror image).

➤ Parts of the business that are mature and simple can be amazingly profitable. Cutting the number of products, customers and suppliers usually leads to higher profits, partly because you can have the luxury of just focusing on the most profitable activities and customers, but partly also because the costs of complexity – in the form of overheads and management – can be slashed.

➤ In different products, firms often have differences in the extent to which they buy in goods and services from the outside (in the jargon, outsourcing). Outsourcing is a terrific way to cut complexity and costs. The best approach is to decide which is the part of the value-adding chain (R&D–manufacturing–distribution–selling–marketing–servicing) where your company has the greatest comparative advantage – and then ruthlessly outsource everything else. This can take out most of the costs of complexity and enable dramatic reductions in headcount, as well as speeding up the time it takes you to get a product to market. The result: much lower costs and often significantly higher prices too.

➤ It can enable you to do away with all central functions and costs. If you are just in one line of business, you don't need a head office, regional head offices or functional offices. And the abolition of the head office can have an electric effect on profits. The key problem with head offices is not their cost. It is the way they take away real responsibility and initiative from those who do the work and add the value to customers. For the first time, corporations can centre themselves around customer needs rather than around the management hierarchy.

Before the head office is abolished, different chunks of business attract different degrees of head office cost and interference. The most profitable products and services are usually those that are left to get on with their own life without any 'help' from the centre. This is why, when 80/20 profitability exercises have been carried out, executives are often staggered to learn that the most neglected areas are the most profitable. It is no accident. (And one of the unfortunate byproducts of 80/20 Analysis is sometimes that the most profitable areas get a lot more attention from managers at the top. As a result, they can begin to drop down the profitability league table.)

➤ Finally, where a chunk of business is simple, the chances are that it is closer to the customer. There is less management to get in the way. Customers can be listened to and feel that they are important. People are willing to pay a lot more for this. For customers, the quest for self-importance is at least as important as the quest for value. Simplicity raises prices as well as lowering costs.

Contribution to overhead: one of the lamest excuses for inaction

Frequently, managers faced with the results of 80/20 Analysis protest that they cannot just focus on the most profitable segments. They point out that the less profitable segments, and even the loss-making segments, make a positive contribution to overheads. This is one of the lamest and most self-serving defence mechanisms ever contrived.

If you focus on the most profitable segments, you can grow them surprisingly fast – nearly always at 20 per cent a year and sometimes even faster. Remember that the initial position and customer franchise are strong, so it's a lot easier than growing the business overall. The need for overhead coverage from unprofitable segments can disappear pretty quickly.

Yet the truth is that you don't need to wait. 'If your eye offends you, pluck it out!' Just remove the offending overhead. If your will is strong, you can always do it. The less profitable segments can sometimes be sold, with or without their overheads, and always be closed. (Do not listen to accountants who bleat about 'exit costs'; a lot of these are just numbers on a page with no cash cost. Even where there is a cash cost, there is normally a very quick payback, one that will be much quicker, because of the value of simplicity, than the bean counters will ever tell you.) A third option, often the most profitable, is to harvest these segments, deliberately losing market share. You let go of the less profitable customers and products, cut off most support and sales effort, raise prices and allow sales to decline at 5–20 per cent while you laugh all the way to the bank.

Go for the most simple 20 per cent

What is most simple and standardized is hugely more productive and cost effective than what is complex. The simplest messages are the most appealing and universal: to colleagues, consumers and suppliers. The simplest structures and process flows are at once the most attractive and the lowest cost. Letting the customer access your business system – as with all forms of self-service – creates choice, economy, speed and spend.

Always try to identify the simplest 20 per cent of any product range, process, marketing message, sales channel, product design, product manufacture, service delivery or customer feedback mechanism. Cultivate the simplest 20 per cent. Refine it until it is as simple as you can make it. Standardize delivery of a simple product or service on as universal and global a basis as possible. Pass up thrills, bells and whistles. Make the simplest 20 per cent as high quality and consistent as imaginable. Whenever something has become complex, simplify it; if you cannot, eliminate it.

Reducing complexity at Corning

How can a business in trouble use the 80/20 Principle to reduce complexity and raise profits? An excellent case study is provided by Corning, which produces ceramic substrates for automobile exhaust systems in Greenville, Ohio, and Kaiserslautern, Germany.[3]

In 1992 the US business was doing badly and the next year the German market fell sharply. Instead of panicking, the Corning executives took a long, hard look at the profitability of all their products.

As in almost every firm around the world, the Corning

executives had used a standard cost approach to decide what to produce. But standard cost systems are one of the most important reasons the 80/20 Principle has so much to add: standard cost systems make it impossible to know true product profitability, largely because they do not differentiate between high- and low-volume products. When variable costs – such as overtime, training, equipment modifications and downtime – were fully allocated at Corning, the results caused astonishment.

Take two products made at Kaiserslautern: a high-volume, simple, symmetrically shaped ceramic substrate, disguised here as the R10; and a much lower-volume product, the R5, an odd-shaped substrate. The standard cost of the R5 was 20 per cent more than that of the R10. But when the extra engineering and shopfloor effort to produce the R5 were fully costed, it turned out to have an incredible cost, around 500,000 per cent greater than the R10!

Yet, on reflection, the data could be believed. The R10 virtually made itself. The R5 required expensive engineers to hover over it, nudging it to keep within specification. Therefore, if only R10s were made, far fewer engineers would be needed. And that is what happened. By eliminating low-volume, unprofitable products, which contributed little to revenues and negative amounts of profit, engineering capacity was reduced by 25 per cent.

The 50/5 Principle

The Corning analysis kept gravitating towards a very useful cousin of the 80/20 Principle – the 50/5 Principle.

The 50/5 Principle asserts that, typically, 50 per cent of a company's customers, products, components and suppliers will add less than 5 per cent to revenues and profits. Getting rid of the low-volume (and negative-value) 50 per cent of items is the key to reducing complexity.

The 50/5 Principle worked at Corning. Out of 450 products produced at Greenville, half produced 96.3 per cent of revenue; the other 50 per cent yielded just 3.7 per cent. Depending on the period analysed, the German plant showed that the low-volume 50 per cent of products produced only 2–5 per cent of sales. In both locations, the bottom 50 per cent made losses.

More is worse

The road to hell is paved with the pursuit of volume. Volume leads to marginal products, marginal customers and greatly increased managerial complexity. Since complexity is both interesting and rewarding to managers, it is often tolerated or encouraged until it can no longer be afforded. At Corning, they had filled up the plants with loss-making, complicating business. The solution was to cut the number of products by more than half. Instead of dealing with 1000 suppliers, purchases were consolidated through the 200 suppliers who comprised 95 per cent of total supplies (a 95/20 Principle). The organization was streamlined and flattened.

At the heart of the market meltdown, Corning turned away business. This might seem perverse, but it worked. A simpler, smaller operation rapidly restored profits. Less was more.

Managers love complexity

At this point it is worth asking: why do supposedly profit-maximizing organizations become complex, when this plainly destroys value?

One important answer, alas, is that managers love complexity. Complexity is stimulating and intellectually challenging; it leavens boring routine; and it creates interesting jobs for managers. Some people believe that complexity obtrudes when no one is looking. No doubt – but complexity is also sponsored by managers, just as it sponsors them. Most organizations, even ostensibly commercial and capitalist ones, are conspiracies of management against the interests of customers, investors and the outside world generally. Unless firms are facing an economic crisis, or have an unusual leader who favours investors and customers rather than his or her own managers, excess management activity is virtually guaranteed. It is in the interests of the managerial class in charge.[4]

Cost reduction through simplicity

There is thus a natural tendency for business, like life in general, to become overcomplex. All organizations, especially large and complex ones, are inherently inefficient and wasteful. They do not focus on what they should be doing. They should be adding value to their customers and potential customers. Any activity that does not fulfil this goal is unproductive. Yet most large organizations engage in prodigious amounts of expensive, unproductive activity.

Every person and every organization is the product of a coalition and the forces within the coalition are always at war. The war is between the trivial many and the vital few. The trivial many comprise the prevalent inertia and ineffectiveness. The vital few are the breakthrough streaks of effectiveness, brilliance and good fit. Most activity results in little value and little change. A few powerful interventions have massive impact. The war is difficult to observe: it is the same person, the same unit and the same organization which produces both a mass of weak (or negative) output and a smattering of highly valuable output. All we can discern is the overall result; we miss both the garbage and the gems.

It follows that any organization always has great potential for cost reduction and for delivering better value to customers: by simplifying what it does and by eliminating low- or negative-value activities.

Be mindful that:

- waste thrives on complexity; effectiveness requires simplicity
- the mass of activity will always be pointless, poorly conceived, badly directed, wastefully executed and largely beside the point to customers
- a small portion of activity will always be terrifically effective and valued by customers; it is probably not what you think it is; it is opaque and buried within a basket of less effective activity
- all organizations are a mix of productive and unproductive forces: people, relationships and assets
- poor performance is always endemic, hiding behind and succoured by a smaller amount of excellent performance

➤ major improvements are always possible, by doing things differently and by doing less.

Always recall the 80/20 Principle: if you study the output your firm generates, the chances are that a quarter to a fifth of the activity accounts for three-quarters or four-fifths of profits. Multiply that quarter or fifth. Multiply the effectiveness of the rest, or cut it out.

Reducing costs using the 80/20 Principle

All effective techniques to reduce costs use three 80/20 insights: *simplification*, through elimination of unprofitable activity; *focus*, on a few key drivers of improvements; and *comparison of performance*. The last two deserve elaboration.

Be selective

Do not tackle everything with equal effort. Cost reduction is an expensive business!

Identify the areas (perhaps only 20 per cent of the whole business) that have the greatest cost-reduction potential. Concentrate 80 per cent of your efforts here.

> *You don't want to get too bogged down in microanalysis. It can help to apply the 80/20 rule. Ask yourself what are the*

major time sinks that you can cut out, where are the 80 per cent of the time delays and costs in your current processes that you could target, and understand how you would attack those.[5]

To be successful, one has to measure what really counts … most organizations fit Pareto's rule: 80 percent of what is important is supported by 20 percent of the costs … For example, a study in Pacific Bell's customer payment center found that 25 percent of the center's work was devoted to processing 0.1 percent of the payments. A third of the payments were processed twice, and occasionally several times.[6]

In reducing cost or raising product and service quality, remember above all that equal cost does not lead to equal customer satisfaction. A few parts of cost are tremendously productive; but most cost has little or no relationship to what customers value. Identify, treasure and multiply the few productive costs; and get rid of the rest.

Using 80/20 Analysis to pinpoint improvement areas

80/20 Analysis can establish why particular problems arise and focus attention on the key areas for improvement. To take a simple example, let's imagine that you are running a book publishing firm and that your production costs are 30 per cent above budget. Your product manager tells you that there are 1001 reasons for the overrun: sometimes the authors are late with the manuscript, sometimes the proofreaders or index compilers take longer than planned, in many cases the book is longer than planned, the charts and other figures often need correction and there are many other special causes.

One thing you can do is to take a particular time period, say three months, and carefully monitor the causes of all the cost overruns. You should record the main reason for each overrun, and also the financial cost penalty involved.

Figure 32 displays the causes in a table, ranking the most frequent cause at the top and so on.

Causes	Number	Percentage	Cumulative percentage
1 Authors late with corrections	45	30.0	30.0
2 Authors late with original manuscript	37	24.7	54.7
3 Authors make too many corrections	34	22.7	77.4
4 Figures need correction	13	8.6	86.0
5 Book longer than planned	6	4.0	90.0
6 Proofreader late	3	2.0	92.0
7 Index compiler late	3	2.0	94.0
8 Permissions received late	2	1.3	95.3
9 Typesetter's computer fault	1	0.67	96.0
10 Typesetter's correction errors	1	0.67	96.6
11 Schedule changed by editor	1	0.67	97.3
12 Schedule changed by marketing	1	0.67	98.0
13 Schedule changed by printer	1	0.67	98.7
14 Fire at typesetter's	1	0.67	99.3
15 Legal dispute with typesetter	1	0.67	100.0
Total	150	100	100

Figure 32 Causes of publisher's typesetting overruns

Figure 33 converts this information to an 80/20 Chart. To construct this, make the causes bars in descending order of importance, put the number of causes per bar on the left-hand vertical axis and put the cumulative percentage of causes on the right-hand vertical axis. This is easily done and the visual summary of the data is quite powerful.

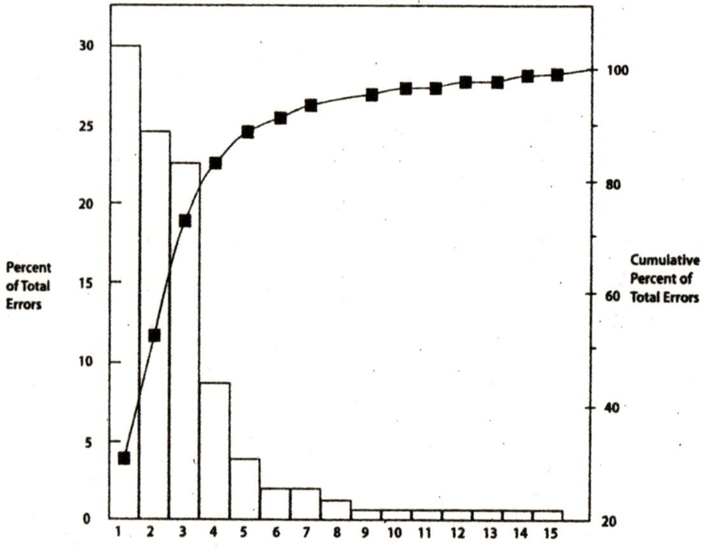

Figure 33 80/20 Chart of causes of publisher's production overruns

We can see from Figure 33 that three of the fifteen problems (exactly 20 per cent) cause nearly 80 per cent of the overruns. The cumulative line flattens out quickly after the first five causes, telling you that you are reaching the 'trivial many' causes.

The major three causes all relate to authors. The publishing house could solve this problem by writing into authors' contracts a clause making them liable for any extra typesetting costs caused by them being late or making too many corrections. A minor change like this would eliminate over 80 per cent of the problem.

Sometimes it is more useful to draw an 80/20 Chart on the basis of the financial impact of the problem (or opportunity) rather than the number of causes. The method is exactly the same.

Compare performance

The 80/20 Principle states that there always are a few high-productivity areas and many low-productivity ones. All of the most effective cost-reduction techniques of the past 30 years have used this insight (often with conscious acknowledgement to the 80/20 Principle) to compare performance. The onus is placed on the majority of laggards to improve performance to the level of the best (sometimes taking the 90th percentile, sometimes the 75th, usually within this range) or else to retire gracefully from the field.

This is not the place to give chapter and verse on cost-reduction/value-improvement techniques such as benchmarking, best demonstrated practice or reengineering. All of these are systematic expansions of the 80/20 Principle and all, if (a big if) pursued relentlessly, can raise value to customers by tremendous amounts. Too often, however, these techniques become the latest, evanescent management fad or self-contained programmes. They stand a much greater chance of success if placed within the context of the very simple 80/20 Principle that should drive all radical action:

- a minority of business activity is useful
- value delivered to customers is rarely measured and always unequal
- great leaps forward require measurement and comparison of the value delivered to customers and what they will pay for it.

Conclusion: simplicity power

Because business is wasteful, and because complexity and waste feed on each other, a simple business will always be better than a complex business. Because scale is normally valuable, for any given level of complexity, it is better to have a larger business. The large and simple business is the best.

The way to create something great is to create something simple. Anyone who is serious about delivering better value to customers can easily do so, by reducing complexity. Any large business is stuffed full of passengers – unprofitable products, processes, suppliers, customers and, heaviest of all, managers. The passengers obstruct the evolution of commerce. Progress requires simplicity; and simplicity requires ruthlessness. This helps to explain why simple is as rare as it is beautiful.

6 Hooking the Right Customers

Those who analyze the reasons for their success know the 80/20 rule applies. Eighty percent of their growth, profitability and satisfaction comes from 20 percent of the clients. At a minimum, firms should identify the top 20 percent to get a clear picture of desirable prospects for future growth.

Vin Manaktala[1]

The 80/20 Principle is essential for doing the right kind of selling and marketing and for relating this to any organization's overall strategy, including the whole process of producing and delivering goods and services. We will show how to use the 80/20 Principle in this way. But first, we have an obligation to clear away a lot of pseudo-intellectual undergrowth about industrialization and marketing. For example, it is often said that we live in a post-industrial world, that firms should not be production led, that they should be marketing led and customer centred. These are, at best, half-truths. A short historical excursion is necessary to explain why.

In the beginning, most firms concentrated on their markets – their important customers – with little or no thought. Marketing as a separate function or activity was not necessary, yet the small business made sure that it looked after its customers.

Then came the Industrial Revolution, which created big business, specialization (Adam Smith's pin factory) and eventually the production line. The natural tendency of big business was to subordinate customer needs to the exigencies of low-cost mass production. Henry Ford famously said that customers could have his Model T in 'any colour as long as it's black'. Until the late 1950s, big business everywhere was overwhelmingly production led.

It is easy for the sophisticated marketeer or businessperson today to sneer at the primitiveness of the production-led approach. In fact the Fordist approach was plainly the right one for its time; the mission to simplify goods and lower their cost, while making them more attractive, is the foundation for today's wealthy consumer society. Products from the low-cost factory progressively made goods in higher and higher categories available (or, in the ghastly phrase, 'affordable') to consumers previously excluded from the market. The creation of a mass market also created spending power that had not previously existed, leading to a virtuous circle of lower-cost production, higher consumption, greater employment, higher purchasing power, greater unit volumes, lower unit costs, higher consumption ... and so on in a progressive, if not unbroken, upward spiral.

Viewed in this light, Henry Ford was not a production-driven troglodite: he was a creative genius who did signal service to ordinary citizens. In 1909, he said that his mission was to 'democratize the automobile'. At the time was laughable: only rich people had cars. But, of course, the mass-produced Model T, provided at a fraction of the cost of earlier cars, set the ball rolling. For good and ill, and on the whole much more good than ill, we enjoy the 'horn of plenty'[2] provided by the Fordist world.

Mass industrialization and innovation did not stop with automobiles. Many products, from fridges to the Sony Walkman or the CD-Rom, could not have been commissioned as a result of market research. Nobody in the nineteenth century would have wanted frozen food, because there were no freezers to keep it in. All the great breakthroughs from the invention of fire and the wheel onward have been triumphs of production that then created their own markets. And it is nonsense to say that we live in a post-industrial world. Services are now being industrialized in the same way that physical products were in the so-called industrial era. Retailing, agriculture, flower production, language, entertainment, teaching, cleaning, hotel provision and even the art of restaurateuring – all these used to be exclusively the province of individual service providers, non-industrializable and non-exportable. Now all these areas are being rapidly industrialized and in some cases globalized.[3]

The 1960s rediscovered marketing and the 1990s rediscovered customers

The success of the production-driven approach, with the focus on making the product, expanding production and driving down costs, eventually highlighted the approach's own deficiencies. In the early 1960s, business school professors like

Theodore Levitt told managers to be marketing led. His legendary *Harvard Business Review* article in 1960 called 'Marketing myopia' encouraged industry to be 'customer satisfying' rather than 'goods producing'. The new gospel was electric. Business people fell over themselves to win the hearts and minds of customers; a relatively new branch of business studies, market research, was vastly expanded in order to discover which new products customers wanted. Marketing became the hot topic at business schools and marketing executives ousted those from production backgrounds as the new generation of CEOs. The mass market was dead; product and customer segmentation became the watchwords of the wise. More recently, in the 1980s and 1990s, customer satisfaction, customer centredness, customer delight and customer obsession became the stated goals of most enlightened and successful corporations.

The customer-led approach is both right and dangerous

It is absolutely right to be marketing led and customer centred. But it can also have dangerous and potentially lethal side effects. If the product range is extended into too many new areas, or if the obsession with customers leads to recruiting more and more marginal consumers, unit costs will rise and returns fall. With additional product range, overhead costs rise sharply, as a result of the cost of complexity. Factory costs are now so low that they comprise only a small part of firms' value added – typically less than 10 per cent of a product's selling price. The vast majority of firms' costs lie outside the factory. These costs can be penal if the product range is too large.

Similarly, chasing too many customers can escalate marketing and selling costs, lead to higher logistical costs and very often, most dangerously of all, permanently lower prevailing selling prices, not just for the new customers, for the old ones too.

The 80/20 Principle is essential here. It can provide a synthesis of the production-led and marketing-led approaches, so that you concentrate only on profitable marketing and profitable customer centredness (as opposed to the unprofitable customer centredness very evident today).

The 80/20 marketing gospel

The markets and customers on which any firm should be centred must be the right ones, typically a small minority of those that the company currently owns. The conventional wisdom on being marketing led and customer centred is typically only 20 per cent correct.

There are three golden rules:

➤ Marketing, and the whole firm, should focus on providing a stunning product and service in 20 per cent of the existing product line – that small part generating 80 per cent of fully costed profits.

➤ Marketing, and the whole firm, should devote extraordinary endeavour towards delighting, keeping for ever and expanding the sales to the 20 per cent of customers who provide 80 per cent of the firm's sales and/or profits.

➤ There is no real conflict between production and

marketing. You will only be successful in marketing if what you are marketing is different and, for your target customers, either unobtainable elsewhere, or provided by you in a product/service/price package that is much better value than is obtainable elsewhere. These conditions are unlikely to apply in more than 20 per cent of your current product line; and you are likely to obtain more than 80 per cent of your true profits from this 20 per cent. And if these conditions apply in almost none of your product lines, your only hope is to innovate. At this stage, the creative marketeer must become product led. All innovation is necessarily product led. You cannot innovate without a new product or service.

Be marketing led in the few right product/market segments

Products accounting for 20 per cent of your revenues are likely to comprise 80 per cent of your profits, once you take into account all the costs, including overheads, associated with each product. It is even more likely that 20 per cent of your products account for 80 per cent of your profits. Bill Roatch, the cosmetics buyer for Raley's, a retailer in Sacramento, California, comments:

> *Eighty percent of your profit comes from 20% of the products. The question [for a retailer] is, how much of the 80% can you afford to eliminate [without the risk of losing stature in cosmetics] ... Ask the cosmetics franchisers and they say it'll hurt. Ask the retailers and they'll say you can cut some.*[4]

The logical thing to do is to expand the area devoted to the 20 per cent of most profitable and best-selling lipsticks and to delist some of the slowest-selling product. Major promotion can then be undertaken in-store on the most profitable 20 per cent, in cooperation with the suppliers of these top products. Note that there are always apparently good reasons trotted out as to why you need the unprofitable 80 per cent of products, in this case the fear of 'losing stature' by having a smaller product line. Excuses like this rest on the strange view that shoppers like to see a lot of product they have no intention of buying which distracts attention from the product they like to buy. Whenever this has been put to the test, the answer in 99 per cent of cases is that delisting marginal products boosts profits while not harming customer perceptions one jot.

A company making automobile appearance products – waxes, polishes and other car-cleaning accessories – marketed its products through car washes. In theory this was logical, since car-wash owners would make incremental profits through each sale of appearance products simply by putting them on display in space that would otherwise serve no useful function. The idea was that they would give the products premium floor space and make an effort to sell them.

But when the auto appearance product business was sold and new management conducted a comprehensive sales analysis, they found that 'the classic 80/20 rule applied – meaning 80 percent of the company's revenues were generated at 20 percent of its retail sites'.[5] When the new CEO turned up at 50 car washes generating minimal sales, he found his display hidden away in corners or other poor locations, allowing the products to be mistreated and often badly understocked.

The CEO harangued the owners of the car washes not selling many of his products. He told them to pull their socks up and manage their point-of-sale displays properly. This didn't work. Instead, he should have concentrated on the best 20 per cent of car washes. What were they doing right? Could they do more of it? What did they have in common? How could more such outlets be found? As the successful outlets were owned by large, professionally run chains, he should have cultivated these outlets rather than trying to improve the performance of the sole-proprietor sites.

Be customer centred for the few right customers

Important as focus on the few best products is, it is much less important than focusing on the few best customers. Many successful marketing professionals have learnt this lesson. A few cases may be cited. In telecoms:

> *Direct your attention where the real threat of competition exists. In most instances, the 80/20 rule still applies – 80% of the revenue comes from 20% of the customers. Know who the top revenue-producing customers are and make sure you meet their needs.*[6]

In contract management:

> *Remember the old 80/20 rule. Keep in closest contact with the 20 percent of your clients who give you 80 percent of your business. Every Sunday evening, go through contract management files and jot a note, send a card, or make a note to call anyone you haven't had contact with for too long.*[7]

Since 1994 American Express has conducted many campaigns to strengthen its franchise with the merchants and their customers who generate the highest volume of Amex sales. Carlos Viera, director of sales for American Express in South Florida, explains:

> *It's the old 80/20 rule: the bulk of your business comes from 20 percent of your market. This campaign is more of a PR campaign to get people to dine out more.*[8]

Successful marketing is all about a focus on the relatively small number of customers who are the most active in consuming your product or service. A few customers buy a great deal while a great number buy very little. The latter can be ignored. It is the core customer group that matters: those that consume heavily and frequently. For example, Emmis Broadcasting, which owns WQHT and WRKS radio stations, has conducted successful marketing campaigns focused exclusively on its core audiences, to increase the time they spend listening:

> *Instead of spending 12 hours a week with their favorite radio station, they are now spending 25 hours a week with it ... we focus on the 80/20 rule of consumption with all of our stations ... we get every single one of the listeners in our target audience and milk every single quarter-hour we can out of them.*[9]

Focusing on 20 per cent of your customers is a great deal easier than focusing on 100 per cent of them. Being customer centred on all of your customers is pretty nigh impossible. But cherishing the core 20 per cent is both feasible and highly rewarding.

Four steps to lock in your core customers

You cannot target the key 20 per cent until you know who they are. Firms with a finite customer base can work this out individual customer by individual customer. Firms selling to ten of thousands or millions of consumers need to know who their key customers are (these might be channels of distribution) and also the profile of the heavy and frequent consumer.

Second, you need to provide quite exceptional or even 'outrageous' service to them. To create a super insurance agency of the future, advises consultant Dan Sullivan, 'you'd build 20 relationships and cover them like a run with service. Not regular service, not good service. Outrageous service. You'd anticipate their needs when you could and you'd rush like a SWAT team when they asked you for anything else.'[10] The real key is to provide surprising service, above and beyond the call of duty and quite out of line with prevailing industry standards. This may have a short-term cost but it will have a long-term reward.

Third, target new products and services at the core 20 per cent of customers, developing them solely for and with this group. In seeking to gain market share, try above all to sell more to your existing core customers. This is not, generally, a matter of sheer selling skills. Nor is it largely a matter of selling more of existing products to them, although frequent-buyer programmes nearly always give a high return and raise both short- and long-term profits. But much more important still is developing improvements to existing products, or developing totally new products, that are wanted by, and if possible developed in liaison with, your core customers. Innovation should be grounded in the relationship with this group.

Finally, you should aim to keep your core customers for ever. Your core customers are money in the bank. If any of them drops out, your profitability will suffer. It follows that quite extraordinary efforts to keep your core customers, which look as though they are depressing profitability, are bound to enhance it substantially over any meaningful time period. Exceptional service may even help short-term profits, by encouraging core customers to buy more. But profitability is only a scorecard providing an after-the-fact measure of a business's health. The real measure of a healthy business lies in the strength, depth and length of its relationship with its core customers. Customer loyalty is the basic fact that drives profitability in any case. If you start to lose core customers, the business is crumbling beneath your feet, whatever you do to dress up short-term earnings. If core customers are deserting, sell the business as fast as you can, or fire the management – fire yourself if you are the boss – and take whatever drastic steps are necessary to win the core customers back or at least stop the attrition. Conversely, if the core customers are happy, the long-term expansion of the business is assured.

Serving the core 20 per cent of customers must be a company-wide obsession

Only a focus on the key 20 per cent of customers can make marketing a firm's central process. We started this section by looking at the shift from being production led to being marketing led. We then observed that the so-called excesses of the marketing approach were a result of focusing on 100 per cent rather than 20 per cent of customers. For the key 20 per cent of customers, no excess can possibly be excessive enough. You can spend up to the limits of your cash and your energy and know that you will obtain an excellent return.

Your organization cannot be centred on 100 per cent of its customers: it can be centred on 20 per cent. To be centred on these is the main job of any marketing person. But this type of marketing is also the main job of everyone in the firm. The customer will see and judge by the efforts of everyone in the firm, seen and unseen. In this sense, the 80/20 Principle breaks new ground. It is central to marketing, it makes marketing central to the firm, but it also makes marketing the job of everyone in any organization. And marketing, for all the organization's members, must mean providing ever higher levels of delight for the key 20 per cent of its customers.

Selling

Sales is marketing's close cousin: the front-line activity to communicate to and, at least as important, to listen to customers. 80/20 Thinking, as we will see next, is just as crucial for sales as for marketing.

The key to superior sales performance is to stop thinking averages and start thinking 80/20. Average sales performance is very misleading. Some sales people earn over £100,000 per annum while a large minority barely beat the minimum wage. Average performance means little to these people or to their employers.

Take any salesforce and perform an 80/20 Analysis. It is

odds on that you will find an unbalanced relationship between sales and salespeople. Most studies find that the top 20 per cent of salespeople generate between 70 and 80 per cent of sales.[11] For those who do not realize the prevalence of 80/20 relationships in life, this is a pretty remarkable result. But for anyone in business, it holds an important key to raising profits in short order. In the short term, profits are tied to sales more closely than to any other variable. Why does the 80/20 Principle apply to sales and what can we do about it?

There are two sets of reasons why sales per salesperson vary so much. The first set relates to pure salesforce performance issues; the second to structural issues of customer focus.

Salesperson performance

Suppose that your analysis duplicates one recent example and you find that 20 per cent of your sales personnel are generating 73 per cent of your sales. What should you do about it?

One obvious but often neglected imperative is to *hang on to the high performers*. You shouldn't follow the old adage: if it ain't broke don't fix it. If it ain't broke, make damn sure it doesn't break. The next best thing to staying close to your customers is to stay close to the top salespeople. Keep them happy; this cannot be done mainly with cash.

Next, *hire more of the same type of salesperson*. This is not necessarily people with the same qualifications. Personality and attitude can be much more important. Put your sales superstars in a room together and work out what they have in common. Better still, ask them to help you hire more people like them.

Third, *try to identify when the top salespeople sell the most and what they did differently then.* The 80/20 Principle applies to time as well as to people: 80 per cent of sales by each of your salespeople were probably generated in 20 per cent of their worktime. Try to identify so-called lucky streaks and why they happened. One commentator makes the point well:

> *If you're in sales, think back to the best streak you ever had. What did you do differently that week? I don't know if ball players or salespeople are more superstitious ... but the successful ones in each field tend to look at the conditions that were present when they were on a hot streak and try, try, try not to change them. Unlike a ball player, however, if you're in sales, and you're on a hot streak, change your underwear.*[12]

Fourth, *get everyone to adopt the methods that have the highest ratio of output to input.* Sometimes it's advertising, sometimes personal sales visits, sometimes focused mail shots, sometimes it's making telephone calls. Do more of what makes best use of time and money. You could decide to analyse this, but it may be quicker and cheaper simply to observe how the top salespeople spend their time.

Fifth, *switch a successful team from one area with an unsuccessful team from another area.* Do this as a genuine experiment: you will soon find out whether the good team can beat the structural difficulties or vice versa. If the good team cracks the problem in the previously difficult area but the other team is foundering, ask the former team what to do: the answer may lie in splitting the teams so that some are left in each area. Recently a client of mine had terrific success in international sales but the domestic team was demotivated and losing market share. I suggested switching teams. The CEO demurred, because the export team had language talents that would be wasted in domestic sales. Eventually he agreed to release one of the international team, fired the sales director of domestic and put the young man from international in charge. Suddenly, the previously unstoppable loss of market share was reversed. Not all such stories will have a happy ending, but in sales it is generally true that nothing fails like failure and vice versa.

Finally, what about *salesforce training*? 'Is it worth investing in training the lower 80% of the salesforce to enhance their performance levels, or is it a waste of time because so many of them are destined to wash out regardless of training?'[13] As on any issue, ask yourself what answer the 80/20 Principle implies. My answer:

➤ Only train those who you are reasonably sure plan to stick around with you for several years.

➤ Get those who are the best salespeople to train them, rewarding the sales superstars according to the subsequent performance of their trainees.

➤ Invest the most training in those who perform best after the first tranche of training. Take the best 20 per cent of the trainees and invest 80 per cent of the training effort in them. Stop training the bottom 50 per cent, unless it is clear that you are obtaining a good payback even on this effort.

Many salesforce performance differentials do derive from pure selling skill, but many do not. These structural factors can also be looked at in 80/20 terms.

Selling is not just having good sales techniques

80/20 Analysis can identify structural reasons that reach far beyond individual competence. These structural factors are often much easier to address, and even more rewarding, than dealing with individual merit. A great deal often depends on the products being sold and the customers being served:

> *Look at the salesforce. We find, for example, that 20 percent of our salespeople are generating 73 percent of our sales; we find that 16 percent of our products are accounting for 80 percent of sales; also, 22 percent of our customers are producing 77 percent of our sales…*
>
> *Looking further at our salesforce, we find that Black has 100 active accounts. 20 of these produce about 80 percent of Black's sales. Green covers 100 counties, and we find that 80 percent of her customers are concentrated in only 24 counties. White sells 30 different products. Six account for 81 percent of her sales.*[14]

We have already highlighted the 80/20 Principle's application to products and customers in the section on marketing. Those in charge of salesforces should therefore:

➤ Focus every salesperson's efforts on the 20 per cent of products that generate 80 per cent of sales. Make sure that the most profitable products attract four times the credit that an equivalent dollar of less profitable products does. The salesforce should be rewarded for selling the most profitable products, not the least profitable.

➤ Focus salespeople on the 20 per cent of customers who generate 80 per cent of sales and 80 per cent of profits. Teach the salesforce to rank their customers by sales and profits. Insist that they spend 80 per cent of their time on the best 20 per cent of customers, even if they have to neglect some of the less important customers.

Spending more time with the minority of high-volume customers should result in higher sales to them. If opportunities to sell more existing products have been exhausted, the salesforce should concentrate on providing superior service, so that existing business will be protected, and on identifying new products that the core customers want.

➤ Organize the highest volume and profit accounts under one salesperson or team, regardless of geography. Have more national accounts and fewer regional ones.

National accounts used to be confined to firms where one buyer had responsibility for purchasing all of one product, regardless of the location to which it went. Here it is plainly sensible to have an important buyer marked by a senior national sales executive. But increasingly, large accounts should be treated as national accounts and served by a dedicated person or team, even where there are many local buying points. Rich Chiarello, former senior vice president of US sales at Computer Associates International, comments:

> *Out of the top 20 percent of organizations, I'm going to get 80 percent of my revenue. I'm going to treat those companies as national accounts. I don't care if a rep flies all over the country, he's going to own the account, and we're going to identify everyone in that organization and put a plan in place to sell them our products.*

➤ Lower costs and use the telephone for less important accounts. A frequent complaint of salesforces is that downsizing or spending more time on large accounts can result in some sales territories having twice as many accounts as can reasonably be covered. One solution is to drop some accounts, but this should only be done as a last resort. A better solution, very often, is to centralize the 80 per cent of smaller accounts and provide a telephone selling and ordering service. This can provide a more efficient service much more cheaply than is possible by face-to-face selling.

➤ Finally, get the salesforce to revisit old customers who have provided good business in the past. This can mean knocking on old doors or calling old phone numbers.

This is an amazingly successful sales technique, amazingly neglected. An old, satisfied customer is very likely to buy from you again. Bill Bain, the founder of strategic consultants Bain & Company, used to sell bibles door to door in the US Deep South. He tells of a lean spell, trudging from door to door and making no new sales, before he had a blinding glimpse of the obvious. He went back to the last customer who had bought a bible and sold her another one! Another man following the same technique is one of the top real estate brokers in the US, Nicholas Barsan, a Romanian emigrant. He wins over $1 million of personal commissions each year and over a third of these come from repeat customers. Mr Barsan literally knocks on old doors and ask the homeowners (who were clients of his) if they're ready to sell.

Making use of these 80/20 structural influences can turn mediocre salespeople into good ones and good ones into superstars. The impact of a better salesforce on a firm's bottom line is immediate. Even more important is the longer-term impact on market share and customer delight of a salesforce pulsating with energy and confidence, determined to deliver the best to the core customer group, but still able to listen to what they really want.

The vital few customers

Some customers are vital. Most are not. Some sales efforts are wonderfully productive. Most are inefficient. Some will lose you money.

Channel marketing and sales effort where you can offer a minority of potential customers something that is unique, better or much better value than they can obtain elsewhere, provided that you can make higher profits in the process. Any successful enterprise draws its success from this simple, and simplifying, principle.

7 The Top 10 Business Uses of the 80/20 Principle

The versatility of the 80/20 Principle is legion: it can be used in almost any area or function to direct strategic and financial improvement. Therefore, my Top 10 applications of the 80/20 Principle, shown in Figure 34, inevitably represent an arbitrary choice. In compiling the list, I took into account the extent to which, historically, the business world has already used the 80/20 Principle and also my own opinion of its potential and underexploited value.

Previous chapters have already covered my top six uses: strategy in Chapters 4 and 5; quality and information technology in Chapter 3; cost reduction and service improvement in Chapter 5; and marketing and sales in Chapter 6. The current chapter provides a summary of the other four applications of the 80/20 Principle in my hit parade.

1	Strategy
2	Quality
3	Cost reduction and service improvement
4	Marketing
5	Selling
6	Information technology
7	Decision taking and analysis
8	Inventory management
9	Project management
10	Negotiation

Figure 34 The Top 10 business applications of the 80/20 Principle

Decision taking and analysis

Business requires decisions: frequent, fast and often without much idea whether they are right or wrong. Since 1950, business has increasingly been blessed, or if you prefer plagued, by management scientists and analytical managers incubated in business schools, accounting firms and consultancies, who can bring analysis (usually linked to extensive and expensive data gathering) to bear on any issue. Analysis has probably been the greatest US growth industry of all in the past half-century and analysis has been instrumental in some of the greatest US triumphs, such as the moon landing.

Anglo-Saxon big business has taken analysis too far

But analysis has had its darker side: the escalation of corporate staffs that are only now being properly dismantled; the infatuation with the latest fads peddled by highly numerate consultants; the stock market's obsession with ever more sophisticated analysis of near-term earnings, despite the fact that these capture only a small part of what a company is really worth; and the withdrawal of intuitive confidence from the forefront of so much of business. The latter has led not just to the pervasive reality behind the cliché of 'analysis paralysis', but also to a change for the worse in those who head the West's great corporations. Analysis has driven out vision, just as analysts have driven out visionaries from the CEO's suite.

In short, you can have too much of a good thing and there is no doubt that the US and the UK exhibit a strange misallocation of analysis: the private sector has far too much and the public sector far too little. Our large corporations need much less, but much more useful, analysis.

The 80/20 Principle is analytical, but puts analysis in its place

Remember the main tenets of the 80/20 Principle:

➤ The doctrine of the vital few and the trivial many: there are only a few things that ever produce important results.

- Most efforts do not realize their intended results.
- What you see is generally not what you get: there are subterranean forces at work.
- It is usually too complicated and too wearisome to work out what is happening and it is also unnecessary: all you need to know is whether something is working or not and change the mix until it is; then keep the mix constant until it stops working.
- Most good events happen because of a small minority of highly productive forces; most bad things happen because of a small minority of highly destructive forces.
- Most activity, *en masse* and individually, is a waste of time. It will not contribute materially to desired results.

Five rules for decision taking with the 80/20 Principle

Rule one says that *not many decisions are very important.* Before deciding anything, picture yourself with two trays in front of you – like the dreaded In and Out trays on a desk – one marked Important Decisions and one Unimportant Decisions. Mentally sort the decisions, remembering that only one in twenty is likely to fall into the Important Decision box. Do not agonize over the unimportant decisions and above all don't conduct expensive and time-consuming analysis. If possible, delegate them all. If you can't, decide which decision has a probability of 51 per cent of being correct. If you can't decide that quickly, spin a coin.

Rule two affirms that *the most important decisions are often those made only by default*, because turning points have come and gone without being recognized. For example, your chief money makers leave because you have not been close enough to them to notice their disaffection or correct it. Or your competitors develop a new product (as competitors to IBM did with the PC) that you think is wrongly conceived and will never catch on. Or you lose a leading market-share position without realizing it, because the channels of distribution change. Or you invent a great new product and enjoy a modest success with it, but someone else comes along and makes billions out of a lookalike rolled out like crazy. Or the nerd working for you in R&D ups and founds Microsoft.

When this happens, no amount of data gathering and analysis will help you realize the problem or opportunity. What you need are intuition and insight: to ask the right questions rather than getting the right answers to the wrong questions. The only way to stand a reasonable chance of noticing critical turning points is to stand above all your data and analysis for one day a month and ask questions like:

- What uncharted problems and opportunities, which could potentially have tremendous consequences, are mounting up without my noticing?
- What is working well when it shouldn't, or at least was not intended to? What are we unintentionally providing to customers that for some reason they seem to appreciate greatly?
- Is there something going badly astray, where we think we know why but where we might be totally wrong?
- Since something important is always happening under-

neath the surface, without anyone noticing it, what could it be this time?

The third rule of 80/20 decision taking is for important decisions: *gather 80 per cent of the data and perform 80 per cent of the relevant analyses in the first 20 per cent of the time available, then make a decision 100 per cent of the time and act decisively as if you were 100 per cent confident that the decision is right.* If it helps you to remember, call this the 80/20/100/100 rule of decision taking.

Fourth, *if what you have decided isn't working, change your mind early rather than late.* The market in its broadest sense – what works in practice – is a much more reliable indicator than tons of analysis. So don't be afraid to experiment and don't persevere with losing solutions. Do not fight the market.

Finally, *when something is working well, double and redouble your bets.* You may not know why it's working so well, but push as hard as you can while the forces of the universe are bending your way. Venture capitalists know this. Most of the investments in their portfolio fail to meet their expectations, but they are redeemed by a few superstar investments that succeed beyond everyone's wildest dreams. When a business keeps performing below its budgets, you may be sure you have a dog. When a business consistently outperforms expectations, there is at least a good chance that it can be multiplied by ten or a hundred times. In these circumstances, most people settle for modest growth. Those who seize the day become seriously rich.

Inventory management

We saw in Chapter 5 that simplicity requires few products. Managing stock is another key discipline flowing from the 80/20 Principle. Good stock keeping, following the 80/20 Principle, is vital to profits and cash; it is also an excellent check on whether a business is pursuing simplicity or complexity.

Nearly all businesses have far too much stock, partly because they have too many products and partly because they have too many variants of each product. Stock is measured in stock-keeping units (SKUs), with one unit for each variant.

Stock almost invariably follows some sort of 80/20 distribution: that is, around 80 per cent of stock only accounts for 20 per cent of volume or revenues. This means that slow-moving stock is very expensive and cash guzzling to keep and probably involves product that is inherently unprofitable in any case.

I can cite two recent examples of stock review. In one of them:

> *Upon analyzing the data, Pareto's 80/20 rule held close to true: 20 percent of the SKUs picked represented 75 percent of the daily volume. These picks were primarily full cases and typically required multiple cases per SKU. The remaining 80 percent of the SKUs represented only 25 percent of the daily volume. These picks amounted to only a few pieces per SKU per day.*[1]

The 20 per cent was very profitable and the 80 per cent unprofitable. Another case comes from a warehouse introducing an electronic system; before doing so it decided to see if it had the right stock in the first place:

> *A preliminary study showed that the 80/20 rule didn't fit. Rather than 20 percent of the SKUs accounting for 80 percent of warehouse activity, only 0.5 percent (just 144 SKUs) account for 70 percent of the activity.*[2]

Again, while I know nothing at all about the product, it is a safe bet that the top 0.5 per cent of SKUs by volume are a great deal more profitable than the other 99.5 per cent.

An example that is very important to me, because correcting it made me a lot of money, is that of Filofax. My business partner at the time, Robin Field, takes up the story.

> *While Filofax design and features had remained static [in the late 1980s], the product line width had expanded beyond all control. The same basic binder was available in a bewildering variety of sizes and a huge assortment of – mainly exotic – skins. Name a creature and Filofax would have ordered several thousand binders made of its hide and proudly placed them in its catalogue and in stock. I don't know what a Karung is, but I inherited an awful lot of its skin in 1990.*
>
> *Similarly, name a subject: bridge, chess, photography, bird watching, windsurfing, and Filofax would have commissioned several specialist inserts, had tens of thousands of them printed and put them in inventory...*
>
> *The result was, of course, not only a huge overhang of worthless stock, not only an administrative burden of vast complexity, but total confusion among our retailers.*[3]

Although good stock management is vital, there are only four key points to it. The most strategic point – cut down radically on your unprofitable product – has already been covered in Chapter 3.

For any given number of products, you should cut down on the number of variants, starting with the slowest movers. Simply cut them out of the product range, as Filofax did. Do not listen to anyone who tells you that the slow movers are really needed. If this were so, they'd move much faster.

Try to export the problem and cost of inventory management to other parts of the value-added chain – to your suppliers or to your customers. The ideal solution is for your stock never to come near your facilities. With modern information technology this is increasingly possible and can raise service standards while simultaneously cutting costs.

Finally, if you must hold a certain amount of stock, there are many tactical ways to use the 80/20 Principle to cut costs and speed up picking and packing:

> *The 80/20 rule is reliable in many applications, meaning that about 80 percent of the activity involves only about 20 percent of the inventory. The areas divided by size and weight … can now also be divided by part number into areas of high or low activity. In general, fast-moving items should be located as close to the shoulder–hip zone as possible, to minimize operator movement and reduce fatigue.*[4]

Inventory management in the future

Despite its historical overtones of the brown coat and the dusty store, inventory management is a fast-moving and exciting area. 'Virtual inventory', with on-line order processing, is becoming widespread, lowering costs but also improving service to distributors and customers. Innovators such as Baxter International's hospital supply business are having great success with 'customer-intimate' inventory systems. In all cases, progress is being driven by focus: focus on the most important customers, focus on a simple product line, simply tracked and simply delivered.

The 80/20 Principle is also alive and well in another increasingly important component of corporate value creation: project management.

Project management

Management structures are being exposed as inadequate and worse. They usually destroy more value than they add. One way of destroying or circumventing structures, so as to create value for valuable customers, is the project. Many of the most energetic people in business, from chief executives down, do not really have a job: rather, they pursue a number of projects.

Project management is an odd task. On the one hand, a project involves a team: it is a cooperative and not a hierarchical arrangement. But on the other hand, the team members usually do not know fully what to do, because the project requires innovation and *ad hoc* arrangements. The art of the project manager is to focus all team members on the few things that really matter.

Simplify the objective

First, simplify the task. A project is not a project: almost invariably, a project is several projects. There may be a central theme in the project and a series of satellite concerns. Alternatively, there may be three or four themes wrapped up in the same project. Think of any project with which you are familiar and you will see the point.

Projects obey the law of organizational complexity. The greater the number of a project's aims, the effort to accomplish the project satisfactorily increases, not in proportion, but geometrically.

80 per cent of the value of any project will come from 20 per cent of its activities; and the other 80 per cent of activities will arise because of needless complexity. Therefore do not start your project until you have stripped it down to one simple aim. Jettison the baggage.

Impose an impossible time scale

This will ensure that the project team does only the really high-value tasks:

> *Faced with an impossible time scale, [project members] will identify and implement the 20 percent of the requirement that delivers 80 percent of the benefit. Again, it is the inclusion of the 'nice to have' features that turn potentially sound projects into looming catastrophes.*[5]

> *Impose stretch targets. Desperate situations inspire creative solutions. Ask for a prototype in four weeks. Demand a live pilot in three months. This will force the development team to apply the 80/20 rule and really make it work. Take calculated risks.*[6]

Plan before you act

The shorter the time allowed for a project, the greater proportion of time that should be allowed for its detailed planning and thinking through. When I was a partner at management consultants Bain & Company, we proved conclusively that the best-managed projects we undertook – those that had the highest client and consultant satisfaction, the least wasted time and the highest margins – were those where there was the greatest ratio of planning time to execution time.

In the planning phase, write down all the critical issues that you are trying to resolve. (If there are more than seven of these, bump off the least important.) Construct hypotheses on what the answers are, even if these are pure guesswork (but take your best guesses). Work out what information needs to be gathered or processes need to be completed to resolve whether you are right or not with your guesses. Decide who is to do what and when. Replan after short intervals, based on your new knowledge and any divergences from your previous guesses.

Design before you implement

Particularly if the project involves designing a product or service, ensure you have the best possible answer in the design phase before you start implementation. Another 80/20 rule says that 20 per cent of the problems with any design project cause 80 per cent of the costs or overruns; and that 80 per cent of these critical problems arise in the design phase and are hugely expensive to correct later, requiring massive rework and in some cases retooling.

Negotiation

Negotiation completes my Top 10 applications of the 80/20 Principle in business. Not surprisingly, negotiation has been much studied. The 80/20 Principle adds just two points, but they can be crucial.

Few points in a negotiation really matter

20 per cent or fewer of the points at issue will comprise over 80 per cent of the value of the disputed territory. You may think this will be obvious to both sides, but people like to win points, even completely unimportant ones. Similarly, they respond to concessions, even trivial ones.

Therefore, build up a long list of spurious concerns and requirements early in a negotiation, making them seem as important to you as possible. These points must, however, be inherently unreasonable, or at least incapable of concession by the other party without real hurt (otherwise they will gain credit for being flexible and conceding the points). Then, in the closing stages of the negotiation, you can concede the points that are unimportant to you in exchange for more than a fair share of the really important points.

For instance, imagine that you are negotiating with a sole supplier for the prices on 100 parts of a key product you make. 80 per cent of the cost of any product rests in 20 per cent of the parts. You should only really be concerned about the prices of these 20 parts. But if you concede the asking price on the other 80 parts too early in the negotiation, you lose valuable bargaining chips. You should therefore construct reasons for the prices on some of the unimportant 80 parts being important to you, perhaps by exaggerating the number of units you are likely to consume.

Don't peak too early

Second, it has often been observed that most negotiations go through a phony war and only get going in earnest when the deadline looms:

> *It also seems true that on account of the incredible pressure that time can put on a negotiation, 80 percent of the concessions ... will occur in the last 20 percent of the time available. If demands are presented early on, neither side may be willing to yield, and the entire transaction can fall apart. But if additional demands or problems surface in the final 20 percent of the time available for the negotiation, both sides will be more flexible.*[7]

Impatient people don't make good negotiators.

How to secure a pay raise

Orten Skinner gives an intriguing example of how to exploit the 80/20 Principle:

> *80 percent of concessions will be made in the last 20 percent of negotiating time. If your appointment to ask for a long-overdue raise is scheduled for 9:00 a.m. and you know your supervisor has another appointment at 10:00, expect the critical moments to occur around 9:50. Pace yourself accordingly.*

Don't make your request too early to permit a gracious compromise on your supervisor's part.[8]

Beyond the Top 10

By now you will have realized that the 80/20 Principle cuts across whatever boxes we create. The insights derive from the living reality behind people, behind business and behind the world in which business operates. The 80/20 Principle is so pervasive because it is a reflection of deeper forces ruling our existence. It is time to draw these strands together.

8 The Vital Few Give Success to You

The 80/20 Principle comprises radar and autopilot. The radar gives us insight: it helps us spot opportunities and dangers. The autopilot allows us to stroll around our business arena and talk to customers and anyone else who might matter, knowing that we are still in control of our destiny. The logic of the 80/20 Principle requires us to grasp and internalize a few simple points; we can then easily 'think 80/20' and 'act 80/20' whatever we are doing.

A few things are always much more important than most things

This is invariably true, yet difficult at first to credit. Unless we have numbers or 80/20 Thinking to guide us, most things always appear more important than the few things that are actually more important. Even if we accept the point in our minds, it is difficult to make the next hop to focused action. Keep the 'vital few' in the forefront of your brain. And keep reviewing whether you are spending more time and effort on the vital few rather than the trivial many.

Progress means moving resources from low-value to high-value uses

Like individual entrepreneurs, the free markets shift resources out of areas of lower productivity into areas of higher productivity and yield. But neither markets nor entrepreneurs, let alone today's overcomplex corporate or government bureaucracies, do this well enough. There is always a tail of waste, usually a very long tail, where 80 per cent of resources are producing only 20 per cent of value. This always creates arbitrage opportunities for genuine entrepreneurs. The scope for entrepreneurial arbitrage is always underestimated.

A few people add most of the value

The best people – meaning the people best fitted to what they are doing and doing the things that make the most money – generate enormous surpluses, usually far beyond what they are allowed to take out. Normally there are very few such people. The majority add little more than they take out. A large minority (still often the majority) take out more than they contribute. This misallocation of resources is greatest in larger and more diversified corporations.

Any large, managed corporation is an organized conspiracy to misallocate rewards. The larger and more complex the firm, the greater the extent and success of the conspiracy. Those who work in corporations, or have extensive dealings with them, know that a few employees are priceless. They add value far beyond their cost. Many employees are passengers adding much less value than they cost. Some, perhaps 10–20 per cent, subtract value, even ignoring their compensation.

There are many reasons for this happening: the difficulty of measuring true performance; the political skill or otherwise of executives; the difficult-to-eradicate tendency to favour those whom we like; the ridiculous but prevalent idea that job role should count for as much or more than individual performance; and the sheer human tendency towards egalitarianism, often buttressed by the legitimate wish to foster team working. Waste and idleness gravitate to where complexity and democracy meet.

I once advised the head of an investment bank on how to divide up his extremely large annual bonus pool. My client is an extremely rich self-made businessman whose delight and source of success lie in spotting and exploiting market imperfections. He believes passionately in the market. He also knows that two people out of the hundreds in the bonus pool made more than 50 per cent of the money in his division last year; in his line of business it is easy to measure. But when I suggested giving more than half the total pool to these two, he was aghast. Later on, we came to the case of one executive who we both knew was subtracting more value than he added (but who was both likeable and an extremely astute politician within the bank). Why not cut his bonus to zero, I suggested. Again, my friend hadn't thought of that: 'Gee, Richard, I've already cut it to a quarter of what it was last year and I daren't go any further.' Yet in this case, the executive should have been paying the bank to work there. Happily, the nettle was grasped. The bonus was set at zero. The executive has now moved to a job where he's adding some value.

Accounting systems are the enemy of fair rewards, because they are absolutely brilliant at obscuring where the money is really being made. This is why, human frailty apart, the imbalance between performance and reward is greater in large and complex firms than in small businesses. The entrepreneur with four employees knows who is making the organization money, and how much, without needing a divisional P&L. The CEO of a large corporation needs to rely on misleading accounting data and the filter provided by the head of human resources (dread phrase!); it is not surprising that in large firms the top performers get less than they should and the mass of mediocre managers end up with more than they deserve.

Margins vary wildly

Margins – between value and cost, between effort and reward – are always highly variable. High-margin activities constitute a small part of total activities but a majority of total margins. If we didn't interfere with the natural allocation of resources, these imbalances would become even more marked. But we bury our heads in the sand (accounting systems conveniently provide endless beaches specifically for this purpose) and refuse to acknowledge the reality that the majority of what we and our firms do is worth much less than the minority of high-margin activities.

Resources are always misallocated

We give too many resources to low-margin activities and too few to high-margin activities. Yet despite our best endeavours, the high-margin activities continue to flourish and the subsidized activities fail to generate their own momentum. If resources are available, because of the slack created by the high-margin activities, the low-margin activities will consume more and more resources while continuing to contribute little, zero or negative surpluses for reinvestment.

We are continually surprised at how well the best activities are doing and at how long it is taking for the problem areas to turn around. Usually, the latter never do. We nearly always take too long to realize this and only the intervention of a new boss, a crisis or a management consultant makes us do what we should have done long ago.

Success is underrated and underfêted

Success is undervalued, undercelebrated and underexploited. Often it is dismissed as a lucky streak. But luck, like accidents, doesn't happen as often as we think. 'Luck' is our word for success that we cannot fathom. Behind luck there is always a highly effective mechanism, generating surpluses regardless of our failure to notice it. Because we cannot believe our 'luck', we fail to multiply and benefit from value-creating virtuous circles.

Equilibrium is illusory

Nothing lasts for ever and nothing is ever in equilibrium. Innovation is the only constant. Innovation is always resisted and often retarded, but rarely extinguished. Successful innovation is hugely more productive than the status quo; it has to be, to overcome it. Beyond a certain point, the momentum of effective innovation becomes irresistible. Personal, corporate and national success resides not in invention, or even in creating the marketable innovation, but in spotting the point at which the innovation is about to become irresistible and then riding it for all it is worth.

Change is necessary for survival. Constructive change requires insight into what is most effective and a focus on that winning way.

The biggest wins all start small

Finally, something big always comes from something that is small to start with. Small causes, small products, small firms, small markets, small systems: all of these are often the start of something big. Yet they are rarely recognized as such. Our attention is usually on the mass of what already exists, not on the trend evident in small phenomena. We usually only notice something after it has already become big, when the growth is already decelerating. Fortunes are made by the very few who latch on to growth when it is still small and accelerating. Even those who are experiencing the growth rarely realize its significance or potential to make a fortune.

Stop thinking 50/50

We need massive reeducation to stop thinking 50/50 and start thinking 80/20. Figure 35 contains some hints.

- Think skewness. Expect 20 per cent to equal 80 per cent. Expect 80 per cent to equal 20 per cent.
- Expect the unexpected. Expect 20 per cent to lead to 80 per cent and 80 per cent to result in 20 per cent.
- Expect everything – your time, your organization, your market and every person or business entity you come across – to have a quality 20 per cent: its essence, its power, its value, a small part with substantially all the goodness hidden away by the mass of mediocrity. Look for the powerful 20 per cent.
- Look for the invisible 20 per cent and the subterranean 20 per cent. It's there – find it. Unexpected successes are one give-away. If a business activity succeeds beyond expectations, that is a 20 per cent activity – and it will have much further to run.
- Expect tomorrow's 20 per cent to be different to today's 20 per cent. Where is the germ, the seed, of tomorrow's 20 per cent? Where are the 1 per cents that will grow to 20 per cents and be worth 80 per cent? Where are the 3 per cents that last year were 1 per cents?
- Develop the facility for mentally blocking out the 80 per cents – the easy answer, the obvious reality, the evident mass, the current incumbent, the conventional wisdom, the prevailing consensus. None of these is what it seems or worth its weight in the basest of base metals. These 80 per cents are huge blots on the landscape, stopping you

seeing the 20 per cents beyond. Look round these ugly blots, look over them, look beneath them, look through them. However you do it, ignore them, pretend they don't exist. Free up your vision for the elusive 20 per cents.

Figure 35 How to think 80/20

Psychologists tell us, however, that thought and attitudes can be changed by appropriate action, as well as the other way round. The best way to start thinking 80/20 is to start acting 80/20, just as the best way to start acting 80/20 is to start thinking 80/20. You have to try them out in tandem. Figure 36 contains hints on how to act 80/20.

- Whenever you spot a 20 per cent activity, run to it, surround yourself with it, immerse yourself in it, patent it, make yourself its expert, worshipper, high priest, partner, creator, propagandist and indispensable ally. Make the most of it. If the most appears to be more than you can imagine, multiply your imagination.

- Use whatever resources you have at your disposal – talent, money, friends, business allies, powers of persuasion, your credit, your organization, whatever you have or can purloin – to seize, magnify and exploit any 20 per cent you come across.

- Use alliances with other people extensively, but only ally yourself to 20 per cent people and to the 20 per cent of them who are powerful allies. Then seek to ally your alliance to other 20 percenters and 20 percentages.

- Exploit 80/20 arbitrage. Whenever you can, move resources from 80 per cent activities to 20 per cent activities. The profit from this is enormous because it is highly leveraged arbitrage. You use what is not very valuable to make something that is enormously valuable, winning at both ends of the exchange.

There are two principal media of 80/20 arbitrage: people and money, or assets that are proxies for money or can be turned into money.

Move 20 per cent people (including yourself) away from 80 per cent activities towards 20 per cent activities.

Move money from 80 per cent activities to 20 per cent activities. If possible and not too risky, use leverage (gearing) in the process. If you really are moving 80 per cent to 20 per cent activities, the risk is much lower than generally perceived. There are two forms of money leverage. One is borrowing. The other is using other people's money (OPM) as equity rather than debt. OPM used for 80 per cent activities is addictive, dangerous and risky. It ends in tears. OPM used for 20 per cent activities creates winners all round and, quite fairly, allows you to be the biggest winner.

➤ Innovate new 20 per cent activities. Steal 20 per cent ideas from elsewhere: other people, other products, other industries, other intellectual spheres, other countries. Apply them in your own 20 per cent backyard.

➤ Ruthlessly prune 80 per cent activities. 80 per cent time drives out 20 per cent time. 80 per cent allies hog space that should go to 20 per cent allies. 80 per cent assets deprive 20 per cent activities of funds. 80 per cent business relationships displace 20 per cent ones. Being in 80 per cent organizations or places stops you spending time in 20 per cent ones. Living in an 80 per cent place prevents you moving to a 20 per cent one. Mental energy expended on 80 per cent activities takes away from 20 per cent projects.

Figure 36 How to act 80/20

So there we have it. Think 80/20 and act 80/20. Those who ignore the 80/20 Principle are doomed to average returns. Those who use it must bear the burden of exceptional achievement.

On to Part Three

The 80/20 Principle has proved its worth in business and in helping business to startling success in the West and in Asia. Even those who do not love business, or know of the 80/20 Principle, have been touched by the progress made by the minority who do.

Yet the 80/20 Principle is a principle of life, not of business. It originated in academic economics. It works in business because it reflects the way the world works, not because there is something about business that particularly fits the 80/20 Principle. In any situation, the 80/20 Principle is either true or not true; whenever it has been tested, inside or outside the business arena, it works equally well. It is just that the principle has been tested far more often within the confines of business enterprise.

It is high time to liberate the power of the 80/20 Principle and use it beyond business. Business and the capitalist system are exciting and important parts of life, but they are basically procedures; the envelope of life, but not its contents. The most precious part of life lies in the inner and outer lives of individuals, in personal relationships and in the interactions and values of society.

Part Three attempts to relate the 80/20 Principle to our own lives, to achievement and to happiness. It is more speculative and less proven than what we have covered thus far, but is potentially even more important. The reader is asked to collaborate in the expedition to the unknown that we are about to begin.

Part Three

Work Less, Earn and Enjoy More

9 Being Free

The 80/20 Principle, like the truth, can make you free. You can work less. At the same time, you can earn and enjoy more. The only price is that you need to do some serious 80/20 Thinking. This will yield a few key insights that, if you act on them, could change your life.

And this can happen without the baggage of religion, ideology or any other externally imposed view. The beauty of 80/20 Thinking is that it is pragmatic and internally generated, centred around the individual.

There is a slight catch. *You* must do the thinking. You must 'editionize' and elaborate what is written here for your own purposes. But this shouldn't be too difficult.

The insights from 80/20 Thinking are few in number but very powerful. Not all of them will apply to every reader, so if you find your experience different, skip along until you meet the next insight that does resonate with your own position.

Become an 80/20 thinker, starting with your own life

My ambition is not just to serve up insights from 80/20 Thinking and have you tailor them to your own life. I am actually much more ambitious than that. I want you to lock on to the nature of 80/20 Thinking so that you can develop your own insights, both particular and general, that have not crossed my mind. I want to enlist you in the army of 80/20 thinkers, multiplying the amount of 80/20 Thinking let loose in the world.

The common attributes of 80/20 Thinking are that it is reflective, unconventional, hedonistic, strategic and non-linear; and that it combines extreme ambition (in the sense of wanting to change things for the better) with a relaxed and confident manner. It is also on the constant look-out for 80/20-type hypotheses and insights. Some explanation of these areas will provide a pointer to how to conduct 80/20 Thinking so you will know when you are on the right track.

80/20 Thinking is reflective

The objective of 80/20 Thinking is to generate action that will make sharp improvements in your life and that of others. Action of the type desired requires unusual insight. Insight requires reflection and introspection. Insight sometimes requires data gathering and we will indulge gently in a little of this as it relates to your own life. Often, insight can be generated purely by reflection, without the explicit need for information. The brain already has much more information than we can imagine.

80/20 Thinking is different from the type of thinking that prevails today. The latter is usually rushed, opportunistic, linear (for example, *x* is good or bad, what caused it?) and incrementalist. The predominant type of thinking in today's world is very closely allied to immediate action and consequently is greatly impoverished. Action drives out thought. Our objective, as 80/20 thinkers, is to leave action behind, do some quiet thinking, mine a few small pieces of precious insight and then act: selectively, on a few objectives and a narrow front, decisively and impressively, to produce terrific results with as little energy and as few resources as possible.

80/20 Thinking is unconventional

80/20 Thinking teases out where conventional wisdom is wrong, as it generally is. Progress springs from identifying the waste and suboptimality inherent in life, starting with our daily lives, and then doing something about it. Conventional wisdom is no help here, except as a counter indicator. It is conventional wisdom that leads to the waste and suboptimality in the first place. The power of the 80/20 Principle lies in doing things differently based on unconventional wisdom. This requires you to work out why most other people are doing things wrongly or to a fraction of their potential. If your insights are not unconventional, you are not thinking 80/20.

80/20 Thinking is hedonistic

80/20 Thinking seeks pleasure. It believes that life is meant to be enjoyed. It believes that most achievement is a byproduct of interest, joy and the desire for future happiness. This may not seem controversial, but most people do not do the simple things that would be conducive to their happiness, even when they know what they are.

Most people fall into one or more of the following traps. They spend a lot of time with people they do not much like. They do jobs they are not enthusiastic about. They use up most of their 'free time' (incidentally an anti-hedonistic concept) on activities they do not greatly enjoy. The reverse is also true. They do not spend most time with the people they like most; they do not pursue the career they would most like; and they do not use most of their free time on the activities they enjoy most. They are not optimists, and even those who are optimists do not plan carefully to make their future lives better.

All this is curious. One could say that it is the triumph of experience over hope, except that 'experience' is a self-created construct that usually owes more to our perception of external reality than to objective external reality itself. It would be better to say that it is the triumph of guilt over joy, of genetics over intelligence or predestination over choice and, in a very real sense, of death over life.

'Hedonism' is often held to imply selfishness, a disregard for others and a lack of ambition. All this is a smear. Hedonism is in fact a necessary condition for helping others and for achievement. It is very difficult, and always wasteful, to achieve something worthwhile without enjoying it. If more people were hedonistic, the world would be a better and, in all senses, a richer place.

80/20 Thinking believes in progress

There has been no consensus for the past 3000 years on whether progress exists, whether the history of the universe and of mankind demonstrates a jagged upward path or something less hopeful. Against the idea of progress are Hesiod (around 800BC), Plato (428–348BC), Aristotle (384–322BC), Seneca (4BC–AD54), Horace (AD65–8), St Augustine (AD354–430) and most living philosophers and scientists. In favour of the idea of progress stand nearly all of the Enlightenment figures of the late seventeenth century and eighteenth century, such as Fontenelle and Condorcet, and a majority of nineteenth-century thinkers and scientists, including Darwin and Marx. Team captain for progress must be Edward Gibbon (1737–94), the oddball historian, who wrote in *The Decline and Fall of the Roman Empire*:

> *We cannot be certain to what height the human species may aspire in their advance toward perfection ... We may therefore safely acquiesce in the pleasing conclusion that every age of the world has increased, and still increases, the real wealth, the happiness, the knowledge, and perhaps the virtue, of the human race.*

Nowadays, of course, the evidence against progress is much stronger than in Gibbon's day. But so too is the evidence for progress. The debate can never be resolved empirically. Belief in progress has to be an act of faith. Progress is a duty.[1] If we did not believe in the possibility of progress, we could never change the world for the better. Business understands this. On the whole, business, in alliance with science, has provided the greatest evidence for progress. Just as we have discovered that natural resources are not inexhaustible, business and science have come along and supplied new dimensions of unnatural inexhaustibility: economic space, the microchip, new enabling technologies.[2] But to be of greatest benefit, progress should not be confined to the worlds of science, technology and business. We need to apply progress to the quality of our own lives, individually and collectively.

80/20 Thinking is inherently optimistic because, paradoxically, it reveals a state of affairs that is seriously below what it should be. Only 20 per cent of resources really matter in terms of achievement. The rest, the large majority, are marking time, making token contributions to the overall effort. Therefore, give more power to the 20 per cent, get the 80 per cent up to a reasonable level and you can multiply the output. Progress takes you to a new and much higher level. But, even at this level, there will still typically be an 80/20 distribution of outputs/inputs. So you can progress again to a much higher level.

The progress of business and science vindicates the 80/20 Principle. Construct a huge computer that can make calculations several times faster than any previous machine. Demand that the computer be made smaller, faster and cheaper, several times smaller, faster and cheaper. Repeat the process. Repeat it again. There is no end in sight to such progress. Now apply the same principle to other provinces of life. If we believe in progress, the 80/20 Principle can help us to realize it. We may even end up proving Edward Gibbon right: real wealth, happiness, knowledge, and perhaps virtue, can be constantly increased.

80/20 Thinking is strategic

To be strategic is to concentrate on what is important, on those few objectives that can give us a comparative advantage, on what is important to us rather than others; and to plan and execute the resulting plan with determination and steadfastness.

80/20 Thinking is non-linear

Traditional thinking is encased within a powerful but sometimes inaccurate and destructive mental model. It is linear. It believes that *x* leads to *y*, that *y* causes *z* and that *b* is the inevitable consequence of *a*. You made me unhappy because you were late. My poor schooling led to my dead-end job. I have been successful because I am very clever. Hitler caused the Second World War. My firm cannot grow because the industry is declining. Unemployment is the price we pay for low inflation. High taxes are necessary if we want to look after the poor, the sick and the old. And so on.

All of these are examples of linear thinking. Linear thinking is attractive because it is simple, cut and dried. The trouble is that it is a poor description of the world and an even worse preparation for changing it. Scientists and historians have long ago abandoned linear thinking. Why should you cling to it?

80/20 Thinking offers you a life raft. Nothing flows from one simple cause. Nothing is inevitable. Nothing is ever in equilibrium or unchangeable. No undesired state of affairs need endure. Nothing desirable need be unobtainable. Few people understand what is really causing anything, good or bad. Causes may be very influential without being particularly noticeable or even (yet) very extensive. The balance of circumstances can be shifted in a major way by a minor action. Only a few decisions really matter. Those that do, matter a great deal. Choice can always be exercised.

80/20 Thinking escapes from the linear-logic trap by appealing to experience, introspection and imagination. If you are unhappy, do not worry about the proximate cause. Think about the times you have been happy and manoeuvre yourself into similar situations. If your career is going nowhere, do not tinker around at the edges seeking incremental improvements: a bigger office, a more expensive car, a grander-sounding title, fewer working hours, a more understanding boss. Think about the few, most important achievements that are yours in your whole life and seek more of the same, if necessary switching jobs or even careers. Do not look for causes, especially not for causes of failure. Imagine, and then create, the circumstances that will make you both happy and productive.

80/20 Thinking combines extreme ambition with a relaxed and confident manner

We have been conditioned to think that high ambition must go with thrusting hyperactivity, long hours, ruthlessness, the sacrifice both of self and others to the cause, and extreme busyness. In short, the rat race. We pay dearly for this association of ideas. The combination is neither desirable nor necessary.

A much more attractive, and at least equally attainable, combination is that of extreme ambition with confidence, relaxation and a civilized manner. This is the 80/20 ideal, but it rests on solid empirical foundations. Most great achievements are made through a combination of steady application and sudden insight. Think of Archimedes in his bath or Newton sitting under a tree being struck by an apple. The immensely important insights thus generated would not have happened if Archimedes had not been thinking about displacement or Newton about gravity, but neither would have occurred if Archimedes had been chained to his desk or Newton frenetically directing teams of scientists.

Most of what any of us achieve in life, of any serious degree of value to ourselves and others, occurs in a very small proportion of our working lives. 80/20 Thinking and observation make this perfectly clear. We have more than enough time. We demean ourselves, both by lack of ambition and by assuming that ambition is served by bustle and busyness. Achievement is driven by insight and selective action. The still, small voice of calm has a bigger place in our lives than we acknowledge. Insight comes when we are feeling relaxed and good about ourselves. Insight requires time – and time, despite conventional wisdom, is there in abundance.

80/20 insights for individuals

The rest of Part Three will explore 80/20 insights for your personal life, some of which can be sampled here as a taster. It only takes action on a few insights to improve greatly the quality of your life.

➤ 80 per cent of achievement and happiness takes place in 20 per cent of our time – and these peaks can be expanded greatly.

➤ Our lives are profoundly affected, for good and ill, by a few events and a few decisions. The few decisions are often taken by default rather than conscious choice: we let life happen to us rather than shaping our own lives. We can improve our lives dramatically by recognizing the turning points and making the decisions that will make us happy and productive.

➤ There are always a few key inputs to what happens and they are often not the obvious ones. If the key causes can be identified and isolated, we can very often exert more influence on them than we think possible.

➤ Everyone can achieve something significant. The key is not effort, but finding the right thing to achieve. You are hugely more productive at some things than at others, but dilute the effectiveness of this by doing too many things where your comparative skill is nowhere near as great.

➤ There are always winners and losers – and always more of the latter. You can be a winner by choosing the right competition, the right team and the right methods to win. You are more likely to win by rigging the odds in your favour (legitimately and fairly) than by striving to improve your performance. You are more likely to win again where you have won before. You are more likely to win when you are selective about the races you enter.

➤ Most of our failures are in races for which others enter us. Most of our successes come from races we ourselves want to enter. We fail to win most races because we enter too many of the wrong ones: their ones, not our ones.

➤ Few people take objectives really seriously. They put average effort into too many things, rather than superior thought and effort into a few important things. People who achieve the most are selective as well as determined.

➤ Most people spend most of their time on activities that are of low value to themselves and others. The 80/20 thinker escapes this trap and can achieve many more of the few higher-value objectives without noticeably more effort.

➤ One of the most important decisions someone can make in life is their choice of allies. Almost nothing can be achieved without allies. Most people do not choose their allies carefully or even at all. The allies somehow arrive. This is a serious case of letting life happen to you. Most people have the wrong allies. Most also have too many and do not use them properly. 80/20 thinkers choose a few allies carefully and build the alliances carefully to achieve their specific objectives.

➤ An extreme case of carelessness with allies is picking the wrong 'significant other' or life partner. Most people have too many friends and do not enjoy an appropriately selected and reinforced inner circle. Many people have the wrong life partners – and even more do not nurture the right life partner properly.

➤ Money used rightly can be a source of opportunity to shift to a better lifestyle. Few people know how to multiply money, but 80/20 thinkers should be able to do so. As long as money is subordinated to lifestyle and happiness, there is no harm in this ability.

➤ Few people spend enough time and thought cultivating their own happiness. They seek indirect goals, like money and promotion, that may be difficult to attain and will prove when they are attained to be extremely inefficient sources of happiness. Not only is happiness not money, it is not even like money. Money not spent can be saved and invested and, through the magic of compound interest, multiplied. But happiness not spent today does not lead to happiness tomorrow. Happiness, like the mind, will atrophy if not exercised. 80/20 thinkers know what generates their happiness and pursue it consciously, cheerfully and intelligently, using happiness today to build and multiply happiness tomorrow.

Time is waiting in the wings

The best place to start 80/20 Thinking about achievement and happiness is the subject of time. Our society's appreciation of the quality and role of time is very poor. Many people intuitively understand this and several hundred thousand busy executives have sought redemption in the form of time management. But these executives are just tinkering around the edges. Our whole attitude towards time needs to be transformed. We don't need time management – we need a time revolution.

10 Time Revolution

But at my back I always hear
Time's wingèd chariot hurrying near;
And yonder all before us lie
Deserts of vast eternity.

Andrew Marvell[1]

Almost everyone, whether ultra busy or ultra idle, needs a time revolution. It is not that we are short of time or even that we have too much of it. It is the way we treat time, even the way we think about it, that is the problem – and the opportunity. For those who have not experienced a time revolution, it is the fastest way to make a giant leap in both happiness and effectiveness.

The 80/20 Principle and time revolution

The 80/20 Principle, when applied to our use of time, advances the following hypotheses:

- Most of any individual's significant achievements – most of the value someone adds in personal, professional, intellectual, artistic, cultural or athletic terms – is achieved in a minority of their time. There is a profound imbalance between what is created and the time taken to create it, whether the time is measured in days, weeks, months, years or a lifetime.
- Similarly, most of an individual's happiness occurs during quite bounded periods of time. If happiness could be accurately measured, a large majority of it would register in a fairly small proportion of the total time and this would apply during most periods, whether the period measured was a day, a week, a month, a year or a lifetime.

We could rephrase these two ideas with spurious precision, but greater snappiness, using 80/20 shorthand:

- 80 per cent of achievement is attained in 20 per cent of the time taken; conversely, 80 per cent of time spent leads to only 20 per cent of output value.
- 80 per cent of happiness is experienced in 20 per cent of life; and 80 per cent of time contributes only 20 per cent of happiness.

Remember that these are hypotheses to be tested against your experience, not self-evident truths or the results of exhaustive research.

Where the hypotheses are true (as they are in a majority of cases I have tested), they have four rather startling implications:

➤ Most of what we do is of low value.

➤ Some small fragments of our time are much more valuable than all the rest.

➤ If we can do anything about this, we should do something radical: there is no point tinkering around the edges or making our use of time a little more efficient.

➤ If we make good use of only 20 per cent of our time, there is no shortage of it!

Spend a few minutes or hours reflecting on whether the 80/20 Principle operates for you in each of these spheres. It doesn't matter what the exact percentages are and in any case it is almost impossible to measure them precisely. The key question is whether there is a major imbalance between the time spent on the one hand and achievement or happiness on the other. Does the most productive fifth of your time lead to four-fifths of valuable results? Are four-fifths of your happiest times concentrated into one-fifth of your life?

These are important questions and should not be answered glibly. It might be an idea to set this book aside and go for a walk. Don't come back until you have decided whether your use of time is unbalanced.

The point is *not* to manage your time better!

If your use of time is unbalanced, a time revolution is required. You don't need to organize yourself better or alter your time allocation at the margins; you need to transform how you spend your time. You probably also need to change the way you think about time itself.

What you need should not, however, be confused with time management. Time management originated in Denmark as a training device to help busy executives organize their time more effectively. It has now become a $1 billion industry operating throughout the world.

The key characteristic of the time management industry now is not so much the training, but more the sale of 'time managers', executive personal organizers, both of the traditional paper-based type and now increasingly electronic. Time management also often comes with a strong evangelical pitch: the fastest-growing corporation in the industry, Franklin, has deep Mormon roots.[2]

Time management is not a fad, since its users are usually highly appreciative of the systems used and they generally say that their productivity has risen by 15–25 per cent as a result. But time management aims to fit a litre into a pint pot. It is about speeding up. It is specifically aimed at business people pressured by too many demands on their time. The idea is that better planning of each tiny segment of the day will help executives act more efficiently. Time management also advocates the establishment of clear priorities, to escape the tyranny of daily events that, although very urgent, may not be all that important.

Time management implicitly assumes that we know what is and is not a good use of our time. If the 80/20 Principle holds, this is not a safe assumption. In any case, if we knew what was important, we'd be doing it already.

Time management often advises people to categorize their list of 'to do' activities into A, B, C or D priorities. In practice, most people end up classifying 60–70 per cent of their activities as A or B priorities. They conclude that what they are really short of is time. This is why they were interested in time management to start with. So they end up with better planning, longer working hours, greater earnestness and usually greater frustration too. They become addicted to time management, but it doesn't fundamentally change what they do, or significantly lower their level of guilt that they are not doing enough.

The name time management gives the game away. It implies that time can be managed more efficiently, that it is a valuable and scarce resource and that we must dance to its tune. We must be parsimonious with time. Given half a chance, it will escape from us. Time lost, the time management evangelists say, can never be regained.

We now live in an age of busyness. The long-predicted age of leisure is taking an age to arrive, except for the unemployed. We now have the absurd situation noted by Charles Handy[3] that working hours for executives are growing – 60 hours a week are not unusual – at the same time as there is a worsening shortage of work to go round.

Society is divided into those who have money but no time to enjoy it and those who have time but no money. The popularity of time management co-exists with unprecedented anxiety about using time properly and having enough time to do one's job satisfactorily.

80/20 time heresy

The 80/20 Principle overturns conventional wisdom about time. The implications of 80/20 time analysis are quite different and, to those suffering from the conventional view of time, startlingly liberating. The 80/20 Principle asserts the following:

- Our current use of time is not rational. There is therefore no point in seeking marginal improvements in how we spend our time. We need to go back to the drawing board and overturn all our assumptions about time.
- There is no shortage of time. In fact, we are positively awash with it. We only make good use of 20 per cent of our time. And for the most talented individuals, it is often tiny amounts of time that make all the difference. The 80/20 Principle says that if we doubled our time on the top 20 per cent of activities, we could work a two-day week and achieve 60 per cent more than now. This is light years away from the frenetic world of time management.
- The 80/20 Principle treats time as a friend, not an enemy. Time gone is not time lost. Time will always come round again. This is why there are seven days in a week, twelve months in a year, why the seasons recur. Insight and value are likely to come from placing ourselves in a comfortable, relaxed and collaborative position towards time. It is our use of time, and not time itself, that is the enemy.
- The 80/20 Principle says that we should act less. Action drives out thought. It is because we have so much time that we squander it. The most productive time on a project is usually the last 20 per cent, simply because the work has

to be completed before a deadline. Productivity on most projects could be doubled simply by halving the amount of time for their completion. This is not evidence that time is in short supply.

Time is the benign link between the past, present and future

It is not shortage of time that should worry us, but the tendency for the majority of time to be spent in low-quality ways. Speeding up or being more 'efficient' with our use of time will not help us; indeed, such ways of thinking are more the problem than the solution.

80/20 Thinking directs us to a more 'eastern' view of time. Time should not be seen as a sequence, running from left to right as in nearly all graphical representations that the culture of business has imposed on us. It is better to view time as a synchronizing and cyclical device, just as the inventors of the clock intended. Time keeps coming round, bringing with it the opportunity to learn, to deepen a few valued relationships, to produce a better product or outcome and to add more value to life. We do not exist just in the present; we spring from the past and have a treasure trove of past associations; and our future, like our past, is already immanent in the present. A far better graphical representation of time in our lives than the left-to-right graph is a series of interlocked and ever larger and higher triangles, as shown in Figure 37.

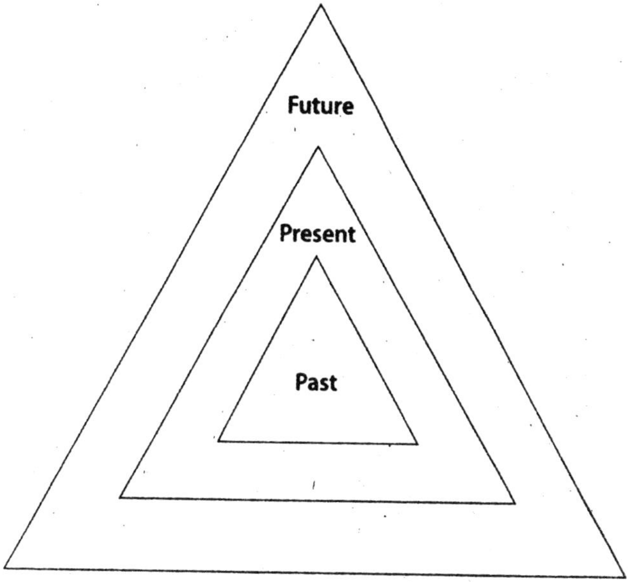

Figure 37 The time triad

The effect of thinking about time in this way is that it highlights the need to carry with us, through our lives, the most precious and valued 20 per cent of what we have – our personality, abilities, friendships and even our physical assets – and ensure that they are nurtured, developed, extended and deepened, to increase our effectiveness, value and happiness. This can only be done by having consistent and continuous relationships, founded on optimism that the future will be better than the present, because we can take and extend the best 20 per cent from the past and the present to create that better future. Viewed in this way, the future is not a random movie that we are halfway through, aware of (and terrified by) time whizzing past. Rather, the future is a dimension of the present and the past, giving us the opportunity to create something better. 80/20 Thinking insists that this is always possible. All we have to do is to give freer rein and better direction to our most positive 20 per cent.

A primer for time revolutionaries

Here are seven steps to detonating a time revolution.

Make the difficult mental leap of dissociating effort and reward

The Protestant work ethic is so deeply engrained in everyone, of all religions and none, that we need to make a conscious effort to extirpate it. The trouble is that we do enjoy hard work, or at least the feeling of virtue that comes from having done it. What we must do is to plant firmly in our minds that hard work, especially for somebody else, is not an efficient way to achieve what we want. Hard work leads to low returns. Insight and doing what we ourselves want lead to high returns.

Decide on your own patron saints of productive laziness. Mine are Ronald Reagan and Warren Buffett. Reagan made an effortless progression from B-film actor to darling of the Republican Right, Governor of California and extremely successful President.

What did Reagan have going for him? Good looks, a wonderfully mellifluous voice which he deployed instinctively on all the right occasions (the high point of which undoubtedly consisted in his words to Nancy when shot, 'Honey, I forgot to duck'), some very astute campaign managers, old-fashioned grace and a Disneyesque view of America and the world. Reagan's ability to apply himself was limited at best, his grasp of conventional reality ever more tenuous, his ability to inspire the US and destroy communism ever more awesome. To maul Churchill's dictum, never was so much achieved by so few with so little effort.

Warren Buffett became (for a time) the richest man in the US, not by working but by investing. Starting with very little capital, he has compounded it over many years at rates far above stock market average appreciation. He has done this with a limited degree of analysis (he started before sliderules were invented) but basically with a few insights that he has applied consistently.

Buffett started his riches rollercoaster with one Big Idea: that US local newspapers had a local monopoly that constituted the most perfect business franchise. This simple idea made him his first fortune and much of his subsequent money has been made in shares in the media: an industry he understands.

If not lazy, Buffett is very economical with his energy. Whereas most fund managers buy lots of stocks and churn them frequently, Buffett buys few and holds them for ages. This means that there is very little work to do. He pours scorn on the conventional view of investment portfolio diversification, which he has dubbed the Noah's Ark method: 'one buys two of everything and ends up with a zoo'. His own investment philosophy 'borders on lethargy'.

Whenever I am tempted to do too much, I remember Ronald Reagan and Warren Buffett. You should think of your own examples, of people you know personally or those in the public eye, who exemplify productive inertia. Think about them often.

Give up guilt

Giving up guilt is clearly related to the dangers of excessively hard work. But it is also related to doing the things you enjoy. There is nothing wrong with that. There is no value in doing things you don't enjoy.

Do the things that you like doing. Make them your job. Make your job them. Nearly everyone who has become rich has had the added bonus of becoming rich doing things they enjoy. This might be taken as yet another example of the universe's 80/20 perversity.

20 per cent of people not only enjoy 80 per cent of wealth but also monopolize 80 per cent of the enjoyment to be had from work: and they are the same 20 per cent!

The curmudgeonly old Puritan, John Kenneth Galbraith (1908–2006), drew attention to a fundamental unfairness in the world of work. The middle classes not only get paid more for their work, but they have more interesting work and enjoy it more. They have secretaries, assistants, first-class travel, luxurious hotels and more interesting working lives too. In fact, you would need to have a large private fortune to afford all the perquisites that senior industrialists now routinely award themselves.

Galbraith advanced the revolutionary view that those who have less interesting jobs should be paid more than those with jobs that are more fun. What a spoilsport! Such views are thought provoking, but no good will come of them. As with so many 80/20 phenomena, if you look beneath the surface you can detect a deeper logic behind the apparent inequity.

In this case the logic is very simple. Those who achieve the most have to enjoy what they do. It is only by fulfilling oneself that anything of extraordinary value can be created. Think, for example, of any great artist in any sphere. The quality and quantity of the output are stunning. Van Gogh never stopped. Picasso ran an art factory long before Andy Warhol, because he loved what he did.

Revel in Michelangelo's prodigious, sexually driven, sublime output. Even the fragments that I can remember – his *David*, *The Dying Slave*, the Laurentian Library, the New Sacristy, the Sistine chapel ceiling, the Pietà in Saint Peter's – are miraculous for one individual. Michelangelo did it all, not because it was his job, or because he feared the irascible Pope Julius II or even to make money, but because he loved his creations and young men.

You may not have quite the same drives, but you will not create anything of enduring value unless you love creating it. This applies as much to purely personal as to business matters.

I am not advocating perpetual laziness. Work is a natural activity that satisfies an intrinsic need, as the unemployed, retired and those who make overnight fortunes rapidly discover. Everyone has their own natural balance, rhythm and optimal work/play mix and most people can sense innately when they are being too lazy or industrious. 80/20 Thinking is most valuable in encouraging people to pursue high-value/satisfaction activities in both work and play periods, rather than in stimulating an exchange of work for play. But I suspect that most people try too hard at the wrong things. The modern world would greatly benefit if a lower quantity of work led to a greater profusion of creativity and intelligence. If much greater work would benefit the most idle 20 per cent of our people, much less work would benefit the hardest-working 20 per cent; and such arbitrage would benefit society both ways. The quantity of work is much less important than its quality; and its quality depends on self-direction.

Free yourself from obligations imposed by others

It is a fair bet that when 80 per cent of time yields 20 per cent of results, that 80 per cent is undertaken at the behest of others.

It is increasingly apparent that the whole idea of working directly for someone else, of having a job with security but limited discretion, has just been a transient phase (albeit one lasting more than two centuries) in the history of work.[4] Even if you work for a large corporation, you should think of yourself as an independent business, working for yourself, despite being on Monolith Inc's payroll.

The 80/20 Principle shows time and time again that the 20 per cent who achieve the most either work for themselves or behave as if they do.

The same idea applies outside work. It is very difficult to make good use of your time if you don't control it. (It is actually quite difficult even if you do, since your mind is prisoner to guilt, convention and other externally imposed views of what you should do – but at least you stand a chance of cutting these down to size.)

It is impossible, and even undesirable, to take my advice too far. You will always have some obligations to others and these can be extremely useful from your perspective. Even the entrepreneur is not really a lone wolf, answerable to no one.

He or she has partners, employees, alliances and a network of contacts, from whom nothing can be expected if nothing is given. The point is to choose your partners and obligations extremely selectively and with great care.

Be unconventional and eccentric in your use of time

You are unlikely to spend the most valuable 20 per cent of your time in being a good soldier, in doing what is expected of you, in attending the meetings that everyone assumes you will, in doing what most of your peers do or in otherwise observing the social conventions of your role. In fact, you should question whether any of these things is necessary.

You will not escape from the tyranny of 80/20 – the likelihood that 80 per cent of your time is spent on low-priority activities – by adopting conventional behaviour or solutions.

A good exercise is to work out the most unconventional or eccentric ways in which you could spend your time: how far you could deviate from the norm without being thrown out of your world. Not all eccentric ways of spending time will multiply your effectiveness, but some or at least one of them could. Draw up several scenarios and adopt the one that allows you the most time on high-value activities that you enjoy.

Who among your acquaintances is both effective and eccentric? Find out how they spend their time and how it deviates from the norm. You may want to copy some of the things they do and don't do.

Identify the 20 per cent that gives you 80 per cent

About a fifth of your time is likely to give you four-fifths of your achievement or results and four-fifths of your happiness. Since this may not be the same fifth (although there is usually considerable overlap), the first thing to do is to be clear about whether your objective, for the purposes of each run through, is achievement or happiness. I recommend that you look at them both separately.

For happiness, identify your *happiness islands*: the small amounts of time, or the few years, that have contributed a quite disproportionate amount of your happiness. Take a clean sheet of paper, write 'Happiness Islands' at the top and list as many of them as you can remember. Then try to deduce what is common between all or some of the happiness islands.

Repeat the procedures for your *unhappiness islands*. These will not generally comprise the other 80 per cent of your time, since (for most people) there is a large no-man's-land of moderate happiness between the happiness and unhappiness islands. Yet it is important to identify the most significant causes of unhappiness and any common denominators between them.

Repeat this whole procedure for achievement. Identify your *achievement islands*: the short periods when you have achieved a much higher ratio of value to time than during the rest of your week, month, year or life. Head a clean sheet of paper with 'Achievement Islands' and list as many as you can, if possible taken over the whole of your life.

Try to identify the achievement islands' common characteristics. Before leaving your analysis, you might want to glance at the list of the Top 10 highest-value uses of time on page 210. This is a general list compiled from many people's experience and may nudge your memory.

List separately your *achievement desert islands*. These are the periods of greatest sterility and lowest productivity. The list of the Top 10 low-value uses of time on page 209 may help you. Again, what do they tend to have in common?

Now act accordingly.

Multiply the 20 per cent of your time that gives you 80 per cent

When you have identified your happiness and achievement islands, you are likely to want to spend more time on these and similar activities.

When I explain this idea some people say there is a flaw in my logic, because spending more time on the top 20 per cent may lead to diminishing returns setting in. Twice as much time on the top 20 per cent may not lead to another 80 per cent of output, perhaps only to another 40, 50, 60 or 70 per cent.

I have two replies to this point. First, since it is impossible (at the moment) to measure happiness or effectiveness with anything approaching precision, the critics may well be right in some cases. But who cares? There will still be a marked increase in the supply of what is best.

But my second answer is that I don't think the critics are generally right. My recommendation is not that you duplicate *exactly* what it is that you are doing today that is in the 20 per cent yielding 80 per cent. The point of examining the common characteristics of your happiness and achievement islands is to isolate something far more basic than what has happened: to isolate what you are uniquely programmed to do best.

It may well be that there are things you should be doing (to realize your full potential achievement or happiness) that you have only started doing imperfectly, to some degree, or even that you have not started to do at all. For example, Dick Francis was a superb National Hunt jockey, but did not publish his first racing mystery until he was nearly 40. His success, money earned and possibly personal satisfaction from the latter activity far exceeded those from the former. Richard Adams was an unfulfilled, middle-aged, middle-level civil servant before he wrote the bestseller *Watership Down*.

It is not at all uncommon for analysis of happiness or achievement islands to yield insight into what individuals are best at, and what is best for them, which then enables them to spend time on totally new activities that have a higher ratio of reward to time than anything they were doing before. There can, therefore, be increasing returns as well as the possibility of diminishing returns. In fact, one thing you should specifically consider is a change of career and/or lifestyle.

Your basic objective, when you have identified both the specific activities and the general type of activity that take 20 per cent of your time but yield 80 per cent of happiness or achievement, should be to increase the 20 per cent of time spent on those and similar activities by as much as possible.

A short-term objective, usually feasible, is to decide to take the 20 per cent of time spent on the high-value activities up to 40 per cent within a year. This one act will tend to raise your 'productivity' by between 60 and 80 per cent. (You will now have two lots of 80 per cent of output, from two lots of 20 per cent of time, so your total output would go from 100 to 160 even if you forfeited all the previous 20 from low-value activities in reallocating some of the time to the high-value activities!)

The ideal position is to move the time spent on high-value activities up from 20 to 100 per cent. This may only be possible by changing career and lifestyle. If so, make a plan, with deadlines, for how you are going to make these changes.

Eliminate or reduce the low-value activities

For the 80 per cent of activities that give you only 20 per cent of results, the ideal is to eliminate them. You may need to do this before allocating more time to the high-value activities (although people often find that firing themselves up to spend more time on the high-value activities is a more efficient way of forcing them to set aside the low-value time sinks).

First reactions are often that there is little scope for escaping from low-value activities. They are said to be inevitable parts of family, social or work obligations. If you find yourself thinking this, think again.

There is normally great scope to do things differently within your existing circumstances. Remember the advice above: be unconventional and eccentric in how you use your time. Do not follow the herd.

Try your new policy and see what happens. Since there is little value in the activities you want to displace, people may not actually notice if you stop doing them. Even if they do notice, they may not care enough to force you to do them if they can see that this would take major effort on their part.

But even if dropping the low-value activities does require a radical change in circumstances – a new job, a new career, new friends, even a new lifestyle or partner – form a plan to make the desired changes. The alternative is that your potential for achievement and happiness will never be attained.

Four illustrations of eccentric and effective time use

My first illustration is William Ewart Gladstone, the dominant Liberal statesman of Victorian Britain who was elected Prime Minister four times. Gladstone was eccentric in many ways, not least his spectacularly unsuccessful attempts to rescue 'fallen women' from prostitution and his not totally unrelated bouts of self-flagellation; but his use of time is the eccentricity on which we shall focus here.[5]

Gladstone was not constrained by his political duties, or, rather, was effective at them because he spent his time pretty much as he pleased in an amazing variety of ways. He was an inveterate tourist, both in the British Isles and overseas, often slipping over to France, Italy or Germany on private business while Prime Minister.

He loved the theatre, pursued several (almost certainly non-physical) affairs with women, read avidly (20,000 books in his lifetime), made incredibly long speeches in the House of Commons (which despite their length were apparently compulsive listening) and virtually invented the sport of modern electioneering, which he pursued with enormous gusto and enjoyment. Whenever he felt even slightly ill, he would go to bed for at least a whole day, where he would read and think. His enormous political energy and effectiveness derived from his eccentric use of time.

Of subsequent British Prime Ministers, only Lloyd George, Churchill and Thatcher came anywhere near to rivalling Gladstone's eccentricity in time use; and all three were unusually effective.

Three highly eccentric management consultants

The other examples of unconventional time management come from the staid world of management consulting. Consultants are notorious for long hours and frenetic activity. My three characters, all of whom I knew quite well, broke all the conventions. They were also all spectacularly successful.

The first, whom I will call Fred, made tens of millions of dollars from being a consultant. He never bothered to go to business school, but managed to set up a very large and successful firm of consultants where almost everyone else worked 70 or more hours a week. Fred visited the office occasionally and chaired partners' meetings once a month, which partners from all over the globe were compelled to attend, but preferred to spend his time playing tennis and thinking. He ruled the firm with an iron fist but never raised his voice. Fred controlled everything through an alliance with his five main subordinates.

The second, alias Randy, was one of these lieutenants. Apart from its founder, he was virtually the only exception to the workaholic culture of the firm. He had himself posted to a far-distant country, where he ran a thriving and rapidly growing office, also staffed by people working unbelievably hard, largely from his home. Nobody knew how Randy spent his time or how few hours he worked, but he was incredibly laid back. Randy would only attend the most important client meetings, delegating everything else to junior partners and if necessary inventing the most bizarre reasons why he could not be there.

Although head of the office, Randy paid zero attention to any administrative matters. His whole energy was spent working out how to increase revenues with the most important clients and then putting mechanisms in place to do this with the least personal effort. Randy never had more than three priorities and often only one; everything else went by the board. Randy was impossibly frustrating to work for, but wonderfully effective.

My third and final eccentric time user was a friend and partner: let's call him Jim. My abiding memory of Jim is of when we shared a small office, together with a handful of other colleagues. It was cramped and full of wild activity: people talking on the phone, rushing round to get presentations done, shouting from one end of the office to the other.

But there was Jim, an oasis of calm inactivity, staring thoughtfully at his calendar, working out what to do. Occasionally, he would take a few colleagues aside to the one quiet room and explain what he wanted everyone to do: not once, not twice, but three times, in life-threateningly tedious detail. Jim would then make everyone repeat back to him what they were going to do. Jim was slow, languid and half-deaf. But he was a terrific leader. He spent all his time working out which tasks were high value and who should do them; and then ensuring that they got done.

The Top 10 low-value uses of time

You can only spend time on high-value activities (whether for achievement or enjoyment) if you have abandoned low-value activities. I invited you above to identify your low-value time sinks. To check that you have not missed some out, Figure 38 lists the 10 that are most common.

Be ruthless in cutting out these activities. Under no circumstances give everyone a fair share of your time. Above all, don't do something just because people ask, or because you receive a phone call or an email. Follow Nancy Reagan's advice (in another context) and Just Say No! – or treat the matter with what Lord George Brown called 'a complete ignoral'.

1	Things other people want you to do
2	Things that have always been done this way
3	Things you're not unusually good at doing
4	Things you don't enjoy doing
5	Things that are always interrupted
6	Things few other people are interested in
7	Things that have already taken twice as long as you originally expected
8	Things where your collaborators are unreliable or low quality
9	Things that have a predictable cycle
10	Answering the telephone

Figure 38 The Top 10 low-value uses of time

The Top 10 highest-value uses of time

Figure 39 gives the other side of the coin.

1. Things that advance your overall purpose in life
2. Things you have always wanted to do
3. Things already in the 20/80 relationship of time to results
4. Innovative ways of doing things that promise to slash the time required and/or multiply the quality of results
5. Things other people tell you can't be done
6. Things other people have done successfully in a different arena
7. Things that use your own creativity
8. Things that you can get other people to do for you with relatively little effort on your part
9. Anything with high-quality collaborators who have already transcended the 80/20 rule of time, who use time eccentrically and effectively
10. Things for which it is now or never

Figure 39 The Top 10 highest-value uses of time

When thinking about any potential use of time, ask two questions:

- Is it unconventional?
- Does it promise to multiply effectiveness?

It is unlikely to be a good use of time unless the answer to both questions is yes.

Is a time revolution feasible?

Many of you may feel that much of my advice is rather revolutionary and pie in the sky for your circumstances. Comments and criticisms that have been made to me include the following:

- I can't choose how to spend my time. My bosses won't allow it.
- I would need to change job to follow your advice and I can't afford the risk.
- This advice is all very well for the rich, but I just don't have that degree of freedom.
- I'd have to divorce my spouse!
- My ambition is to improve my effectiveness 25 per cent, not 250 per cent. I just don't believe the latter can be done.
- If it were as easy as you say, everyone would do it.

If you find yourself saying any of these things, time revolution may not be for you.

Don't start a time revolution unless you are willing to be a revolutionary

I could encapsulate (or at least caricature) these responses as follows: 'I'm not a radical, let alone a revolutionary, so leave me alone. I'm basically happy with my existing horizons.' Fair enough. Revolution is revolution. It is uncomfortable, wrenching and dangerous. Before you start a revolution, realize that it will involve major risks and will lead you into uncharted territory.

Those who want a time revolution need to link together their past, present and future, as suggested above by Figure 37. Behind the issue of how we allocate time lurks the even more fundamental issue of what we want to get out of our lives.

11 You Can Always Get What You Want

Things that matter most
Must never be at the mercy of things that matter least.
Johann Wolfgang von Goethe

Work out what you want from life. In the 1980s phrase, aim to 'have it all'. Everything you want should be yours: the type of work you want; the relationships you need; the social, mental and aesthetic stimulation that will make you happy and fulfilled; the money you require for the lifestyle that is appropriate to you; and any requirement that you may (or may not) have for achievement or service to others. If you don't aim for it all, you'll never get it all. To aim for it requires that you know what you want.

Most of us don't work out what we want. And most of us end up with lopsided lives as a result. We may get work right and relationships wrong or the other way round. We may strive after money or achievement, but find after we achieve our goal that the victory is hollow.

The 80/20 Principle records this sorry state. 20 per cent of what we do leads to 80 per cent of the results; but 80 per cent of what we do leads to only 20 per cent. We are wasting 80 per cent of our effort on low-value outcomes. 20 per cent of our time leads to 80 per cent of what we value; 80 per cent of our time disappears on things that have little value to us. 20 per cent of our time leads to 80 per cent of happiness; but 80 per cent of our time yields very little happiness.

But the 80/20 Principle does not always apply and need not apply. It is there as a diagnostic, to point out an unsatisfactory and wasteful state of affairs. We should aim to frustrate the 80/20 Principle, or at least translate it to a higher plane where we can be much happier and more effective. Remember the promise of the 80/20 Principle: if we take note of what it tells us, we can work less, earn more, enjoy more and achieve more.

To do this, we must start with a rounded view of everything we want. That is what this chapter deals with. Chapters 12, 13 and 14 then deal in more detail with some of the components – with relationships, careers and money respectively – before we revert in Chapter 15 to the ultimate goal: happiness.

Start with lifestyle

Do you enjoy your life? Not part of it, but most of it: at least 80 per cent of it? And whether you do or not, is there a lifestyle that could suit you better? Ask yourself:

- Am I living with the right person or people?
- Am I living in the right place?
- Am I working the right hours and do they match my ideal work/play rhythm, and suit my family and social needs?
- Do I feel in control?
- Can I exercise or meditate when I want?
- Am I nearly always relaxed and comfortable with my surroundings?
- Does my lifestyle make it easy for me to be creative and fulfil my potential?
- Do I have enough money and are my affairs organized so that I don't have to worry about them?
- Does the lifestyle facilitate whatever contribution I want to make to enriching the lives of people I want to help?
- Do I see my close friends enough?
- Is the extent of travel in my life just right, not too much or too little?
- Is the lifestyle right for my partner and family too?
- Do I have everything that I need right here: do I have it all?

What about work?

Work is a key part of life, one which should be neither overdone nor underdone. Almost everyone needs to work, whether it is paid or not. Almost no one should allow work to take over their lives, however much they claim to enjoy it. Hours of work should not be dictated by social convention. The 80/20 Principle can provide a good measure here and a good way to say whether you should work more or less. It is the idea of arbitrage: if on average you are happier outside work than at work, you should work less and/or change your job. If you are on average happier at work than outside work, you should work more and/or change your non-work life. You haven't got it right until you are equally happy at work and outside work; and until you are happy at least 80 per cent of the time at work and 80 per cent of the time outside work.

Career alienation

Many people don't like their work much. They don't feel it's them. But they feel that they 'must' do it because it provides their livelihood. You may also know people who, while it would be wrong to say that they dislike their jobs, still have an ambivalent view of them: sometimes, or some parts, they enjoy; on other occasions, or other parts, they definitely do not. Many, perhaps most, of the people you know would rather be doing something else, if they could be paid the same for doing that as for their current job.

Career is not a separate box

The career that you and/or your partner pursue should be viewed in terms of the total quality of the life implied by that career: where you live, the time you spend together and with friends and the satisfaction that you get from actually working, as well as whether your after-tax incomes can support that lifestyle.

You probably have more choices than you think. Your present career may be the right one and you can use it as a benchmark. But think creatively about whether you might not prefer a different career and lifestyle. Construct various different options for your current and future lifestyle.

Start from the premise that there does not have to be any conflict between your work life and the things you enjoy outside work. 'Work' can be many things, especially as leisure industries now comprise a large slice of the economy. You may be able to work in an area that is your hobby or even turn your hobby into a business. Remember that enthusiasm can lead to success. It is often easier to make an enthusiasm into a career than to become enthusiastic about a career dictated by others.

Whatever you do, be clear about the optimum point you are trying to reach and view it within your life's total context. This is easier said than done: old habits die hard and the importance of lifestyle is easily relegated to the demands of conventional career thinking.

For instance, when two colleagues and I set up our own management consulting business in 1983, we were aware of the negative effects on our lives of the long hours and extensive travelling previously required by our bosses. So we decided that we would institute a 'total lifestyle approach' in our new business and stress the quality of life as much as the earnings. But when work started flooding in, we ended up working the usual 80-hour week and, what was worse, we required our professional staff to do the same (I couldn't understand, at first, what he meant when an anguished consultant accused me and my partners of 'ruining people's lives'). In the pursuit of money, the total lifestyle approach had quickly gone out of the window.

Which type of career will make you happiest?

Am I advocating here that you 'drop out' of the rat race? Not necessarily. It may be that you will be happiest in the rat race; perhaps, like me, you are basically a rat.

You should certainly be clear about what you enjoy doing, and try to include this in your career. But 'what' you do is only one element in the equation. You also need to consider the work context within which you should operate and the importance to you of professional achievement. These may be at least as important in determining your professional happiness.

You should be clear where you stand on two dimensions:

➤ Do you have a high drive for achievement and career success?

➤ Would you be happiest working for an organization, as a self-employed and self-contained individual (a 'sole trader') or employing other people?

Figure 40 shows this choice. Which box describes you best?

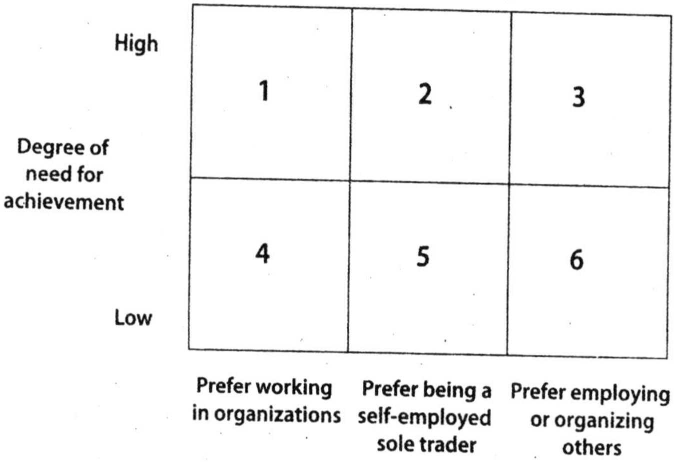

Figure 40 Desired career and lifestyle

Box 1 people are highly ambitious but prefer to work in a context organized and provided by others. The archetypal 'organization man' (and woman) falls in this box. The number of these roles is falling, as large organizations employ fewer people and also as large organizations lose market share to smaller ones (the former trend will continue, the latter may not). But if the supply of these posts is falling, so too is the demand for them. If you want this type of role, you should recognize the fact and pursue your ambition, however unfashionable it may become. Large organizations still provide structure and status even if they can no longer provide security.

Box 2 people are typically professionals who have a drive for recognition by their peers or who want to be the best in their field. They want to be independent and do not fit well into organizations, unless the latter (like most universities) are extremely permissive. These people should ensure that they become self-employed as quickly as possible. Once they are, they should resist the temptation to employ other people, even if this offers high financial rewards. Box 2 people are sole traders, who want to avoid professional dependence on others as far as possible.

Box 3 people have high drive and ambition, hate being employed but do not want the lonely life of the sole trader. They may be unconventional, but they are builders: they want to build a web or a structure around themselves. They are tomorrow's entrepreneurs.

Bill Gates, one of the richest men in America, was a college dropout who was obsessed with personal computer software. But Bill Gates is not a sole trader. He needs to have other people, large numbers of them, working for him. Many people are like this. The ideology of empowerment has obscured this need and made the desire to build businesses slightly unfashionable. If you want to work with other people, but not for them, you are a Box 3 person. You had better recognize this fact and do something about it. Many frustrated professionals are Box 3 people who like what they do but are operating in Box 1 or 2. They do not recognize that the source of their frustration is not professional but organizational.

Box 4 people do not have a high drive for career achievement but do enjoy working with others. They should ensure that they spend many hours a week doing so, either in a conventional job or in a voluntary role.

Box 5 people are not ambitious but do have a strong desire for autonomy in their work. Rather than set up their own firm, the best role for Box 5 people is as freelances, working on particular projects for other firms to suit their own convenience.

Box 6 people are individuals whose need for career achievement is low but who enjoy the process of organizing and developing others. Many teachers, social workers and charity workers are Box 6 people and are well suited to their roles. For Box 6 people the journey is everything; there is no need to arrive.

Many people gravitate towards their 'right' box, but where alienation at work exists it is often because the person is in the wrong box.

What about money?

What indeed! Most people have got peculiar views about money. They think it's more important than it is. But they also think it's more difficult to get than it is. Since most people want to have more money than they currently have, let's deal with the second point first.

My view is that money is not difficult to obtain and, once you have even a little of it to spare, it is not difficult to multiply.

How do you obtain money in the first place? The best answer, one that works surprisingly often, is to do something that you enjoy.

The logic runs as follows. If you enjoy something you are likely to be good at it. You are likely to be better at that than at things you don't enjoy (this is not always true, but the exceptions are rare). If you are good at something, you can create something that will satisfy others. If you satisfy others, they will generally pay you well for it. And since most people do not do things they enjoy, and will not be as productive as you are, you will be able to earn above the going rate in your vocation.

But the logic is not foolproof. There are some professions, such as acting, where supply vastly exceeds demand. What do you do in these circumstances?

What you shouldn't do is to give up. Instead, find a profession where supply and demand are more equally matched, but which is close in its requirements to your preferred vocation. Such adjacent professions usually exist, although they may not be immediately apparent. Think creatively. For example, the requirements of politicians are very close to those of actors. The most effective politicians, like Ronald Reagan, John F Kennedy, Winston Churchill, Harold Macmillan or Margaret Thatcher, either were or could have been successful actors. Charlie Chaplin was a dead ringer for Adolf Hitler and this was not accidental; sadly, Hitler was one of the century's best and most charismatic actors. This may all seem pretty obvious. But few would-be actors seriously contemplate a career in politics, despite the weaker competition and superior rewards.

What if what you enjoy most has a poor employment market and you can't find an adjacent profession that has good prospects? Then go to your next most preferred vocation and repeat the process until you find one that you like and that pays well.

Once in your profession, if making money is really important to you and if you are any good at what you do, you should aim to become self-employed as soon as possible and, after that, to start to employ others.

I arrive at this conclusion from the 80/20 Principle's argument about arbitrage. 80 per cent of the value in any organization or profession comes from 20 per cent of the professionals. The workers who are above average will tend to be paid more than those who are below average, but nowhere near enough to reflect the differential in performance. It follows that the best people are always underpaid and the worst people always overpaid. As an above-average employee, you cannot escape from this trap. Your boss may think you are good, but will never credit your true value relative to others. The only way out is to set up in business yourself and, if you are so inclined, to employ other above-average workers. Don't take either of these steps, however, if you aren't comfortable with being self-employed or a boss (see Figure 40).

Money is easy to multiply

The other thing to remember is that once you have a little spare cash, it can easily be multiplied. Save and invest. This is what capitalism is all about. To multiply money, you don't need to be in business. You can simply invest in the stock market, using the 80/20 Principle as your guide. Chapter 14 will elaborate.

Money is overrated

I would like you to have a lot more money, but don't go overboard on this. Money can help you gain the lifestyle you want, but beware: all those nasty fables about Midas and the like are rooted in truth. Money can buy you happiness, but only to the extent that you use money to do what is really right for you in the first place. Also, money can bite back.

Remember that the more money you have, the less value an extra dollop of wealth creates. In economist speak, the marginal utility of money declines sharply. Once you have adjusted to a higher standard of living, it may give you little or no extra happiness. It can even turn negative, if the extra cost of maintaining the new lifestyle causes anxiety or piles on extra pressure to earn money in non-satisfying ways.

More wealth also requires more management. Looking after my money irritates me. (Don't offer to relieve me of it; it irritates me less than giving it away would!)

The tax authorities also make money inefficient. Earn more, pay disproportionately more tax. Earn more, work more. Work more and you have to spend more: on living close to work in an expensive metropolitan area or alternatively on commuting; on labour-saving devices; on contracting out housework; and on ever-more expensive leisure compensations. Spend more and you have to work more. You can end up with an expensive lifestyle that controls you rather than vice versa. You might get much better value and happiness out of a simpler and cheaper lifestyle.

What about achievement?

There are people who want to achieve – and then there are sane people. All motivational writers fall into the trap of telling you that you need direction and purpose in life. Then they tell you that you don't have it. Then they put you through the agony of deciding what it should be. Finally, they tell you what they think you ought to do.

So if you don't want to achieve anything specific and are happy enough going through life having it all (minus achievement), count yourself lucky (and skip to the end of this chapter).

But if, like me, you feel guilty and insecure without achievement and want to increase it, the 80/20 Principle can help with your affliction.

Achievement should be easy. It shouldn't be '99 per cent perspiration and 1 per cent inspiration'. Instead, see if it's true that 80 per cent of your achievement to date – measured by what you yourself value – has come from 20 per cent of your inputs. If true or nearly true, then think carefully about this top 20 per cent. Could you simply repeat the achievements? Upgrade them? Reproduce similar ones on a grander scale? Combine two previous achievements to compound the satisfaction?

➤ Think about your past achievements that have had the most positive 'market' response from others, those that have led to the greatest critical acclaim: the 20 per cent of your work and play that has led to 80 per cent of the praise others have given you. How much real satisfaction did this give you?

➤ What methods worked best for you in the past? Which collaborators? Which audiences? Again, think 80/20. Anything that just yielded an average degree of satisfaction for the time or effort should be discarded. Think of the exceptional highs achieved exceptionally easily. Do not constrain yourself to your work history. Think of your time as a student, a tourist or with friends.

➤ Looking forward, what could you achieve that would make you proud, that no one else could do with the same ease? If there were 100 people around you trying to do something, what could you do in 20 per cent of the time that it would take

80 of them to finish? Where would you be in the top 20? Even more stringently, what could you do better than 80 per cent but in only 20 per cent of the time? These questions may initially seem like riddles but, believe me, there are answers! People's abilities in different spheres are incredibly diverse.

➤ If you could measure the enjoyment derived from anything, what would you enjoy more than 95 per cent of your peers? What would you do better than 95 out of 100? Which achievements would fulfil both conditions?

It is important to focus on what you find easy. This is where most motivational writers go wrong. They assume you should try things that are difficult for you; on the same grounds, one suspects, that grandparents used to urge the consumption of cod liver oil before capsules were invented. The inspirationalists quote such worthies as T J Watson, who said that 'success lies on the far side of failure'. My view is that normally failure lies on the far side of failure. Also, success lies on the near side of failure. You are already very successful at some things and it matters not a whit if those things are very few in number.

The 80/20 Principle is clear. Pursue those few things where you are amazingly better than others and that you enjoy most.

What else do you need to have it all?

We've dealt with work, with lifestyle, with money and with achievement. To have it all, you also need a few satisfying relationships. This requires a separate chapter.

12 With a Little Help From Our Friends

Relationships help us to define who we are and what we can become. Most of us can trace our successes to pivotal relationships.

Donald O Clifton and Paula Nelson[1]

Without relationships we are either dead to the world – or dead. Although banal, this is true: our friendships are at the heart of our lives. It is also true that our professional relationships are at the heart of our success. This is a chapter about both personal and professional relationships. We start with personal relationships, with friends, lovers and loved ones. Then we consider professional relationships in their own right.

What on earth has this got to do with the 80/20 Principle? The answer is quite a lot. There is a trade-off between quality and quantity and we consistently undercultivate what is most important.

The 80/20 Principle provides three provocative hypotheses:

- 80 per cent of the value of our relationships comes from 20 per cent of the relationships.
- 80 per cent of the value of our relationships comes from the 20 per cent of close relationships that we form first in our lives.
- We devote much less than 80 per cent of our attention to the 20 per cent of relationships that create 80 per cent of the value.

Compile your Top 20 personal relationships chart

At this stage, write down the names of your Top 20 friends and loved ones, those with whom you have the most important relationships, ranked from most important to least important to you. 'Important' means the depth and closeness of the personal relationship, the extent to which the relationship helps you in life and the extent to which the relationship enhances your sense of who you are and what you can become. Do this now, before reading on.

As a matter of interest, where did your lover/partner come on the list? Above or below your parents or children? Be honest (but you should probably destroy the list when you are through with this chapter!).

Next, allocate a total of 100 points between the relationships in terms of their importance to you. For example, if the first person on the list is exactly as important as the next 19 down the list combined, allocate 50 points to him or her. You may need to have more than one run at the numbers to make them add up to 100 by the time you're finished.

I don't know what your list looks like, but a typical pattern in line with the 80/20 Principle would have two characteristics: the top four relationships (20 per cent of the total) would score most of the points (maybe 80 per cent); and there would tend to be a constant relationship between each number and the next one down. For example, number two may be two-thirds or half as important as number one; number three may similarly be two-thirds or half as important as number two; and so on. It is interesting to note that if the number one relationship is twice as important as number two and so on, relationship number six is only about 3 per cent as important as number one!

Complete this exercise by noting against each name the proportion of time that you actively spend with the person, talking or doing something together (exclude time spent with someone where they are not the main focus of attention, for example when watching television or a movie). Take the total amount of time spent with the 20 people as 100 units and then allocate these. Typically, you will find that you spend much less than 80 per cent of the time with the few people who comprise 80 per cent of 'relationship value' to you.

The action implications should be plain. Go for quality rather than quantity. Spend your time and emotional energy reinforcing and deepening the relationships that are most important.

But there is another wrinkle, to do with the chronology of the relationships in our life. It turns out that our capacity for close relationships is far from infinite. There is another trade-off between quality and quantity of which we should be aware.

The village theory

Anthropologists stress that the number of exhilarating and important personal relationships that people can establish is limited.[2] Apparently, the common pattern of people in any society is to have two important childhood friends, two significant adult friends and two doctors. Typically, there are two powerful sexual partners who eclipse the others. Most commonly, you fall in love only once and there is one member of your family whom you love above all others. The number of significant personal relationships is remarkably similar for everyone, regardless of their location, sophistication or culture.

This has led to the anthropologists' 'village theory'. In an African village, all these relationships happen within a few hundred metres and are often formed within a short period of time. For us, these relationships may be spread all over the planet and over a whole lifetime. They nonetheless constitute a village that we each have in our heads. And once these slots are filled, they're filled for ever.

The anthropologists say that if you have too much experience, too early, you exhaust your capacity for further deep relationships. This may explain the superficiality often observed in those whose profession or circumstances force them to have a great number of relationships, such as salespeople, prostitutes or those who move house very frequently.

J G Ballard quotes a case example of a rehabilitation project in California for young women who mixed with criminals. The women were young, 20 or 21, and the programme aimed to introduce them to new social backgrounds, basically to middle-class volunteers, who befriended them and invited them to their homes.

Many of these girls had been married at an incredibly early age. Many had had their first children at 13 or 14. Some had been married three times by the time they were 20. They had often had hundreds of lovers and sometimes had close relationships or children by men who were then shot or jailed. They'd been through everything – relationships, motherhood, break-ups, bereavements – and experienced the whole gamut of human experience while still in their teens.

The project was a total failure. The explanation was that the women were incapable of forming any deep new relationships. They were all used up. Their relationship slots had been filled, for ever.

This sad story is salutory. It also fits in with the 80/20 Principle: a small number of relationships will account for a large proportion of emotional value. Fill your relationship slots with extreme care and not too early!

Professional relationships and alliances

We now turn to your relationships and alliances related to your work. Here the importance of a few close allies can hardly be overstated.

Individuals may appear to do amazing things – and they do. But exceptional individual performance requires allies.

You alone cannot make yourself successful. Only others can do that for you. What you can do is to select the best relationships and alliances for your purposes.

You badly need allies. You must treat them well, as an extension of yourself, as you treat yourself (or should). Do not assume your friends and allies are all of roughly equal importance. Focus your attention on nurturing the key alliances of your life. If this seems obvious or banal, ask yourself how many of your friends follow these lines. Then ask yourself whether you do.

All spiritual leaders had many allies. If they needed them, so do you. To take one example: Jesus Christ depended on John the Baptist to draw him to public attention; then on the 12 disciples; then on other apostles, notably St Paul, arguably the greatest marketing genius in history.[3]

Nothing is more important than your choice of alliances and how you build them. Without them you are nothing. With them, you can transform your life, often the lives of those around you and occasionally, in small or large ways, the course of history.

We can best appreciate the importance of alliances by a brief historical excursion.

History is driven by individuals who form effective alliances

Vilfredo Pareto, the 'bourgeois Karl Marx', claimed that history was essentially a history of the succession of élites.[4] The objective of energetic individuals or families was therefore devoted to rise into the élite or to be part of one élite that displaced another (or, if already in the élite, to stay there and keep the élite in place).

If you turn a Paretian or Marxian, class-based view of history on its head, you can conclude that alliances within élites or would-be élites are the driving forces of progress. The individual is nothing except as part of a class, certainly; but equally, the individual allied with other individuals of the same class (or possibly, with individuals from another class) is everything.

The importance of individuals, allied to others, is apparent from some of history's turning points. Would there have been a Russian Revolution in 1917 without the pivotal role of Lenin? Probably not at all; and certainly not one that diverted the course of world history for the next 72 years. Would the Russian Revolution of 1989 that reversed the one of 1917 have succeeded and been maintained without the presence of mind and bravery of Boris Yeltsin? If he had not climbed on a tank outside the Russian White House, the Communist gerontocrats would probably have cemented their shaky coup.

We can play the game of historical what-ifs repeatedly to demonstrate the importance of individuals. There would have been no Holocaust and no Second World War without Hitler. Without Roosevelt and Churchill, Hitler would probably have united Europe rather earlier and more thoroughly and in a considerably more vexacious way than his successors have done. And so on. But the key point often overlooked is that none of these individuals could have turned the course of history without relationships and alliances.

In almost any sphere of achievement,[5] you can identify a small number of key collaborators, without whom individuals could not have succeeded but with whom individuals have had massive impact. In government, in mass ideological movements, in business, in medicine, in the sciences, in philanthropy or in sport, the pattern is the same. History is not composed of blind, non-human forces. History is not run by classes or élites operating according to some pre-programmed economic or sociological formula. History is determined and changed by dedicated individuals who form effective alliances with a small number of close collaborators.

You need a few key allies

If you have had any success in life, you will (unless you are a blind egotist headed for a fall) recognize the crucial importance of allies in your achievements. But you will also detect the hand of the 80/20 Principle here. The key allies are few in number.

It is generally a safe assertion that at least 80 per cent of the value of your allies comes from fewer than 20 per cent of their number. For anyone who has done anything, the list of allies, when you come to think of it, is incredibly long. But of the hundreds or more involved, the value is highly skewed. Usually half a dozen key allies are far more important than all the rest.

You don't need many allies but you need the right ones, with the right relationships between you and each of them and between themselves. You need them at the right time, in the right place and with a common interest in advancing your interests. Above all, the allies must trust you and you must be able to trust them.

Make a list of your Top 20 business relationships, of people that you consider to be important allies, and compare it with an estimation of the total number of contacts with whom you would be on first-name terms – if you have a Rolodex, a Filofax or a telephone list, this is the total number of active contacts on that list. 80 per cent of the value to you of alliances is likely to be comprised in 20 per cent of the relationships. If this is not the case, the alliances (or some of them) are likely to be of poor quality.

Achievement alliances

If you are well into your career, make a list of the people who have helped you the most to date. Rank them from top to bottom and then assign 100 points between the top 10.

In general, the people who have helped you the most in the past will also be the people who can do so in the future. Sometimes, however, a good friend who is some way down the list becomes a much more important potential ally: perhaps because he or she has gained a new and highly influential post, has made a killing through an investment or secured valuable recognition. Go through the exercise again, ranking your allies from one to ten and allocating another 100 points to them, this time on the basis of their future ability to help you.

People help you because there is a strong relationship between you. The best relationships are built on five attributes: mutual enjoyment of each other's company, respect, shared experience, reciprocity and trust. In successful business relationships these attributes become entwined and are impossible to untangle, but we can think of them separately.

Mutual enjoyment

The first of our five attributes is the most obvious. If you do not enjoy talking to someone, in their office, a restaurant, at a social occasion or on the phone, you will not build a strong relationship. They have to enjoy your company too.

If this seems terribly obvious, reflect for a moment on the people with whom you mix socially, but basically for professional purposes. How many of them do you really like? A surprising number of people spend a lot of time with people they don't like. This is a complete and utter waste of time. It's not enjoyable, it's tiring, it's often expensive, it prevents you doing better things and it will get you absolutely nowhere. Stop doing it! Spend more time with the contacts you enjoy, particularly if they can also be useful to you.

Respect

There are people whose company I enjoy immensely, but whom I do not greatly respect professionally; and vice versa. I would never advance someone's career if I didn't respect their professional abilities.

If someone is to help you professionally, they must be impressed by you! Yet very often we hide our light under a bushel. A good friend, Paul, who was in a position to advance my career considerably, once remarked in a board meeting where we were both outside directors that he was prepared to believe that I was competent professionally, although he had never seen the slightest evidence of it! I resolved to find a context where I could show some evidence. I did – and Paul moved sharply up my list of business allies.

Shared experience

Just as in the primitive village, we have a limited number of slots for important professional experiences. Shared experience, especially if it involves struggle or suffering, is very bonding. One of my greatest relationships, both as business ally and friend, came from being a new recruit in my first job alongside another recruit in the same situation. I am sure we would not have developed such rapport if we had not both hated our jobs in the oil refinery so much.

The implication is that if you are in a difficult job, develop one ally whom you like and respect. Make it a deep and fruitful alliance. If you don't, you are missing a big opportunity!

Even if you are not suffering, find one person who has a great deal of shared experience and make him or her a key ally.

Reciprocity

For alliances to work, each ally must do a great deal for the other party – repeatedly, consistently, over a long period of time.

Reciprocity requires that the relationship is not one sided.

Equally, reciprocity should come naturally and not be too finely calculated. The important thing is that you do whatever you possibly can, consistent with high ethical standards, to help the other person. This requires time and thought! You should not wait until they ask a favour.

What surprises me in reviewing business relationships is how infrequently true reciprocity is built up. Even if all the other ingredients – friendship, respect, shared experience and trust – are present, people very often neglect to be pro-active in helping their allies. This, again, is a massive wasted opportunity to deepen the relationship and store up future help.

The Beatles told us that 'in the end, the love you take is equal to the love you make'. Similarly, in the end, the professional help you receive is equal to that you provide

Trust

Trust cements relationships. Lack of trust can unwind them very quickly. Trust requires total honesty at all times. If there is even a suspicion that you are not saying what you think, even for the most high-minded reasons or to remain diplomatic, trust can be undermined.

If you do not trust someone totally, don't try to build up an alliance. It shouldn't work and it won't.

But if you do have total trust, it makes business relationships so much faster and more efficient. A lot of time and cost can be eliminated. Never forfeit trust by being capricious, cowardly or cunning.

If you are in the early stages of your career, fill your ally slots carefully

A good rule of thumb is that you should develop up to six or seven absolutely gilt-edged business alliances, composed as follows:

- one or two relationships with mentors, people more senior than you
- two or three relationships with peers
- one or two relationships where you are the mentor.

Relationships with mentors

Choose your one or two mentors carefully. Do not let them choose you: they might deprive a much better mentor of the slot. The mentors you choose should have the following two characteristics:

- You must be able to build up the 'five ingredient' relationship comprising mutual enjoyment, respect, shared experience, reciprocity and trust.
- The mentor should be as senior as possible or, even better, relatively junior but clearly destined for the top. The best mentors are extremely able and ambitious.

It may seem strange to say that relationships with mentors should be reciprocal, since inevitably the mentor will have more to offer than the mentee. But mentors must be rewarded or else they will lose interest. The mentee must provide fresh ideas, mental stimulation, enthusiasm, hard work, knowledge of new technologies or some other attribute of value to the mentor. Wise mentors very often use younger allies to keep them up to date with emerging trends and potential opportunities or threats that may not be apparent from the top.

Relationships with peers

With peers, you are very often spoilt for choice. There are many potential allies. But remember that you have only two or three slots to fill. Be very selective. Make a list of all potential allies who have the 'five ingredients' or potential for them. Pick the two or three from the list who you believe will be the most successful. Then work hard at making them allies.

Relationships where you are the mentor

Do not neglect these. You are likely to get the most out of your one or two mentees if they work for you, preferably for quite a long period of time.

Multiple alliances

Alliances very often build up into webs or networks, where many of the same people have relationships with each other.

These networks can become very powerful, or at least seem so from the outside. They are often great fun.

But do not get carried away, smug in the knowledge that you are 'in with the in crowd'. You may just be a fringe player. Don't forget that all true and valuable relationships are bilateral. If you have a strong alliance with both X and Y and they have one between each other, that is excellent. Lenin said that a chain is as strong as its weakest link. However strong the relationships between X and Y, the ones that really matter for you are yours with X and yours with Y.

Conclusion

For both personal and professional relationships, fewer and deeper is better than more and less deep. One relationship is not as good as another. Seriously flawed relationships, when you spend a lot of time together but the result is unsatisfying, should be terminated as soon as possible. Bad relationships drive out good. There is a limited number of slots for relationships; don't use up the slots too early or on low-quality relationships.

Choose with care. Then build with commitment.

A fork in the book

We have now reached an optional fork in this book's progress. The next two chapters (13 and 14) are, respectively, for those who want to know how to advance their careers or multiply their money. Readers for whom these are not important concerns should advance to Chapter 15, where the seven habits of happiness await.

13 Intelligent and Lazy

There are only four types of officer. First, there are the lazy, stupid ones. Leave them alone, they do no harm... Second, there are the hard-working intelligent ones. They make excellent staff officers, ensuring that every detail is properly considered. Third, there are the hard-working, stupid ones. These people are a menace and must be fired at once. They create irrelevant work for everybody. Finally, there are the intelligent lazy ones. They are suited for the highest office.

General Von Manstein on the German Officer Corps

This is a chapter for the truly ambitious. If you do not suffer from the insecurity that fuels the desire to be rich or famous, move on to Chapter 15. But if you want to win the rat race, here is some advice that may surprise you.

General Von Manstein captures the essence of this chapter, which is the 80/20 Principle's guidance on how to have a successful career. If the general had been a management consultant, he would have made a fortune out of the matrix shown in Figure 41.

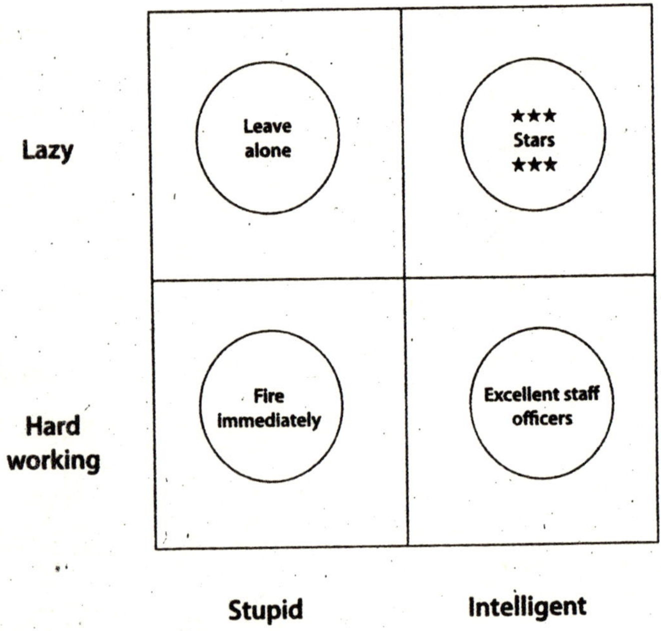

Figure 41 The Von Manstein matrix

This advice is what to do about other people. But what about yourself? It might be thought that intelligence and propensity to work are fixed properties, in which case the Von Manstein matrix, although interesting, is useless. But the position advanced in this chapter is slightly different. Even if you are hard working, you can learn to become lazy. And even if you or other people think you are stupid, you are intelligent at something. The key to becoming a star is to simulate, manufacture and deploy lazy intelligence. As we will see, lazy intelligence can be worked at. The key to earning more and working less is to pick the right thing to do and to do only those things that add the highest value.

First, however, it is instructive to see how the 80/20 Principle distributes rewards to those who work. Rewards are both unbalanced and unfair. We can either complain about this or align ourselves to take advantage of the Von Manstein matrix.

Imbalance is rampant in professional success and returns

The 80/20 Principle is nowhere more evident today than in the very high and increasing returns enjoyed by very small numbers of élite professionals.

We live in a world where the returns for top talent, in all spheres of life, have never been higher. A small percentage of professionals obtain a disproportionate amount of recognition and fame and usually also a high percentage of the spoils available.

Take any sphere of contemporary human endeavour, in any country or globally. Whether the sphere be athletics, baseball, basketball, football, golf, rugby, tennis or any other popular sport; or architecture, sculpture, painting or any other visual art; or music of any category; the movies or the theatre; novels, cookery books or autobiography; or even hosting TV chat shows, reading the news, politics or any other well-defined area, there will be a small number of pre-eminent professionals whose names spring to mind.

Considering how many people there are in each country,

it is a remarkably small number of names, and usually a small percentage – typically well under 5 per cent – of the professionals active in the relevant sphere. The fraction of any profession who are recognized 'names' is very small, but they hog the limelight. They are always in demand and always in the news. They are the human equivalent of consumer goods brands, obtaining instant recognition as known quantities.

The same concentration operates with regard to popularity and financial rewards. More than 80 per cent of novels sold are from fewer than 20 per cent of novel titles in print. The same is true of any other category of publishing: of pop CDs and concerts, of movies, even of books about business. The same applies to actors, TV celebrities or any branch of sports. 80 per cent of prize money in golf goes to fewer than 20 per cent of professional golfers; the equivalent is true in tennis; and in horseracing, more than 80 per cent of winnings go to fewer than 20 per cent of owners, jockeys and trainers.

We live in an increasingly marketized world. The top names can command enormous fees – but those who are not quite as good or well known make relatively little.

There is a big difference between being at the top, and well known to all; and being almost at the top, and well known only to a few enthusiasts. The best-known baseball, basketball or football stars can make millions; those just below the top rank, only a comfortable living.

Why do the winners take all?

The distribution of incomes for superstars is even more unbalanced than for the population as a whole and provides excellent illustrations of the 80/20 Principle (or in most cases, 90/10 or 95/5). Various writers[1] have sought economic or sociological explanations of the superreturns to superstars.

The most persuasive explanation is that two conditions facilitate superstar returns. One is that it is possible for the superstar to be accessible to many people at once. Modern communications enable this to happen. The incremental cost of 'distributing' Janet Jackson, J K Rowling, Steven Spielberg, Oprah Winfrey, Paris Hilton, Roger Federer, Mariah Carey or David Beckham to additional consumers can be almost nothing, since the additional cost of broadcasting, making a CD or printing a book is a very small part of the total cost structure.

The additional cost of making these superstars available is certainly no more than for a second-rate substitute, except in so far as the superstars themselves take a higher fee. Although the fee may be many millions or tens of millions, the incremental cost per consumer is very low indeed, often a matter of cents or fractions of a cent.

The second condition for superstar returns is that mediocrity must not be a substitute for talent. It must be important to obtain the best. If one house cleaner is half as quick as another, the market will clear by paying her half as much. But who wants someone who is half as good as Tiger Woods, Celine Dion or Andrea Bocelli? In this case, the non-superstar, even working for nothing, would have vastly inferior economics to the superstar. The non-superstar would attract a smaller audience and, for a tiny decrease in the total cost, bring in very much lower revenues.

Winner takes all is a modern phenomenon

What is intriguing is that this disparity between top returns and the rest has not always existed. The best basketball or football champions of the 1940s and 1950s, for example, did not make much money. It used to be possible to find a prominent politician who died fairly poor. And the further back we go, the less true it was that the winner took all.

For instance, William Shakespeare was absolutely preeminent in terms of talent among his contemporaries. So was Leonardo da Vinci. By rights or, rather, by today's standards, they should have been able to exploit their brilliance, creativity and fame to become the richest men of their times. Instead, they made do with the sort of income that is enjoyed today in relative terms by millions of moderately talented professionals.

The imbalance of financial rewards for talent is becoming more and more pronounced over time. Today, income is more closely linked to merit and marketability, so that the 80/20 connection, because it can be clearly demonstrated in money terms, becomes easily apparent. Our society is clearly more meritocratic than that of a century, or even a generation, ago. This is particularly so in Europe generally and the UK in particular.

If top footballers like Bobby Moore had made fortunes in the 1940s or 1950s, it would have provoked fury among the British Establishment; it would have been unseemly. When the leader writers of the 1960s discovered that the Beatles were millionaires, it caused astonishment. Today the fact that Madonna is worth at least $325m, J K Rowling $1bn, and Oprah Winfrey $1.5bn causes no surprise or outrage. Nowadays we have less respect for rank and more for markets.

The other new element is, as mentioned above, the technological revolution in broadcasting, telecommunications and consumer products like the CD and CD-Rom. The key consideration now is to maximize revenue, which superstars can do. The extra cost of hiring them may be a huge amount of money for an individual, but the cost per consumer is trivial.

Achievement has always obeyed the *80/20 Principle*

Yet if we set money aside and deal in the more enduring and important matters (at least for everyone except the superstars themselves), we can see that the concentration of achievement and fame in very few people, whatever the profession, has always been true. Constraints that seem odd to our eyes – such as class or the absence of telecommunications – stopped Shakespeare and Leonardo da Vinci becoming millionaires. But lack of wealth did not diminish their achievements or the fact that a huge proportion of impact came from a tiny proportion of creators.

80/20 returns also apply to non-media professionals

Although it is most noticeable and exaggerated with respect to media superstars, it is significant that 80/20 returns are not confined to the world of entertainment. In fact, celebrities comprise only 3 per cent of multimillionaires. The majority of the 7 million or so Americans in the $1–10m bracket are professionals of one sort or another: executives, Wall Street types, top lawyers and doctors and the like. Moving up to the 1.4 million Americans who own $10–100m, there are twice as many entrepreneurs as in the 'poorer millionaire' category. When we reach the much smaller number (some thousands) of Americans worth $100m–1bn, entrepreneurs and money managers predominate. The same is true in the billionaire category, where *Forbes* magazine counted 946 in 2007, including no fewer than 178 new entries and 17 re-entries.

Talent has probably always followed an 80/20 pattern. The effect of technology may be, roughly, to move talent to a curve approximating 90/10 or 95/5. Rewards used to follow, perhaps, a 70/30 curve, but for the most famous they must surely now be close to 95/5 or an even more unbalanced curve.

The distribution of wealth along 80/20 or even 99/1 lines seems to have become an inexorable and even frightening trend. Between 1990 and 2004, the top 1 per cent of American earners saw their earnings fatten by 57 per cent. For the top one-tenth of 1 per cent, earnings soared by 85 per cent. Billionaires have fared even better. Their combined wealth was a staggering $439bn in 1995, but now it has multiplied eight times to $3.5 *trillion*. In the year to 2007, it went up by no less than 26 per cent. Two-thirds of the 2007 billionaires were significantly richer than the previous year, and only 17 per cent were poorer.

What does all this mean for the ambitious?

What are the rules for success in this 80/20 world? You may want to give up and refuse to compete in a world where the odds against megasuccess are so long. But I believe this is the wrong conclusion. Even if you do not aim to become a world-beating millionaire (but especially if you do), there are 10 golden rules for successful careers in an increasingly 80/20 world (see Figure 42).

1. Specialize in a very small niche; develop a core skill
2. Choose a niche that you enjoy, where you can excel and stand a chance of becoming an acknowledged leader
3. Realize that knowledge is power
4. Identify your market and your core customers and serve them best
5. Identify where 20 per cent of effort gives 80 per cent of returns
6. Learn from the best
7. Become self-employed early in your career
8. Employ as many net value creators as possible
9. Use outside contractors for everything but your core skill
10. Exploit capital leverage

Figure 42 10 golden rules for career success

Although these principles are more valuable the more ambitious you are, they apply to any level of career and ambition. As we elaborate, put on your 80/20 thinker cap to editionize the text to your own career. Recall the Von Manstein matrix: find the place where your name is already inscribed, where you can be intelligent, lazy and highly rewarded.

Specialize in a very small niche

Specialization is one of the great, universal laws of life. This is how life itself evolved, with each species seeking out new ecological niches and developing unique characteristics. A small business that does not specialize will die. An individual who does not specialize will be doomed to life as a wage slave.

In the natural world the number of species is unknown, but it is almost certainly an astonishingly large number. The number of niches in the business world is very much larger than generally appreciated; hence many small businesses, apparently in competition in a broad market, can actually all be leaders in their own niches and avoid head-to-head competition.[2]

For the individual, too, it is better to know a few things well, or preferably one thing exceptionally well, than it is to know many things superficially.

Specialization is intrinsic to the 80/20 Principle. The reason that it operates – that 20 per cent of inputs can result in 80 per cent of outputs – is that the productive fifth is much more specialized and suited to the task at hand than are the unproductive four-fifths.

Whenever we observe the 80/20 Principle working, this is evidence both of a waste of resources (on the part of the unproductive four-fifths) and of the need for further specialization. If the unproductive 80 per cent specialized in what they are good at, they could become the productive 20 per cent in another sphere. This in turn would produce another 80/20 relationship, but at a higher level. What used to be the unproductive 80 per cent, or some of it, will now be the productive 20 per cent in another distribution.

This process, what the German nineteenth-century philosopher G W F Hegel called a 'dialectic',[3] can go on and on, constituting the engine of progress. Indeed, there is evidence that this is precisely what has happened over time, both in the natural world and in society. Higher living standards have been driven by greater and greater specialization.

The computer evolved from a new specialization within electronics; the personal computer from a further specialization; modern user-friendly software from further specializations; the CD-Rom from yet another stage of the same process. Biotechnology, which will revolutionize food production, has evolved in a similar way, with each new advance requiring and feeding on ever more progressive specialization.

Your career ought to evolve in a similar way. Knowledge is the key. One of the most marked tendencies in the world of work over the past generation has been the increasing power and status of technicians, formerly often blue-collar workers but now empowered by specialist knowledge in league with ever more specialized information technology.[4] These experts are now often more powerful and well paid than the technologically more primitive managers who purported to add value by organizing the technicians.[5]

At the most basic level, specialization requires qualifications. More than 80 per cent of qualifications in most societies are held by 20 per cent of the workforce. Increasingly, the most important class distinction in advanced societies is not ownership of land or even of wealth, but ownership of information. 80 per cent of information is the property of 20 per cent of people.

The American economist and statesman Robert Reich has divided the US workforce into four groups. The top group he calls 'symbolic analysts', people who deal with numbers, ideas, problems and words. They include financial analysts, consultants, architects, lawyers, doctors and journalists, indeed all workers whose intelligence and knowledge are the source of power and influence. Interestingly, he calls this group the 'fortunate fifth' – in our terms the top 20 per cent – whom he says hold 80 per cent of information and 80 per cent of wealth.

Anyone who has any recent experience of intellectual disciplines knows that knowledge is undergoing a profound and progressive fragmentation. In some ways this is worrying, since there is almost nobody in the intelligentzia or society as a whole who can integrate different advances in knowledge and tell us what it all means. But in other ways, the fragmentation is further evidence of the need for and value of specialization.

And for the individual, observing the increasing trend of rewards going to the top dogs, this is an extremely hopeful process. You may have no hope of becoming Albert Einstein or even Bill Gates, but there are literally hundreds of thousands, if not millions, of niches where you can choose to specialize. You could even, like Gates, invent your own niche.

Find your niche. It may take you a long time, but it is the only way you will gain access to exceptional returns.

Choose a niche that you enjoy and in which you can excel

Specialization requires very careful thought. The narrower an area, the more important it is to choose it with extreme care.

Specialize in an area in which you are already interested and which you enjoy. You will not become an acknowledged leader in anything that cannot command your enthusiasm and passion.

This is not as demanding a requirement as you may think. Everyone is excited by something; if not, they are dead or dying. And almost every hobby, every enthusiasm, every vocation can these days be turned into a business activity.

You can also look at it from the other end. Almost anyone who has made it to the top has done so with great enthusiasm for what they are doing. Enthusiasm drives personal achievement and also infects others with enthusiasm, creating a multiplier effect. You cannot feign or manufacture enthusiasm.

If you are not enthusiastic about your current career, and are ambitious, you should stop doing it. But before you take this step, work out a better career. Write down all the things about which you are enthusiastic. Then work out which of these could be made into a career niche. Then choose the one about which you are most enthusiastic.

Realize that knowledge is power

The key to making a career out of an enthusiasm is knowledge. Know more about an area than anybody else does. Then work out a way to marketize it, to create a market and a set of loyal customers.

It is not enough to know a lot about a little. You have to know more than anybody else, at least about something. Do not stop improving your expertise until you are sure you know more, and are better in your niche, than anybody else. Then reinforce your lead by constant practice and inveterate curiosity. Do not expect to become a leader unless you really are more knowledgeable than anyone else.

Marketization is a creative process: you will need to work out for yourself how to do this. Perhaps you can follow the example of others who have marketized their knowledge in an adjacent area. But if this option is not available, follow the guidelines below.

Identify your market and your core customers and serve them best

Your market is those people who might pay for your knowledge. The core customers are those who would value your services most.

The market is the arena within which you will operate. This requires you to define how the knowledge you have can be sold. Are you going to work for an established firm or an individual as an employee, to work for a number of corporations or individuals as a freelance, or to set up a business marketing services (derived from the labour of yourself and others) to individuals or to firms?

Are you going to supply raw knowledge, to process it for specific situations or to use the knowledge to create a product? Are you going to invent the product, to add value to someone else's semi-finished product or to be a retailer of finished products?

Your core customer or customers are the specific individuals or corporations that may place the highest value on your activity and that may provide a stream of well-paid work.

Whether you are employed, self-employed, a small or large employer or even the head of state, you have core customers on whom your continued success depends. This is true whatever the level of your past achievement.

It is surprising, incidentally, how often leaders forfeit their position by neglecting or even abusing their core customer group. Tennis star John McEnroe forgot that his customers were the spectators and even the professional tennis organizers. Mrs Thatcher (as she then was) forgot that her most important customers were her own Conservative Members of Parliament. Richard Nixon forgot that his core customer group was Middle America, with its requirement for integrity.

Serving customers is key, but they must be the right customers for you, those whom with relatively little effort you can make extremely happy.

Identify where 20 per cent of effort gives 80 per cent of returns

There is no fun in work unless you can achieve a lot with a little. If you have to work 60 or 70 hours a week in order to cope, if you feel that you are always behind, if you are struggling to keep up with work's requirements: then you are in the wrong job, or doing it completely the wrong way! You are certainly not benefiting from the 80/20 Principle, or from the Von Manstein matrix.

Keep reminding yourself of some of the golden 80/20

insights. In any sphere of activity, 80 per cent of people are only achieving 20 per cent of results; and 20 per cent of people are achieving 80 per cent of results. What are the majority doing wrong and the minority doing right? Come to that, who are the minority? Could you do what they do? Could you take what they do and do it in an even more extreme form? Could you invent an even more clever and efficient way to do it?

Is there a good fit between yourself and your 'customers'? Are you in the right corporation? The right department? The right job? Where could you impress your 'customers' with relatively little effort? Do you enjoy what you do and are you enthusiastic about it? If not, begin planning today to switch to a job where you can be.

If you like your job and your 'customers' but are not coasting to glory, you are probably spending your time in the wrong way. What is the 20 per cent of your time when you achieve 80 per cent of your results? Do more of it! What is the 80 per cent of your time when you achieve little? Do less of it! The answer can be as simple as that, although implementing the change will require you to break all your normal habits and conventions.

In every market, for every customer, in every firm, in all professions, there is a way to things more efficiently and effectively: not just a bit better, but a step-function better. Look beneath the surface for 80/20 truths in your profession or industry.

In my own profession, that of management consulting, the answers are clear. Big clients, good. Big assignments, good. Large case teams with many cheap junior members, good. Close client relationships – between individuals – good. Relationships with the top person, the CEO, very good. Long client relationships, very good. Long and close client relationships with the top people in large corporations, with large budgets and the use of many junior consultants – laughing all the way to the bank!

What are the 80/20 truths in your line of business? Where do corporations make supranormal, even obscene, profits? Which of your colleagues is riding high while always seeming relaxed, with time to indulge themselves in their favourite hobbies? What are they doing that's so cute? Think, think, think. The answer is there somewhere. All you have to do is find it. But don't ask the industry Establishment what the answer is, don't do a survey of your colleagues and don't try to find the answer in print. All you will find is the conventional wisdom, repeated a zillion ways. The answer will lie with the industry heretics, the professional mavericks and the eccentric individuals.

Learn from the best

The winners in any field have, almost by definition, found ways to make 20 per cent of effort yield 80 per cent of results. This does not mean that the leaders are lazy or lacking in dedication. Leaders usually work very hard. But their output, for no more time than is put in by the merely competent in their field, is several times more valuable than the output of the merely competent. The leaders produce results that, in both quality and quantity, knock spots off the competition.

Put another way, leaders do things differently. Leaders are usually outsiders; they think and feel differently. Those who are best in any sphere do not think and act in similar ways to the average performers. The leaders may not be conscious of what they do differently. Very rarely do they think about it and articulate it. But, if leaders do not generally explain the secrets of their success, these can often be deduced by observation.

Previous generations understood this well. The disciple sitting at the feet of the master, the apprentice learning a trade from a craftsman, the student learning by assisting a professor with research, the artist serving time with an accomplished artist: all learnt by observing the best in their field at work, by assisting and by imitating.

Be willing to pay a high price to work for the best. Find any excuse to spend time with them. Work out what their characteristic ways of operating are. You will find that they see things differently, spend time differently and interact with other people differently. Unless you can do what they do, or something even more different from the average *modus vivendi* in the profession, you will never rise to the top.

Sometimes, it is not just a matter of working for the best individuals. Key knowhow can be located within the collective culture of the best firms. The key is in the differences. Arguably, you should work for one of the average firms, then for one of the very best, and observe the differences. For instance, I worked for Shell and wrote lots of memos. I then went to work for one of the Mars companies and learnt to talk to people face to face until I got the desired answers. The latter was a 20/80 practice: 20 per cent of effort leading to 80 per cent of results. Leaders have many such 20/80 practices.

Observe, learn and practise.

Become self-employed early in your career

Leverage your own time so that you focus on the things where you add five times more value than elsewhere. The second step is to ensure that you capture as much of this value for yourself. The ideal position, one that you should aim to reach early in your career, is to capture all of the value of your work for yourself.

Karl Marx's theory of surplus value states that the workers produce all value and excess value is appropriated by the capitalists who employ the workers. Put crudely, profits are the excess value stolen from the workers.

The theory is nonsense, but can usefully be stood on its head. The ordinary employee who produces average results may actually be exploiting the corporation more than he or she is exploited: corporations typically have far too many managers and the net value added by a majority of them is actually negative. Yet the employee who uses the 80/20 Principle properly will probably be many times more effective than the average. The 80/20 employee is most unlikely to be paid several times what his or her peers are. The 80/20 employee will therefore probably obtain a better deal by becoming self-employed.

When you are self-employed, you get paid by results. For those who use the 80/20 Principle, this is good news.

The one circumstance in which it may not be appropriate to become self-employed yet is when you are still in the rapid learning stage. If a corporation or professional firm is teaching you a great deal, the value of this learning may exceed the differential between the value you add and what you are paid. This is typically the case during the first two or three years of a professional career. It can also be the case when more experienced professionals join a new firm that has higher standards than the ones in which they have previously worked. In this case, the period of super-learning usually lasts for a few months only, or a year at the most.

When these periods are over, become self-employed. Do not worry overmuch about security. Your professional expertise and use of 80/20 precepts constitute your security. In any case, firms can no longer deliver security.

Employ as many net value creators as possible

If the first stage of leverage is the best use of your time and the second stage is to ensure that you capture for yourself the value you create, the third stage is to leverage the power of other people.

There is only one you, but there are a very large number of people whom you could potentially employ. A minority of these people – but the minority from which the 80/20 practitioner will choose to hire – add a great deal more value than they cost.

It follows that the greatest source of leverage is other people. To some extent, you can and should leverage off other people whom you do not employ: your allies. But you can obtain the most direct and complete leverage from the people you employ.

A simple numerical illustration may help to focus the mind on the enormous value of employment leverage. Let us assume that by using the 80/20 Principle you become five times more effective than the average professional in your line of business. Let us also assume that you are self-employed and so capture all of this value. The best that you will do, therefore, is to get results 500 per cent of the average. Your 'surplus' over the average is therefore 400 units.

But let us now assume that you can identify 10 other professionals, each of whom is, or can be trained to become, three times better than the average. They are not as good as you are, but they still add much more value than they cost. Let us also assume that in order to attract and retain these people, you pay them 50 per cent more than the going rate. Each one of them will produce 300 units of value and cost 150 units. You therefore make a 'profit', or capitalistic surplus, of 150 units for each employee. By hiring the 10, you therefore have another 1500 surplus units to add to the 400 extra units that you yourself are creating. Your total surplus is now 1900 units, nearly five times as much as before you started hiring.

Naturally, you do not have to stop at 10 employees. The only constraints are your ability to find employees who add surplus value and your ability (and theirs) to find customers. The latter constraint should not normally operate in the absence of the former, since professionals who add excess value should normally find a ready market for their services.

Clearly, it is crucial to hire only net value creators: those whose value comfortably exceeds their cost. But it would be wrong to say you should only hire the best. The most excess value is created by employing as many excess value creators as possible, even if some of them are only twice as good as the average whereas others may be five times (or even more) as effective. Within your own workforce, there is still likely to be an 80/20 or 70/30 distribution of effectiveness. The greatest absolute surplus value may co-exist with a fairly skewed distribution of talent. The only requirement is that your least supereffective employee still adds more value than he or she costs.

Use outside contractors for everything but your core skill

The 80/20 Principle is a principle of selectivity. You achieve maximum effectiveness by concentrating on the fifth of activities at which you are the best. This principle applies not just to individuals but to firms as well.

The most successful professional firms and corporations are those that outsource everything but what they are best at. If their skill is marketing, they do not manufacture. If their real advantage is in research and development, they use third parties not just for making the goods, but for marketing and selling them. If they are best at volume manufacture of standardized products, they do not make 'specials' or up-market varieties. If they are best at high-margin specials, they do not try their hand in the mass market. And so on.

The fourth stage of leverage is to use outside contractors as much as possible. Keep your own firm as simple as possible and purely focused on those areas where it is several times better than the competition.

Exploit capital leverage

So far we have advocated labour leverage, but you can also benefit from capital leverage.

Capital leverage is using money to capture additional surplus value. At its most basic, it means buying machines to replace labour whenever the machines are more cost effective. Today the most interesting examples of capital leverage involve the use of money to 'roll out' good ideas that have already proven themselves in particular local circumstances. In effect, the capital is used to multiply frozen knowhow captured in a particular formula. Examples include all forms of software distribution, the rollout of fast-food (and increasingly not-so-fast-food) restaurant formulae such as McDonald's and the globalization of soft drinks supply.

Summary

Rewards increasingly demonstrate the 80/20 Principle: the winners take all. Those who are truly ambitious must aim for the top in their field.

Choose your field narrowly. Specialize. Choose the niche that is made for you. You will not excel unless you also enjoy what you are doing.

Success requires knowledge. But success also requires insight into what delivers the greatest customer satisfaction with the least use of resources. Identify where 20 per cent of resources can be made to deliver 80 per cent of returns.

Early in your career, learn all there is to be learnt. You can only do this by working for the best firms and the best individuals within them, 'best' being defined with reference to your own narrow niche.

Obtain the four forms of labour leverage. First, leverage your own time. Second, capture 100 per cent of its value by becoming self-employed. Third, employ as many net value creators as possible. Fourth, contract out everything that you and your colleagues are not several times better at doing.

If you do all this, you will have built your career into a

firm, your own firm. At this stage, use capital leverage to multiply its wealth.

Multiplying money

If you are interested in a successful career, you are probably also interested in multiplying your money. As we shall see in Chapters 14 and 15 respectively, this is both easier, and less worthwhile, than is commonly thought.

14 Money, Money, Money

To every one who has will more be given, and he will have abundance; but from him who has not, even what he has will be taken away.

Matthew 25:29

This is another optional chapter, designed for those who have some money and wish to know how to multiply it.

If the future is at all like the past, it is quite easy to multiply money. All you need to do is put it in the right place and then leave it there.

Money obeys the 80/20 Principle

It is no accident that Vilfredo Pareto discovered what we now know as the 80/20 Principle when he was researching the distribution of incomes and wealth. He found that there was a predictable and highly unbalanced distribution of money. Money, it seems, dislikes being equally distributed:

- Unless redistributed by progressive taxation, incomes tend to be unequally distributed, with a minority gaining most of aggregate income.
- Even with progressive taxation, wealth follows an even more unequal pattern than incomes; it is even harder to make wealth equal than to make incomes equal.
- This is because the majority of wealth is created from investment rather than from income; and because investment returns tend to be even more unbalanced than income returns.
- Investment creates high amounts of wealth because of the phenomenon of compounding. For example, the value of shares may increase by 12.5 per cent per annum, on average. This means that £100 invested in 1950 would be worth around £239,795 in 2017. In general, real investment returns (after taking out the effects of inflation) are highly positive, except when inflation is rampant.
- The compounding returns of investment are highly differential: some investments are much better than others. This helps to explain why wealth becomes so unequally distributed. It makes a huge amount of difference whether you compound wealth at annual rates of, say, 5, 10, 20 or 40 per cent. £1000

compounded over 10 years at these rates would produce, respectively, £1629, £2593, £6191 or £28,925! For eight times the annual return, compounding at 40 per cent produces a return nearly 18 times higher than compounding at 5 per cent; and the results become even more skewed the longer we go on.

Oddly enough, certain categories of investment, and certain investment strategies, are predictably much better than others at creating wealth.

80/20 insights into making money

➤ You are more likely to become wealthy, or to obtain the greatest increase in wealth, from investment income rather than from employment income. This means that there is a premium on accumulating enough money early on to fund investment. Accumulating your stake for entry to the investment world usually requires hard work and low spending: for a period, net income must be higher than spending.

The only exceptions to this rule are acquisition of money from legacies or other gifts, marrying into a wealthy family, windfalls from lotteries or other forms of gambling, and crime. The first cannot easily be predicted, the third is so unlikely that it should be totally discounted, the fourth is not recommended, so only the second can be consciously planned and even then the outcome is uncertain.

➤ Because of the compounding effects of investment, you can become rich either by starting to invest early in life, or by living a long time, or both. Starting early is the most controllable strategy.
➤ As early as possible, develop a consistent, long-term investment strategy, based on principles that have worked well in the past.

How, then, do we obtain 80 per cent of investment returns with 20 per cent of the money? The answer[1] is to follow Koch's 10 commandments of investment, as recorded in Figure

1	Make your investment philosophy reflect your personality
2	Be proactive and unbalanced
3	Invest mainly in the stock market
4	Invest for the long term
5	Invest most when the market is low
6	If you can't beat the market, track it
7	Build your investments on your expertise
8	Consider the merits of emerging markets
9	Cull your loss makers
10	Run your gains

Figure 43 Koch's 10 commandments of investment

Make your investment philosophy reflect your personality

A key to successful personal investing is to match your personality and skills to one of a number of proven techniques. Most private investors fail because they use techniques that, while perfectly valid, are not suited to them as individuals. The investor should choose from a menu of perhaps 10 successful strategies, to suit his or her own temperament and knowledge. For example:

➤ If you like playing with numbers and are analytical, you should become a devotee of one of the analytical methods of investment. Of these, the ones that I like best are value investing (but see the next point), detecting earnings acceleration and specialist investments such as warrants.

➤ If you veer more towards optimism than pessimism, avoid an excessively analytical approach such as those above. The optimist often makes a poor investor, so be sure that your investments really are beating the index; if not, sell them and hand the money over to an index-tracking fund.

Sometimes optimists, who in this case deserve the epithet 'visionaries', make great investors, because they select two or three shares that they know have enormous potential. But if you are an optimist, try to restrain your enthusiasm and write down as carefully as possible why the shares you like are so attractive. Try to be rational before you buy. And be sure to sell any loss-making shares even if you are emotionally committed to them.

➤ If you are neither analytical nor 'visionary' but a practical sort of person, you should either specialize in an area about which you know a great deal or follow successful investors who have a clear track record of beating the index.

Be proactive and unbalanced

Being proactive means that you take charge of your investment decisions yourself. The danger of advisers and money managers is not so much that they cream off a lot of the profit, but even more that they are unlikely to recommend or implement the sort of unbalanced portfolio that is the route to superior returns. Risk, it is said, is minimized by having a broad spread of investments in a wide range of different media, such as bonds, stocks, cash, real estate, gold and collectibles. But risk minimization is overrated. If you want to become rich enough to change your future lifestyle, you need to attain above-average returns. The chances of doing this are much higher if you adopt an unbalanced portfolio. This means that you should have few investments: those that you are convinced will give high returns. And it also means that you should invest in one medium…

Invest mainly in the stock market

Unless you happen to be an expert in a very esoteric investment medium, such as nineteenth-century Chinese silk screens or toy soldiers, the best investment medium is the stock market.

Over the long haul, investing in stocks (also called shares

or equities) has produced returns stunningly higher than putting the money in a bank or investing in interest-bearing instruments like government or corporate bonds. For example, I calculated in the UK that if you had invested £100 in a building society in 1950, you could have taken out £813 by 1992; but the same £100 invested in the stock market would have returned £14,198, more than 17 times as much.[2] Similar calculations can be made for the US and nearly every other major stock market.

Anne Scheiber, a private American investor with no particular expertise in the stock market, put $5000 into blue-chip stocks just after the Second World War. She then sat on them. By 1995 the $5000 had turned into $22 million: 440,000 per cent of the original!

The stock market, happily, is a relatively easy investment medium for the non-expert.

Invest for the long term

Do not move in and out of individual stocks, or your share portfolio as a whole, very often. Unless they are clear losers, keep your stocks for many years. Buying and selling stocks is expensive as well as time consuming. If you possibly can, take a 10-year view or, even better, a 20-, 30- or 50-year view. If you put money into stocks for the short term, you are really gambling rather than investing. If you are tempted to take the money out and spend it, you are deferring expenditure rather than investing.

At some stage, of course, you may want to enjoy your wealth rather than wait for your heirs to do so. The best use of wealth is usually to create a new lifestyle where you can choose how to spend your time, to pursue a career or work activity that you would most enjoy. Then the investment period is over. But until you have enough money to make this shift, continue to accumulate.

Invest most when the stock market is low

Although its value goes up over time, the stock market is cyclical, partly as a function of the economic cycle but mainly because moods fluctuate. It is amazing, but irrational concerns driven by fashion, animal spirits, hope and fear can drive prices up or down. Pareto himself observed this phenomenon:

> *There is a rhythm of sentiment which we can observe in ethics, in religion, and in politics as waves resembling the business cycle…*
>
> *Whereas during the upward trend every argument produced in order to demonstrate that an enterprise will produce money is received with favour; whereas such an argument will be absolutely rejected during the downward trend … A man who during the downward trend refuses to underwrite certain stocks believes himself to be guided exclusively by reason and does not know that, unconsciously, he yields to the thousand small impressions which he receives from the daily economic news. When, later, during the upward trend, he will underwrite those same stocks, or similar shares offering no better chance of success, he will again think that he is following only the dictates of reason and will remain unaware of the fact that his transition from distrust to trust depends on sentiments generated by the atmosphere around him…*
>
> *It is well known at the Stock Exchange that the public*

> *at large buys only in a rising market and sells in a declining market. The financiers who, because of their greater practice in this business, use their reason to a greater extent, although they sometimes allow themselves to be swayed by sentiment, do the opposite, and this is the main source of their gains. During a boom period any mediocre argument to the effect that this boom must continue has great persuasive power; and if you tried to tell man that, after all, prices cannot continue to go up indefinitely, be sure he would not listen to you.*[3]

A whole school, that of value investing, has grown up around this philosophy: buy when the stock market as a whole, or an individual share, is low and sell when it is high. One of the most successful investors of all time, Benjamin Graham, wrote the rule book for value investing, and his rules have been vindicated time and time again.[4]

There are many rules to guide you in value investing. Simplifying greatly, but capturing perhaps 80 per cent of their value in well under 20 per cent of the space, here are three rules to help you:

➤ Do not buy when everyone else is and when everyone is convinced that the stock market can only go up. Instead, buy when everyone else is pessimistic.

➤ Use the price/earnings ratio (P/E) as the best single benchmark for deciding whether shares are expensive or cheap. The P/E of a share is its price divided by its after-tax earnings. For example, if a share is 250 cents and its earnings per share are 25 cents, the share is on a P/E of 10. If the share price goes up, in a period of optimism, to 500 cents, but the earnings per share are still 25 cents, the P/E is now 20.

➤ In general, a P/E of over 17 for the stock market as a whole is a danger signal. Do not invest heavily when the market is this high. A P/E of under 12 is a buy signal; one of under 10 a definite buy signal. Your stockbroker or a good financial newspaper should tell you what the current market average P/E is. If asked which P/E you mean, say learnedly 'the historic P/E, bozo'.[5]

If you can't beat the market, track it

It is quite possible to develop an investment approach that is superior to the stock market average by following certain precepts and developing an approach tailored to your own personality and skills. These possibilities are explored below. But it is more likely that selecting your own investments will lead you to performance inferior to that of the stock market indices.

In the latter case, or if you don't even wish to experiment with your own approach in the hope of beating the market, you should 'track the index'.

Index tracking, also called market tracking, means buying the shares that are in the stock market index. You then only sell shares when they drop out of the index (this happens to underperforming shares) and you only buy new shares when they are first included in the index.

You can track the index yourself, at the cost of some effort in following the financial press. Alternatively, you can put your money into a 'tracker fund' run by fund managers who, for a small annual fee, will do it for you.

You can choose different funds depending on which market you choose to track. Generally, it is safest to choose your home market and to go for a fund tracking the index comprised of the largest and best-quality shares (called 'blue chips').

Index tracking is fairly low risk and yet, over the long term, should deliver high returns. If you decide to follow this approach, you need read no further than these first six commandments. It can be more fun and more rewarding, although at higher risk, to make your own selections. The next four commandments apply in that case. Remember, however, that this commandment requires you to go back to index tracking unless your own investment strategy generally beats the index. If it doesn't, cut your losses and track the index.

Build your investments on your expertise

The whole essence of the 80/20 philosophy is to know a few things well: to specialize.

This law applies particularly to investment. If you are deciding yourself which shares to buy, specialize in an area in which you are a relative expert.

The great thing about specialization is that the possibilities are almost endless. You could, for example, specialize in shares of the industry in which you work, or of your hobby, your local area or anything else in which you are interested. If you like shopping, for example, you might decide to specialize in the shares of retailers. Then if you notice a new chain springing up, where each new store seems to be full of keen shoppers, you might want to invest in those shares.

Even if you do not start out as an expert, it may pay to specialize in a few shares, for example those in a particular industry, so that you can learn as much as possible about that area.

Consider the merits of emerging markets

Emerging markets are stock markets outside the developed countries: in countries where the economy is growing fast and where the stock market is still developing. Emerging markets include most of Asia (but not Japan), Africa, the Indian subcontinent, South America, the ex-communist countries of Central and Eastern Europe, and the fringes of Europe such as Portugal, Greece and Turkey.

The basic theory is very simple. Stock market performance is highly correlated with the growth of an economy as a whole. Therefore, invest in countries that have the fastest current and expected GNP growth – the emerging markets.

There are other reasons emerging markets can be very good investments. They have the lion's share of future privatizations and these are generally good homes for money. The strange and sudden death of Communism around 1990 forced many emerging countries to adopt more free-market economic policies, which are likely to work their way through, after the inevitable initial social disruption, into higher returns for investors. And emerging-country shares are often very good value, because they tend to have quite low P/E ratios. As the market develops and matures, and individual companies become larger, the P/Es are likely to go up, boosting the share prices considerably.

But investing in emerging markets is definitely riskier than investing at home. The companies are younger and less stable, the whole country's stock market could fall as a result of political changes or reductions in commodity prices, the currency could depreciate (and with it the value of your shares) and you may find it much more difficult to take your money out than you did to put it in. Also, the cost of investing in terms of spreads and commissions is much higher than in developed markets. The chances of getting ripped off by a market maker are much higher.

Three policies must be followed by an investor in emerging markets. One is to invest only a small part of your total portfolio, up to 20 per cent, in emerging markets. The second is to invest most of your emerging market funds only when the market is relatively low and the average P/E for the countries you are investing in is under 12. The third is to invest for the long term and only pull money out when the P/Es are relatively high.

But, with these caveats, emerging markets are, over the long haul, likely to outperform and it can be wise as well as fun to have some investment in them.

Cull your loss makers

If any share falls by 15 per cent (of the price you paid), sell it. Follow this rule rigorously and consistently.

If you want to buy it back later at a lower price, wait until the price has stopped falling, for at least a number of days (and preferably weeks), before you reinvest.

Apply the same 15 per cent rule to the new investment: stop the loss after 15 per cent.

The only acceptable exception to this commandment is if you are a very long-term investor who does not want to be bothered with the swings in markets and does not have the time to monitor investments. Those who stayed in stocks during and after the 1929–32, 1974–5 and 1987 crashes will have done well over the long term. Those who sold after the first 15 per cent declines (where this was possible) and returned after the market had risen 15 per cent from its lows would have done even better.

The key point about the 15 per cent rule is to do with individual stocks, not with the market. If an individual stock falls by 15 per cent, which is much more common than the market falling by the same amount, it should be sold. Whereas few, if any, fortunes have been lost by sticking to the stock market (or a broad portfolio of stocks) over the long term, a large number of fortunes have been lost by mistaken loyalty to one or a few declining stocks. For individual stocks, the best indication of the future trend is the current one.

Run your gains

Cut your losses, but do not cut your gains. The best long-term indicator of a great investment is a short-term gain, repeated over and over again! Resist the temptation to take profits too early. This is where many private investors make their worst mistakes: they take nice profits, but forfeit much fatter ones. Nobody ever went broke by taking a profit, but many people never got rich by following the same procedure!

There are two further 80/20 rules of investment that we have not yet explored:

- Comparing a large number of investment portfolios held over a long period of time, it is usually true that 20 per cent of the portfolios contain 80 per cent of the gains.
- For an individual holding a portfolio over a long period of time, 80 per cent of the gains will usually come from 20 per cent of the investments. In a portfolio composed exclusively of equities, 80 per cent of the gains will come from 20 per cent of the shares held.

The reason these rules hold true is that a few investments are usually stunningly good performers, while the majority are not. These few superstar shares can give phenomenal returns. It is absolutely crucial, therefore, to let the superstars stay within the portfolio throughout the process: to let the profits ride. In the dying words of a character from one of Anita Brookner's novels: 'never sell Glaxo'.

It would have been easy to lock in a 100 per cent gain on IBM, McDonald's, Xerox or Marks & Spencer in the 1950s or 1960s, on Shell, GE, Lonrho, BTR or the Swedish pharmaceuticals firm Astra in the 1970s, on American Express, Body Shop or Cadbury Schweppes early in the 1980s, or on Microsoft later that decade. Investors who took these gains would have missed out on several times that appreciation later.

Good businesses tend to produce a virtuous cycle of consistent out-performance. Only when this momentum is reversed, which may take several decades, should you consider selling. Again, one good rule of thumb is not to sell unless the price falls by 15 per cent from its recent high price.

To do this, set a 'lock-gain' price at which you will sell, 15 per cent below the high. A 15 per cent reduction may indicate a change in the trend. Otherwise, continue to hold until circumstances force you to sell.

Conclusion

Money begats money. But some methods of breeding have much more prolific results. Samuel Johnson said that a man was never so innocently employed as when making money. His observation pitches the accumulation of wealth, whether through investment or a successful professional career or both, at the right moral level. Neither pursuit is to be denigrated but, equally, neither is a guaranteed passport to serving society or personal happiness. And both money making and professional success carry the dangers that they become ends in themselves.

A success hangover is quite possible. Wealth creates the need to administer it, to deal with lawyers, tax advisers, bankers and other profoundly stimulating contacts. The logic of professional success outlined in the preceding chapter leads almost inexorably to ever-greater professional demands. To succeed, you must aim for the top. To get there, you must turn yourself into a business. To obtain maximum leverage, you must employ a large number of people. To maximize the value of your business, you must use other people's money and exploit capital leverage – to become even larger and more profitable. Your circle of contacts expands and the time for friends and relationships contracts. On the giddy roundabout of success, it is easy to lose focus, perspective and personal values. It is a perfectly rational response to say, at any stage, stop success: I want to get off!

This is why it is sensible to stand back from careers and money making and consider the most important subject of all: happiness.

15 The Seven Habits of Happiness

Temperament is not destiny. Daniel Goleman[1]

Aristotle said that the goal of all human activity should be happiness. Down the ages, we haven't listened much to Aristotle. Perhaps he should have told us how to be happier. He could usefully have started by analysing the causes of happiness and unhappiness.

Can the 80/20 Principle really apply to happiness? I believe it can. It appears to be true for most people that the majority of perceived happiness occurs in a minority of the time. One 80/20 hypothesis would be that 80 per cent of happiness occurs in 20 per cent of our time. When I have tried this hypothesis on friends and asked them to divide their weeks into days and parts of days, or their months into weeks, or their years into months, or their lives into years, about two-thirds of the respondents show a marked pattern of imbalance, approximating to the 80/20 pattern.

The hypothesis does not work for everyone. About a third of my friends don't exhibit the 80/20 pattern. Their happiness is much more equally distributed over time. What is fascinating is that this latter group seem to be markedly happier overall than the larger group whose happiness peaks in small amounts of their lives.

This fits in with common sense. Those who are happy with most of their lives are more likely to be happier overall. Those whose happiness is highly concentrated in short bursts are likely to be less happy with life overall.

It also fits in with the idea advanced throughout this book that 80/20 relationships imply waste and great scope for improvement. But, more significantly, it suggests that the 80/20 Principle might help us to be happier.

Two ways to be happier

- Identify the times when you are most happy, and expand them as much as possible.
- Identify the times when you are least happy, and reduce them as much as possible.

Spend more time on the type of activities that are very effective at making you happy and less time on other activities. Start by cutting off the 'valleys of unhappiness', the things that tend to make you actively unhappy. The best way to start being more happy is to stop being unhappy. You have more control over this than you imagine, simply by avoiding situations where experience suggests you are likely to become unhappy.

For activities that are very ineffective at making you happy (or effective at making you unhappy), think systematically of ways that you could enjoy them more. If this works, fine. If it doesn't, think how to avoid these situations.

But aren't people powerless to deal with unhappiness?

You might object, particularly if you have some experience of people who are chronically unhappy (and are often consigned to the seemingly objective, but terribly slippery and unhelpful, category of the 'mentally ill', which has perhaps brought the world more misery than most categorizations), that this analysis is far too simplistic and assumes a degree of control over our own happiness that, for deep-rooted psychological reasons, many or most or all people do not have. Isn't our capacity to be happy largely predestined, by heredity and childhood experience? Do we really have any control over our happiness?

There is no doubt that there are people who are temperamentally more inclined to happiness than others. For some the glass is always half full, for others half empty. Psychologists and psychiatrists believe that capacity for happiness is determined by the interaction between genetics, childhood experiences, brain chemistry and important life events. Clearly, adults can do nothing about their genes, childhood experiences or past misfortunes in life. It is all too easy for those inclined to evade responsibility to blame their defeatism on forces outside their control, particularly if they are easily overawed by medical Jeremiahs.

Happily, common sense, observation and the latest scientific evidence all indicate that, while everyone is dealt a different hand of cards in respect of happiness just as for every other blessing, there is a great deal that can be done to play our hand better and to improve it during the game of life. Adults are differently endowed with athletic ability, as a result of genetics and the extent of training and exercise during childhood, youth and subsequently. Yet everyone can markedly improve their fitness by sensible, regular exercise. Similarly, we may through hereditary influences and background be thought more or less intelligent, but everyone can train their mind and develop it. We may be more or less inclined, through our genes and environment, to become overweight, but healthy eating and exercise can make most fat people considerably thinner. Why, in principle, should our ability to become happier be any different, whatever our starting point in terms of temperament?

Most of us have seen examples where the lives of acquaintances or friends have been materially changed, and happiness permanently enhanced or reduced, as a result of actions freely taken by those individuals. A new partner, a new career, a new place to live, a new lifestyle or even a conscious decision to adopt a different attitude to life: any of these can make all the difference to an individual's happiness and all of them are under the individual's control. Predestination is an unconvincing hypothesis if it can be shown that only those who believe in predestination are subject to its sway. Evidence that some people can freely change their destiny ought to be persuasive and encourage us to emulate those exercising free will.

The freedom to be happy is at last supported by science

At last, the field of psychology and psychiatry (which, more than economics, has deserved the epithet of the dismal science), prodded by the findings of other scientific disciplines, is producing a more cheerful picture consistent with our common sense and observations of life. Geneticists used to be excessively deterministic, reducing complex human behaviour to the whim of inherited genes. As a more enlightened geneticist, Professor Steve Jones of University College, London, points out: 'There have been announcements of the discovery of single genes for manic depression, schizophrenia and alcoholism. All have been withdrawn.'[2] More recently we have been told by an eminent neuropsychiatrist, 'the new field of psychoneuro-immunology is telling us ... that a human being acts as an integrated whole ... The evidence suggests that there is a delicate balance between what we think and feel on a daily basis and our physical and mental health.'[3] In other words, within limits, you can choose to make yourself happy or unhappy and even to make yourself healthy or unhealthy.

Sensitive dependence on initial conditions

This does not mean that we should discard earlier research about the importance of childhood experiences (or later misfortunes). We saw in Part One that chaos theory highlights 'sensitive dependence on initial conditions'. This means that early in the life of any phenomenon, chance events and apparently small causes can cause a large deviation in the eventual outcome.

Something analogous appears to happen in childhood, producing beliefs about ourselves – that we are loved or unloved, intelligent or unintelligent, highly valued or of low worth, able to take risks or constrained to obey authority – that are then often played out through life. The initial belief, which may be arrived at with no objective foundation whatever, acquires a life of its own and becomes self-fulfilling. Later events – poor examination results, a lover who leaves, failure to get the job we want, a career that moves sideways, being fired, a setback in health – may blow us off course and reinforce negative views about ourselves.

Putting the clock back to find happiness

So, is this a chilling world where unhappiness is the path laid out for us? I do not think so.

The humanist Pico of Mirandola (1463–93) pointed out that human beings are not entirely like other animals.[4] All other creatures have a definite nature that they cannot change. Humans have been given an indefinite nature and thus the ability to mould themselves. The rest of creation is passive; humans alone have an active nature. They were created; we could create.

When unhappiness strikes, we can recognize what is happening to us and refuse to accept it. We are free to change the way in which we think and act. To invert Jean-Jacques Rousseau, man is everywhere in chains yet everywhere can be free. We can change the way that we think about external events, even where we cannot change them. And we can do something more. We can intelligently change our exposure to events that make us either happy or unhappy.

Making ourselves happy by strengthening emotional intelligence

Daniel Goleman and other writers have contrasted academic intelligence or IQ with *emotional* intelligence: 'abilities such as being able to motivate oneself and delay gratification; to regulate one's moods and to keep distress from swamping the ability to think; to empathize and to hope'.[5] Emotional intelligence is more crucial for happiness than intellectual intelligence, yet our society places little emphasis on the development of emotional intelligence. As Goleman aptly remarks:

> *Even though a high IQ is no guarantee of prosperity, prestige, or happiness in life, our schools and our culture fixate on academic abilities, ignoring emotional intelligence, a set of traits – some might call it character – that also matters immensely for our personal destiny.*[6]

The good news is that emotional intelligence can be cultivated and learnt: certainly as a child, but also at any stage in life. In Goleman's wonderful phrase, 'temperament is not destiny': we can change our destiny by changing our temperament. Psychologist Martin Seligman points out that 'moods like anxiety, sadness and anger don't just descend on you without your having any control over them … you can change the way you feel by what you think'.[7] There are proven techniques for exiting feelings of incipient sadness and depression before they become damaging to your health and happiness. Moreover, by cultivating habits of optimism you can help to prevent disease as well as have a happier life. Again, Goleman shows that happiness is related to neurological processes in the brain:

> *Among the main biological changes in happiness is an increased activity in a brain center that inhibits negative feelings and fosters an increase in available energy, and a quieting of those that generate worrisome thought ... there is ... a quiescence, which makes the body recover more quickly from the biological arousal of upsetting emotions.*[8]

Identify personal levers that can magnify positive thoughts and cut off negative ones. In what circumstances are you at your most positive and most negative? Where are you? Who are you with? What are you doing? What is the weather like? Everyone has a wide range of emotional intelligence, depending on the circumstances. You can start to build up your emotional intelligence by giving yourself a break, by skewing the odds in your favour, by doing the things where you feel most in control and most benevolent. You can also avoid or minimize the circumstances where you are at your most emotionally stupid!

Making ourselves happier by changing the way we think about events

We have all experienced the trap of self-reinforced depression, when we think in a gloomy and negative way and simply make things worse, so that we can imagine no way out of the box. When we come out of the depression, we see that the way out was always there. We can train ourselves to break the self-reinforcing pattern of depression by simple steps, such as seeking out company, changing our physical setting or forcing ourselves to exercise.

There are many examples of people exposed to the worst misfortunes, like those in concentration camps or with fatal diseases, who react in a positive way that changes their perspective and strengthens their ability to survive.

According to Dr Peter Fenwick, a consultant neuropsychiatrist, 'the ability to see silver linings in clouds is not simply Pollyannaism; it is a healthy self-protective mechanism with a good biological basis'.[9] Optimism, it seems, is a medically approved ingredient for both success and happiness; and the greatest motivator on earth. Hope has been defined specifically by C R Snyder, a psychologist at the University of Kansas, as 'believing you have both the will and the way to accomplish your goals, whatever they may be'.[10]

Making ourselves happier by changing the way we think about ourselves

Do you think of yourself as successful or unsuccessful? If you opt for unsuccessful, you may be sure that there are many people who have achieved less than you have and would be described by most people as less successful than you are. Their perception of self-success contributes both to their success and their happiness. Your feeling of being unsuccessful limits your success and your happiness.

The same applies to whether you think you are happy or unhappy. Richard Nixon ended the Vietnam War by declaring that America's objectives had been achieved. He was economical with the truth, but who cared? The rebuilding of

America's self-esteem could begin. Similarly, you can make yourself happy or unhappy just by the way that you decide to feel.

Make the choice that you want to be happy. You owe it to yourself and you owe it to other people too. Unless you are happy, you will make your partner and anyone else with prolonged exposure to you less happy. Therefore you have a positive duty to be happy.

Psychologists tell us that all perceptions about happiness relate to our sense of self-worth. A positive self-image is essential to happiness. A sense of self-worth can and should be cultivated. You know you can do it: give up guilt, forget about your weaknesses, focus and build on your strengths. Remember all the good things you have done, all the small and big achievements to your credit, all the positive feedback you have ever received. There is a lot to be said for yourself. Say it – or at least think it. You will be amazed at the difference it makes to your relationships, your achievements and your happiness.

You may feel that you are deceiving yourself. But in fact, by having a negative perception of yourself you are at least as guilty of self-deception. All the time we tell ourselves stories about ourselves. We have to: there is no objective truth. You might as well choose positive rather than negative stories. By doing so you will increase the sum of human happiness, starting with yourself and radiating out to others.

Use all the willpower at your disposal to make yourself happy. Construct the right stories about yourself – and believe them!

Making ourselves happier by changing events

A further route to superior happiness is to change the events you encounter in order to increase your happiness. None of us can ever have complete control over events but we can have much more control than we think.

If the best way to start being happy is to stop being unhappy, the first thing we should do is to avoid situations and people that tend to make us depressed or miserable.

Making ourselves happier by changing the people we see most

There is medical evidence that high levels of stress can be coped with provided that we have a few excellent personal relationships. But relationships of any kind that take up a large part of our time and are part of the daily fabric of our lives, whether at home, at work or in our social lives, will powerfully influence both our happiness and our health. To quote John Cacioppo, an Ohio State University psychologist:

> *It's the most important relationships in your life, the people you see day in and day out, that seem to be crucial for your health. And the more significant the relationship is in your life, the more it matters for your health.*[11]

Think about the people you see every day. Do they make you happier or less happy? Could you change the amount of time you spend with them accordingly?

Avoid the snake-pits

There are many situations with which each of us typically copes badly. I have never seen the point in training people not to be scared of snakes. The more sensible action is to avoid the jungle (or the pet shop).

What upsets us, of course, varies from person to person. I cannot stop myself getting angry when confronted with pointless bureaucracy. I can feel stress building up when exposed to lawyers for more than a few minutes. I am anxious in traffic jams. I often become mildly depressed when days go by without seeing the sun. I hate being jammed into the same space with too many of my fellow humans. I cannot abide listening to people making excuses and detailing problems beyond their control. If I were to become a rush-hour commuter, working with lawyers and living in Sweden, I am sure I would become depressed and quite possibly top myself. But I have learnt to avoid, as far as practicable, such situations. I do not commute, avoid mass transit systems in the rush hour, spend at least a week a month in the sun, pay someone else to deal with bureaucracy, drive around jams even if it takes longer, avoid having anyone of a negative disposition report to me and find that my telephones mysteriously disconnect five minutes after I am called by lawyers. As a result of all these actions, I am significantly happier.

No doubt you have your own pressure points. Write them down – now! Consciously engineer your life to avoid them: write down how – now! Check each month how far you are succeeding. Congratulate yourself on each small avoidance victory.

In Chapter 10 you identified your unhappiness islands. Analysis or reflection on when you have been least happy very often leads to obvious conclusions. You hate your job! You get depressed by your spouse! Or perhaps more precisely, you hate one-third of your job, you cannot abide being with your spouse's friends or in-laws, you suffer mental torture from your boss, you detest housework. Great! You've finally had a blinding glimpse of the obvious. Now do something about it...

Daily happiness habits

After you have removed – or at least, set in motion plans to remove – the causes of unhappiness, concentrate most energy on the positive seeking of happiness. For this, there is no time like the present. Happiness is profoundly existential. Happiness only exists now. Past happiness may be remembered or future happiness planned, but the pleasure this gives can only be experienced in the 'now'.

What we all need is a set of daily happiness habits, similar to (and in fact partially related to) our daily fitness or healthy eating regime. My seven daily happiness habits are summarized in Figure 44.

One essential ingredient of a happy day is *physical exercise.* I always feel good after (even if not during) exercise. Apparently this is because exertion releases endorphins, natural anti-depressants that are similar to certain exhilarating drugs (but with none of the dangers or expense!). Daily exercise is an essential habit: if you don't make it a habit, you will do it far less often than you should. If it is a workday, I always exercise before going to work, to ensure that my exercise time is not blown away by unexpected work pressures. If you travel a lot, ensure that you plan when you will exercise at the same time that you order the tickets, if necessary changing the schedule to accommodate the exercise. If you are a high-powered executive, do not let your secretary put any meetings in the calendar before 10 am, so that you will have plenty of time to exercise and prepare yourself for the day ahead.

1	Exercise
2	Mental stimulation
3	Spiritual/artistic stimulation/meditation
4	Doing a good turn
5	Taking a pleasure break with a friend
6	Giving yourself a treat
7	Congratulating yourself

Figure 44 Seven daily happiness habits

Another key component of a happy day is *mental stimulation*. You may obtain this at work but, if not, ensure that there is some intellectual or mental exercise each day. There are a huge number of ways to obtain this, depending on your interests: crossword puzzles, certain newspapers and magazines, reading part of a book, talking for at least 20 minutes to an intelligent friend about an abstract topic, writing a short article or journal entry, in fact, doing anything that requires active thought on your part (watching television, even of the high-brow kind, does not qualify).

A third essential daily regime is *spiritual or artistic stimulation.* This need not be as forbidding as it sounds: all that is required is at least half an hour's food for the imagination or spirit. Going to a concert, art gallery, theatre or movie all qualify, as do reading a poem, watching the sun rise or set, looking at the stars or attendance at any event where you are stimulated and excited (this can even include a ball game, race meeting, political rally, church or park). Meditation also works well.

Daily happiness habit number four is *doing something for another person or people.* This does not have to be a major work of benevolence; it can be a random act of kindness such as paying for someone else's parking meter or going out of your way to direct someone. Even a brief altruistic act can have a great effect on your spirits.

The fifth habit is to *share a pleasurable break with a friend.* This must be an uninterrupted *tête-à-tête* lasting at least half an hour, but the form of the occasion is up to you (a cup of coffee, a drink, a meal or a leisurely walk are all appropriate).

Habit number six is to *give yourself a treat.* To prompt you each day, write down now a list of all the pleasures in which you could indulge yourself (don't worry, you don't have to show the list to anyone!). Ensure that you chalk up at least one of these each day.

The final habit, at the end of each day, is to *congratulate yourself* on having followed your daily happiness habits. Since the point is to make yourself happy rather than unhappy, you can count a score of five or more (including this number seven) as a success. If you haven't notched up five habits, but have still achieved something significant or enjoyed yourself, congratulate yourself anyway on a day's worthwhile living.

Medium-term stratagems for happiness

In addition to your seven happiness habits, Figure 45 distils seven short cuts to a happy life.

Short cut number one is to *maximize control over your life.* Lack of control is the root cause of much unease and uncertainty. I would rather drive a long way round a complex city route, with which I am familiar, than try to navigate a potentially shorter course that I do not know. Bus drivers are more frustrated than bus conductors, and more liable to heart attacks, not just because of the lack of exercise on the job but because they have much more limited control over when the bus moves. Working in the classic large bureaucracy leads to alienation because one's working life cannot be controlled. Self-employed people who can determine their working hours and work scheduling are happier than employed people who cannot.

1	Maximize your control
2	Set attainable goals
3	Be flexible
4	Have a close relationship with your partner
5	Have a few happy friends
6	Have a few close professional alliances
7	Evolve your ideal lifestyle

Figure 45 Seven short cuts to a happy life

Maximizing the proportion of your life under your own control requires planning and often risk taking. The happiness dividends, however, should not be underestimated.

Setting reasonable and attainable goals is the second short cut to happiness. Psychological research has shown that we are likely to achieve most when we have reasonably challenging but not too difficult goals. Objectives that are too easy will leads us to be complacent, accepting mediocre performance. But objectives that are too tough – the sort of objectives set by those of us laden with guilt or burdened with high and punitive expectations – are demoralizing and lead us to self-fulfilling self-perceptions of failure. Remember that you are trying to become happier. If in doubt, when setting yourself goals, err on the soft side. It is better for your happiness to set soft goals and succeed than it is to set tough goals and fail, even if the latter would have led you to objectively superior performance. If there is a trade-off between achievement and happiness, choose happiness.

The third short-cut is to *be flexible when chance events interfere with plans and expectations*. John Lennon once remarked that life is what happens while we're making other plans. Our objective must be to make our plans stick so that we happen to life rather than the other way round, but we must be prepared for life to insert its quota of objections and diversions. Life's interjections should be cheerfully and playfully accepted as a counterpoint to our plans. If possible, life's unplanned contribution should be incorporated into our own plan, so that it can proceed to an even higher level. If imagination fails us here, life's objection should be worked around or quashed. If neither of these tactics works, we should accept what we cannot control with grace and maturity and get on with moulding what we can control. On no account should we let life's objections ruffle us, or make us angry, self-doubting or bitter.

Fourthly, *develop a close relationship with a happy partner.* We are programmed to develop a close living relationship with one person. This selection of the partner is one of the few decisions in life (one of the 20 per cent) that will help determine whether we are happy or not. Sexual attraction is one of the universe's great mysteries and demonstrates an extreme form of the 80/20 Principle: the real chemistry can occur in fleeting seconds, so that you feel 99 per cent of the attraction in 1 per cent of the time and you know at once that this is the person for you![12] But the 80/20 Principle should put you on your guard: danger and wasted happiness could lie ahead. Bear in mind that there are many people with whom you could, in theory, bond; this rush of blood to the head (or the heart) will happen again.

If you have not yet selected a partner, remember that your happiness will be greatly influenced by the happiness of your partner. For the sake of your happiness, as well as for love, you will want to make your partner happy. But this is a great deal easier if your partner has, to start with, a happy temperament and/or if he or she consciously adopts a pro-happiness daily regime (such as my happiness habits). Team up with an unhappy partner and the odds are that you yourself will end up unhappy. People with low self-esteem and self-confidence are a nightmare to live with, however much mutual love abounds. If you are a very happy person, you might just make an unhappy person happy, but it is a hell of a trick to pull. Two mildly unhappy people who are deeply in love might just, with strong determination to be happy and a good happiness regimen, manage to attain mutual happiness; but I would not bet on it. Two unhappy people, even in love, will drive each other nuts. If you want to be happy, choose to love a happy partner.

You may, of course, already have a partner who is not happy and, if so, you will probably be seriously subtracting from your own happiness. If so, it should be a major project for both of you to make your partner happy.

The fifth short cut is to *cultivate close friendships with a few happy friends.* The 80/20 Principle predicts that most of the satisfaction you draw from all of your friends will be concentrated in your relationship with a small number of close friends. The principle also indicates that you are likely to misallocate your time, spending too much with the not-so-good friends and too little with the very good friends (although you may allocate more time per friend to the good friends, there are more of the not-so-good variety in most people's friendship portfolio, so that in aggregate the not-so-good friends take more time than the good ones). The answer is to decide who the good friends are and give them 80 per cent of the time allocated to friends (you should probably increase this absolute amount of time as well). You should try to build these good friendships as much as possible, because they will be a great source of mutual happiness.

Short cut six is similar to five: *develop strong professional alliances with a small number of people whose company you enjoy.* Not all your work or professional colleagues should become your friends; if so, you would spread your friendship too thinly. But a few should become close friends and allies; people whom you will go out of your way to support and who will do the same for you. This will not only enhance your career. It will also immeasurably enrich the pleasure you take at work; it will help to prevent you feeling alienated at work; and it will provide a unifying link between your work and play. This unity, too, is essential for full happiness.

The final short cut to lasting happiness is to *evolve the lifestyle you and your partner want.* This requires a harmonious balance between your work life, home life and social life. It means that you live where you want to work, have the quality of life that you want, have time to attend to family and social affairs and are equally happy at work and outside it.

Conclusion

Happiness is a duty. We should choose to be happy. We should work at happiness. And in doing so, we should help those closest to us, and even those who just stumble across us, to share our happiness.

16 Your Hidden Friend

The power to move the world is in your subconscious mind
William James, pioneering American psychologist[1]

Below the surface-stream, shallow and light,
Of what we say we feel – below the stream,
As light, of what we think we feel – there flows
With noiseless current strong, obscure and deep,
The central stream of what we feel indeed.[2]
Matthew Arnold, Victorian poet

Our hidden friend is something we all possess. It gives fantastic results for almost no effort. Our hidden friend largely determines our success and happiness – and yet very few of us use our friend to anything like its potential. I speak of the mind, and in particular the most powerful and 80/20 part of it, our subconscious friend, which can be our greatest ally, if we learn to appreciate and program it properly.

What is the subconscious?

The first person to identify and name it was Pierre Janet (1859–1947) the great (and now totally neglected) French psychologist. He called it the *subconscient* – beneath the conscious mind of thought and reason, he said, lay a powerful part of the mind (or brain) which strongly influences our emotions and behaviour.[3] Sigmund Freud was very sniffy about the term 'subconscious' preferring the word 'unconscious'. 'The only trustworthy antithesis', he claimed, 'is between conscious and unconscious [mind].'[4] As is well known, Freud held that the unconscious was a storehouse of unpleasant memories, desires and neuroses – in short, anything socially unacceptable which the conscious mind repressed. Carl Jung took a much more pragmatic and positive view of the unconscious, saying that without this vast store of memories and knowledge our minds 'would become impossibly cluttered'.[5]

Modern psychology sides with Jung in taking a constructive view of the unconscious or subconscious (the terms are interchangeable) mind – I will use 'subconscious' throughout. Dr Paul MacLean, Chief of the Laboratory of Brain Research and Behavior at the (US) National Institute of Mental Health, has developed the 'Triune Model' of the brain. According to him, the conscious part of the human brain is the most recent – this is the *cortex*, which is at least 40,000 years old, and still evolving. Much older, some 50 million years old, is the *mammalian brain*, which directs feelings and emotions, and enables mammals to look after their young. Even older is the *reptilian brain*, which evolved 250 million years ago, to enable reptiles to survive. The reptilian brain – also present in mammals including humans – controls all bodily functions, such as heart rate, breathing and reproduction. The reptilian brain is usefully paranoid, resulting in awareness of threats to our existence and 'fight or flight' responses. It is this part of the brain that warned me on a recent vacation in Provence not to step out into the road, as I was about to do, when a car immediately hurtled past at great speed.

Our conscious mind, then, deals with the peculiarly human qualities of reasoning and thought; while the subconscious mind comprises our reptilian and mammalian capabilities, dealing with all the bodily functions that keep us alive (reptilian) and with our emotions and memories (mammalian).

There are some vital differences between our conscious and our subconscious minds

➤ The subconscious is much bigger, comprising an estimated 92 per cent of total brain size.

➤ The conscious mind can only do one thing at a time, which is why you should *never* text or use a phone and drive. The subconscious can perform trillions of operations simultaneously.

➤ The conscious mind has limited memory but the subconscious has virtually unlimited memory – though our conscious recall of it may be small.

➤ The subconscious does not have the directive intelligence of the conscious mind. The subconscious does not apply a filter to information – it is literal-minded, and accepts everything as true or valid. It is therefore a weighing machine for views rather than a thinking machine. When there is contradictory information – for example, the view that I am a 'strong' rather than a 'weak' person – the subconscious appears to be influenced by the *intensity*, '*recency*', and *frequency* of inputs:

Intensity means how strongly views are held and how imbued they are with emotion. When we really care about something, this gets communicated to our subconscious.

Recency means how recent the views are – current views seem to 'sit on top' of the subconscious, much as they do for the conscious mind.

Frequency means how often the same view is expressed, compared with contrary views. The subconscious is heavily influenced by repetition.

Like the conscious mind, the subconscious suffers from 'cognitive dissonance' – that is, it cannot entertain opposite views simultaneously, but has to plump for one consistent view.

Where the subconscious differs from the conscious mind, though, is that the latter – when well trained – can discriminate between good and bad information, between truth and falsehood.

➤ The subconscious deals with pictures and emotions; the conscious mind with reason and logic. For example, we may know that a television commercial is biased and has little genuine information on the value of a product, but ads are directed at the subconscious mind, and the use of emotion can be highly effective. It's interesting that changes in technology in the past half-century or so are increasingly changing the 'terms of trade' between the conscious mind and the subconscious, in favour of the latter. Marshall McLuhan argued that the electronic age of images and appeals to emotion – kick-started by the advent of television – is replacing the centuries-old dominance of print technology and therefore of reason.[6]

Joseph LeDoux, a brain researcher, says that decisions are nearly always made on emotional grounds – 'The brain states and bodily responses are the fundamental facts of an emotion, and the conscious feelings are the frills that have added icing to the emotional cake.[7]

Yet, other researchers have demonstrated that our conscious thoughts – as expressed in what we say and write – largely determine our emotions. There are feedback loops all over the place between the conscious and subconscious mind. We must be careful what we think!

➤ Let's disaggregate the two components of the word 'willpower' – the conscious mind has the 'will'; but the subconscious mind has the 'power'. Trying to exercise willpower through our conscious mind is self-defeating. As the theologian Harry Williams said, 'I don't think for one minute that I can summon up this strength [to improve myself] by simple willpower. The very idea of willpower implies division – two things pushing each other in opposite directions.'[8]

The way to change is to split the word 'willpower' – by the conscious mind (the will) directing the subconscious (the power). I'll show how this may be done.

➤ Another way of exploring the same tension between the will of the conscious mind and the power of the subconscious, is to juxtapose 'will' against 'imagination'. Emile Coué (1857–1926), the famous French psychologist and inventor of autosuggestion, said, 'When *will* and *imagination* are in conflict, imagination always wins.'[9] Will comes from the conscious mind, and imagination from the subconscious. Rather than use willpower to get its way, the conscious mind needs to deploy imagination derived from the subconscious.

➤ The conscious mind is the seat of knowledge, but the subconscious is the seat of creativity. Where else, for example, could surrealist art come from? Salvador Dalí made a habit of sitting down, relaxing, and daydreaming in order to conjure up the weird images he painted. To recall them, he trained himself to hold a solid object in his hand, and relax his grip when he saw the images in his mind. The crash of the object on the floor would wake him and he would paint what he had imagined.[10]

➤ The conscious mind can remember the past and plan for the future, but the subconscious lives only in the eternal present. (More on this later.)

Finally, the conscious mind is effortful – thinking almost hurts, which is why so many people avoid it – whereas the subconscious mind requires no effort and works away in the background incessantly.

Why the subconscious is so *very* 80/20

First, the subconscious yields enormous results with no conscious effort. It keeps us healthy; and it supplies the emotion and memories that make us creative and allow us to transform the world. What else does so much, with so little effort? And if we try to exert effort, we crowd out the subconscious – less is more, and more is less.

Second, if we access the subconscious astutely, as Dalí did, we can attain fantastic goals and output with a little clever manipulation.

Third, the *incidence of the use of the subconscious* follows a classic 80/20 – or rather 99/1 – distribution. I hope this will not always be the case, but currently fewer than 1 per cent of people use their subconscious deliberately. Yet, this tiny fraction of people achieves a majority of results.

There are myriad examples of how scientists have used their subconscious mind to make breakthroughs. They follow the same pattern. The scientist is stumped for an answer to a problem. He works for years, without progress. In frustration he sets his work aside. Then one day – out of the blue – the answer comes when the scientist is doing something mundane, not thinking at all; or in a dream, waking up in the middle of the night.

For the French mathematician Henri Poincaré, it was while boarding a bus in Paris and chatting to a friend. 'I went on with the conversation,' he recounted, 'but I felt a perfect certainty that the problem had been solved.'[11] For the philosopher and mathematician Bertrand Russell, it was while buying a pouch of tobacco for his pipe in Cambridge.

August Kekulé (1829–96), the German organic scientist and Nobel Prize winner, worked for years to identify a theory of chemical structures. Eventually he gave up. In the late summer of 1858, he was daydreaming on the upper deck of a horse-drawn omnibus in London, and had a vision of dancing atoms and molecules that led to his theory of structure.[12] Subsequently, he worked on the specific issue of how carbon atoms combined to form benzene, and again couldn't figure it out. But in 1862 he had a dream of snakes catching their tails, which led him to posit that the carbon atoms in benzene form a ring.[13]

Apparently, Thomas Edison, Guglielmo Marconi, Charles F Kettering, Albert Einstein, the American naturalist Louis Agassiz, James Watt, and many other scientists had similar experiences.[14] The historian of science Thomas S Kuhn, charted the way the scientists would notice more and more discrepancies between their data and the generally accepted theory. Kuhn noted that a new theory almost never emerges through the application of conscious reasoning:

> *Instead, the new paradigm, or a sufficient hint to permit later articulation, emerges all at once,* sometimes in the middle of the night, *in the mind of a man deeply immersed in crisis. What the nature of that final stage is – how an individual invents* (or finds he has invented) *a new way of giving order to data now all assembled – must here remain inscrutable and may be permanently so.*[15]

What Kuhn is describing – whether he realized it or not – is the operation of the subconscious mind, sorting all the data in the memory of the scientist and coming up with a compelling new pattern, which could not be arrived at by the conscious mind.

TIP FOR STUDENTS

When you go into an exam, read ALL the questions you plan to answer before you start writing your first answer. That way, your subconscious will be plugging away organizing what you should say to all the later questions while your conscious mind answers the first one. When you write the later answers they will flow thick and fast.

Three cardinal uses of the subconscious

Creative solutions

'Creativity', Einstein famously said, 'is more important than knowledge.' If you want a creative solution to *any* issue, the subconscious can supply it. Here are just a few applications:

- Any form of creative expression, including painting and sculpture, poetry, song-writing (lyrics and music), book-writing (fiction and non-fiction), and broadcasting
- The invention of new games (online or off)
- Creating a new business
- Scientific and technological innovation

- New product development
- Breakthroughs in social theory and practice
- Theories of management, and how to gain competitive advantage.

As David Brooks has written:

> *The unconscious is a natural explorer ... It naturally weighs the importance of various factors as they come into view. It restlessly scurries about – many parallel processes at a time – as the conscious mind is busy with other things, trying to match new situations with old models or trying to rearrange the pieces of a problem until they create a harmonious whole. It chases vibes and metaphors in search of connections, patterns, and similarities. It uses the whole panoply of psychological tools – emotions as well as physical sensations.*[16]

Attaining personal goals

People who write down their goals and review them frequently are much more likely to attain them. It is a separate question whether or not you *should* set goals for yourself. This is what I think:

- Goals are great if you really want to make a dent in the cosmos, if you are interested in extraordinary achievement, or if you want to make a lot of money.
- Goals are a potential source of tyranny if you don't *truly* want to realize them, but you just think you ought to have

them. Maybe if you don't have a goal or goals shouting at you, you should wait until you do.

If you do want to attain goals, mobilizing the subconscious is the surest and easiest way to get there.

Serenity

Peace of mind and tranquillity are near-universal wants. We all want to recover the primitive dream of Eden, a life of harmony and joy where we can be ourselves and yet also united with the world. The Romantic poet William Wordsworth (1770–1850) said that he felt nature to be an integral part of his own being: 'I was often unable to think of external things as having external existence, and I communed with all that I saw as something not apart from, but inherent in, my own immaterial nature.'[17] To restore the unity between our conscious mind and our subconscious, and between our mind and those of our neighbours and all humankind, requires some kind of immersion in truth, beauty, and the quest for individual and mutual good.

If we are what we think, we need to bring our noblest and most creative thoughts to the surface of our conscious mind and to the depths of our subconscious. This quest does not have to be in any way religious, but it has to have some *moral* quality, because this is the only way that internal peace and external unity can be attained.

'Be sure that you think on whatever things are true, whatever things are honest, whatever things are just, whatever things are pure, whatever things are lovely, whatever things are of good report: if there be any virtue, and if there be any praise, think on these things'[18] – this is good advice for all of us, believers, agnostics or atheists alike, not because it is what we *should* do, but because it is the way to amity within and between ourselves.

A new model of how to tap the subconscious

Most books about the subconscious manage to make tapping the subconscious quite a complicated thing. But I think it is very simple. As the chart below shows, there are three stages:

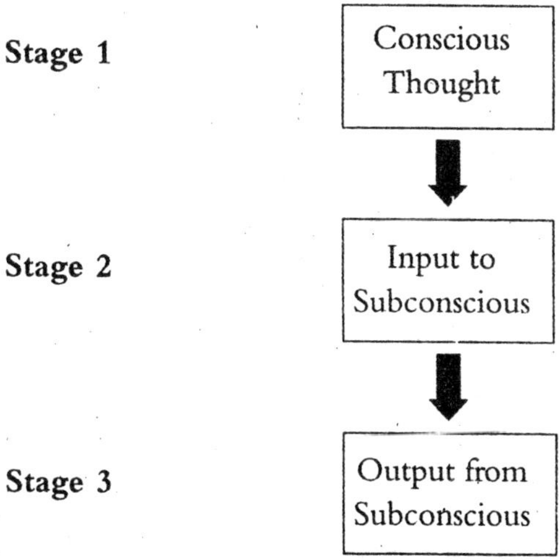

The first stage is conscious thought to identify what we want the subconscious to do for us, and how to present it to the subconscious. This stage is not complicated but it is the hardest of the three – we have to think seriously about what we want the subconscious to do.

The second stage is getting our thoughts over to our subconscious mind. For all the fuss made about this in many books, this stage is extremely quick and simple.

The third stage is to get the answer or output back from the subconscious. This stage is also very easy, if we allow the subconscious to get through to us.

If you doubt that using the subconscious in the second and third stages is quick and effective, think about the times you have set your alarm clock for, say, seven in the morning, and woken up at one minute to seven, just before the alarm goes off. What part of your mind did that?

It couldn't have been the conscious mind, because you were asleep just before you woke up. It was the subconscious that did it. Many people don't bother with alarm clocks but instruct their subconscious that 'I am wide awake at precisely seven a.m.' (I will explain later why it is better to use the present tense.) If you have any doubts at all, try it.

If you read books on the subconscious or 'mindfulness', you will find a lot of detailed and complex instruction about reaching the subconscious through 'getting in the alpha state', 'meditation', and various other techniques. But all that is unnecessary. The second and third stages could hardly be easier, and they need no equipment except your mind.

Stage 1: conscious thought

As with any powerful mental process, to get the most out of it with very little energy requires careful *thought* about *what precisely you want to achieve.* And this is why the first stage needs some guidance. This is different for each of the three cardinal uses of the subconscious:

For *creative solutions*, here are the rules:

- So as to put a clear request to the subconscious, select only one issue at a time.
- The problem or issue must be something that you really care about – sorting it out must be important to you. It can involve your work, career, or personal life.
- It may well be something that you have tried and failed to work out using your conscious mind.
- Chances are it's a 'how to' issue – for example:
    - How to reconcile the conflicting interests of work and family life.
    - How to come up with the words of a song you are writing.
    - How to invent a specific new product which is much better or cheaper than anything currently available.
    - How to avoid conflict with specific friends, family members, or work colleagues.
- You are seeking a solution that is good not just for yourself but for everyone else involved.

For *goal-setting*:

- The goal must be something that you really want to attain.
- You must believe that you can attain the goal, however

unlikely it might seem to other people. If you don't believe it, your subconscious won't glide into action.

➤ The goal must be precise and specific.

➤ You must be emotionally committed to the goal and believe that it will make you happy and fulfilled.

➤ Visualize yourself attaining the goal, making it as specific and joyous as possible. Use all your senses to imagine and describe achieving the goal – what does your life look like, what sights and smells do you associate with it, how will you celebrate having the goal and with whom, what will your daily life be like, and who else will benefit from your attainment?

➤ You must know and believe that the goal is absolutely made for you and tailored to your individual characteristics – the goal is your destiny.

➤ Though the goal may not be realised for many years, you must imagine having attained the goal in the present moment. As I mentioned earlier, the subconscious abides in the eternal present – the future and the past exist for the subconscious as some kind of data that are forever in the present.

This is hard to explain, so let's take an imperfect but helpful illustration. When you watch a movie, it too has a past and a future but they are compressed into ninety minutes. At any given moment you are part way through the life of the people in the movie, yet it is always the present for you. If you can ignore the fact that there are ninety minutes of your life involved, and imagine you are viewing it all at one moment – that is how the subconscious operates.

I find this mysterious – how can the subconscious be aware of a goal in the future, and help you attain it, without realizing that there is a future in your life? But for the subconscious, all time is flat; all time is the present. Everything is an instant movie, one that takes no time to unfold.

To manipulate your subconscious, you must present data in the form it can understand. So to attain the future, you must imagine and feel that it is the present. If you could see the future perfectly, it would be as real and 'present' as the present. That is how it is for the subconscious – time stands still and is not a dimension of reality. For the subconscious, too, reality is imagination and imagination is reality. View it from the perspective of the subconscious, and it can help you make the future the present, and your imagination your reality. After all, once you have seen a great movie, every scene you remember from it is forever in your present, regardless of the date in the movie. It is the intensity of the impact the scenes in the movie made on you, and your ability to re-imagine those scenes, that matter; not the dimension of time, which is irrelevant.

For *serenity*:

➤ If we make positive declarations about ourselves, and we believe them, these register with our subconscious. Here are some of the assertions or affirmations that can help to put us where we want to be:

- ➤ I am thankful for …
- ➤ I am feeling strong, generous, joyful, happy, at one with the world, in a good mood …
- ➤ I am creative because …
- ➤ My work is important and useful because …
- ➤ I am lucky to be able to help other individuals – be specific: who and how and when?
- ➤ I am enjoying good health.

- I have good friends whose company I enjoy and whom I can count on.
- I am lucky in having a great romantic partner – *or* I am going to meet someone soon who will be my mate for life.
- I am fortunate to live in such a beautiful place – *or* I am about to visit somewhere beautiful (or have just done so).
- I am really enthusiastic about this …
- The book I am reading is fantastic … and so on and on.

The 'I am' statements can be made many times a day, whenever there is a half-reasonable excuse – 'how are you today?' – whenever you have a chat with a friend, or even when you are alone. The statements seem to work better if you say them aloud, or write them down in a journal.

Now, there are some cultural issues here. I am British and we Brits find these things a little – how can I put this – brazen? Immodest? Flaky? Unsophisticated? Maybe you do too, whatever your nationality. Yet if we really desire serenity, calmness, composure, tranquillity, and peace of mind, this is the way. Optimistic assertions work!

It is not just our circumstances which we should deem good, whenever we reasonably can, but also ourselves. We are all 'crooked timber'. For peace of mind, however, we should be confident that we have something to offer the world, and that we are making life better, that we are trying to improve ourselves, and that our intentions are good. Without such beliefs life is bleak indeed, and who wants to live in a bleak landscape?

It sounds corny, but the following statements are effective:

- 'Every day, in every way, I'm getting better and better.' (Emile Coué)
- 'Think of yourself as you want to be.' (Harry Carpenter)
- 'I am becoming the best possible version of myself.' (Matthew Kelly)
- 'With all my shortcomings, I am a force for good in the world.'
- 'My quest is for truth and beauty.'

Stage 2: Input to subconscious

Here are three effortless ways to send messages to your subconscious:

1 Relax and daydream

- Sit in a comfortable chair in a quiet and private spot, preferably outdoors.
- Relax.
- Put all thoughts (apart from the message you are about to send) out of your head.
- Send the message to your subconscious – silently is OK, but say it aloud if you can.

2 Daydream during 'automatic' exercise

- Get into a routine form of exercise you are familiar with and can do without thinking about it (ideally something you do very often).
- The exercise must be something you can do easily,

with no stress or strain, alone. I find cycling or walking at a moderate pace work well.

- Before the exercise, read out or think of the message to the subconscious. If you remember, repeat the message while you are exercising and daydreaming. At the end of the exercise, repeat the message again.

3 Before sleep

- Listen to some relaxing or trance-like music for some minutes while in bed. (I listen to the same CD every night – it's called *el-Hadra*, the 'Mystik Dance', published by Edition Akasha in Munich. This seems to cue me up for a good sleep and ease in talking to my subconscious.)
- In the minute or two before you go to sleep, while you are winding down or drowsy, say the message aloud or in your head.
- Look forward to a good sleep and happy dreams.
- Repeat the message as the last thing you say or think before falling asleep.

Stage 3: Output from subconscious

Your subconscious will try to communicate its answer or message to you – you will get it, unless you crowd it out with vigorous activity or a restless mind. To help the subconscious get through to you, relax and daydream at times during the day, as per the suggestions in Stage 2.

The answer often comes at night or during the morning in that period of light sleep or semi-slumber during the hour or so before you fully wake up. To capture any insight before you fall asleep again and forget it, have a notebook and pen on your bedside table.

Conclusion

Once you learn the power of the subconscious, help your friends and family to do the same. Give them a copy of this book or lend it to them. Never will such little effort reap such great benefits.

Part Four

The 80/20 Future

17 Success Through 80/20 Networks

Network society represents a qualitative change in the human experience.

Manuel Castells, Spanish sociologist

When I wrote the first two editions of this book, I had no idea *why* the principle worked so well. I quoted the economist Josef Steindl – 'For a very long time, the Pareto law has lumbered the economic scene like an erratic block on the landscape: an empirical law which nobody can explain.' But now I'm excited, because I think I know the explanation, and it also explains why 80/20 is becoming even more prevalent, affecting our lives in mysterious and perplexing ways.

The answer is in the burgeoning power of networks. The number and influence of networks has been growing for a long time, at first a slow increase over the past few centuries, but since about 1970 the increase has become faster and more dramatic. Networks also behave in an 80/20 way – in the way characteristic of 80/20 distributions. And often in an *extremely* lopsided way. So the principle is becoming more pervasive because the same is true of networks. More networks, more 80/20 phenomena.

As the influence of networks rises, so does that of 80/20.

The importance of the sentence above can scarcely be exaggerated. As Manuel Castells says, network society marks a *qualitative* change in the human experience. And the nature of that change is rooted in the nature of 80/20. There is no type of organization or experience *so characteristically and thoroughly 80/20 as are networks.*

It's vital for us to understand networks, why they are increasing in importance, how they exhibit 80/20 trademarks, *and how we can turn that to our advantage.* If we don't understand 80/20 and networks, we don't understand the most profound change in business and society happening in our lifetimes.

So – what is a network?

Kevin Kelly, the former editor of *Wired*, puts it well:

> *The network is the least structured organization that can be said to have any structure at all.*

Facebook and Twitter are networks; so are terrorist organizations, criminal gangs, political groupings, football teams, the

Internet, the United Nations, a group of friends, and the world's financial system. Nearly all of the web- or app-based organizations that have burst upon the scene and built wealth to an extraordinary extent – firms such as Apple, Google, eBay, Uber, Amazon, Netflix, and Airbnb – are either networks, or have networks nestling within their ecosystems.

How are networks different from traditional top-down organizations?

Well, let's start with one defining difference. The growth of ordinary organizations – those we have been used to for centuries, starting with state bureaucracies and army-based empires, then extending to organized agriculture and commerce, to mills and factories, and to all the business and social organizations of the previous three centuries – *depends on initiative from the top of those organizations.*

Traditional organizations cannot grow without planning from the top, often in minute detail. The plans are then implemented by such activities as product design, manufacturing, marketing, and selling. All of these are expensive and painstaking. It used to take a long time, and a huge amount of effort, manpower and money, for organizations to grow to their maximum size and influence.

But networks are different. Their growth comes not from *inside* the organization (if there is one) which owns or sponsors the network, but from *outside.* It is the network itself that grows, as a result of actions by the network members themselves – if the network is owned by a business, the 'members' are also 'customers' or potential customers. The network grows because of its own internal dynamics and because it is in the interests of the network members that it should grow.

Let me give an example of a network I was involved in

almost from its beginning. This network was started by a group of young and inexperienced but very enthusiastic people. It was *Betfair*. You could call the founders entrepreneurs, and you would be right, but they were really sports and betting enthusiasts, wanting to bet without paying a king's ransom to the old-style bookmakers, who would take around 10 per cent of each bet's value as a margin. The idea behind Betfair was that anyone who wanted to bet could do so with another person, who took the opposite view, about whether a horse or team would or would not win an event. Betfair created an online electronic market – similar to the stock market for shares – and then took a small commission for organizing the market.

I invested in Betfair in 2001, a few months after it started. At that stage the company was valued at £15 million – not a great deal, really. It was still tiny – and very few industry observers noticed it, or if they did, they didn't think the idea would work. Yet the exciting thing about Betfair – what attracted me to it – was that it was growing incredibly fast. In the early years, it grew at 10, 20, 30, even sometimes 60, per cent *each month*.

Where did this growth come from? I can tell you where it didn't come from. It didn't come from sales and marketing effort, because initially there was almost none. It came from the network itself – from the users of Betfair, the customers, who liked it so much they advised their friends who liked to bet to join the network. And this wasn't just because they liked the system or wanted to be kind to their friends. The network users recommended Betfair because they wanted it to get bigger, for their own benefit. They wanted to place more and bigger bets, and get them matched by other members taking the opposite view.

This brings me on to the second cardinal aspect of a network – a network becomes more valuable as it grows in size. Not only that. The growth in value – to the members, and if there are any to the network owners – is *geometric* rather than linear. Think of a dating platform with 1,000 members, all based in a particular town or region, and all interested in potential dates with other members. Would you join such a network? It's unlikely – it's too small.

But imagine that the size of the network doubles, to 2,000 members. Does the value of the network also double? No, it doesn't. The value of the network actually goes up about four times. That is because the number of possible permutations between the network members increases from 499,500 to 1,999,000.[1] For the same reason, as the number of Betfair users grew, the value to users of the network multiplied exponentially. The punters were able to place far more bets, in larger amounts, and get them matched. And the value to Betfair's owners increased enormously too. In February 2016 the firm merged with Paddy Power and the combined firm is now valued at £7,200 million. Betfair shareholders own £3,456 million of that total – about 230 times the value at the time I invested.

If we put together the first two points about networks – the growth coming relatively easily from member activity; and the exponential increase in value from growing in size – we reach a third conclusion: network organizations can gain value super-fast, far faster than other organizations. That's why network-based ventures such as Amazon, eBay, Facebook, Alibaba, Airbnb and Uber have become so valuable, so quickly. No non-network-based businesses have ever matched this rate of value explosion.

There's a fourth and final reason why the number and

force of networks have proliferated: the fuel driving networks is information. Networks multiply, become denser, and more commanding as information technology – in the broadest sense – expands its reach and capabilities. App-based firms such as Airbnb and Uber, for example, just could not have existed in their current form without the invention of the smartphone.

So we have the cascading effect that one immensely valuable network innovation spawns and enables many other immensely valuable network innovations. Given that the cost of information technology keeps going down and its performance keeps getting mightier and more manifold, it is hard to see where all this is going to end. We really are in a brave new world – for good and ill – that is touching the lives of billions and changing the rules of business and society.

Since the 1960s, networks have been noted by academics, business people and commentators. But the link between networks and 80/20 is not yet widely understood. To uncover this link, let's ponder two instances of how networks follow the principle.

The World Wide Web

An obvious example is the online world. The word 'cyberspace' was invented by science-fiction writer William Gibson in 1984. 'I was trying', he said, 'to describe an unthinkable present. Science-fiction's best use is the exploration of contemporary reality.' He defined cyberspace as 'a consensual hallucination experienced daily by billions in every nation … Unthinkable complexity. Lines of light ranged in the non-space of the mind, clutters and constellations of data.'

Certainly the World Wide Web is a strange country we visit without leaving our terrestrial locations, a network transforming our work and social lives, as well as the face of business; and a network that has exploded in size and power. It is democratic in structure, permitting the uninvited to opine on Twitter, allowing all of us to post the fabric of our daily lives on Facebook and other specialist sites. The web grows because it is open to all and because it provides extraordinary value for money. It excludes nobody. It welcomes everybody. Everyone has access to the riches of Wikipedia and the insights from millions of articles.

Yet there is a paradox at the heart of cyberspace. The Internet is open and without barriers, yet also the epitome of 80/20. For example, there are more than two hundred search engines listed by Wikipedia. Yet four of them worldwide – Google, Baidu, Bing, and Yahoo – take 96 per cent of the market. So 2 per cent of search engines hog 96 per cent of search engine enquiries and therefore advertising – a 96/2 relationship.

Google alone has a massive 66 per cent. So 1 out of 200 search engines – less than 1 per cent – commands two-thirds of this incredibly lucrative business – a 66/0.5 relationship. And as I'll show in the next chapter, this is actually a huge underestimate of the profit relationship between Google and the also-rans. Google also captures 82 per cent of mobile operating systems – and 94 per cent of mobile search. In Chinese e-commerce, one site – Alibaba – takes a staggering 75 per cent of *all* transactions. Since there is a huge number of Chinese websites, this is a 75/0 relationship (to the nearest round number, Alibaba comprises 0 per cent of those sites).

How many Betfairs are there? I will tell you – there is only one betting exchange that matters. I estimate that Betfair has more than a 95 per cent share of its market. How many Facebooks are there? There used to be two dominant social platforms – in fact Facebook was much smaller than MySpace at one time. But now there really is only one – Facebook. How many Twitters are there? Only one that matters.

Talking of Twitter, here are some Pareto-like relationships *within* the Twitter system. Research by *Silicon Valley Insider* implied that 10 per cent of 'heavy followers' – the people who follow a lot of Twitter tweeters – accounted for 85 per cent (85/10) of the total number of people followed.[2]

What about the other way round? Researchers in 2011 showed that the amazingly small number of 20,000 prolific tweeters attracted almost half of followers. At that time those top tweeters comprised less than one twentieth of 1 per cent of all tweeters – a 50/0 pattern.[3]

Finally how many Ubers are there? At the moment there is Uber, and there is a bunch of challengers who really operate in different segments of the market. If what you want is what Uber offers, you really have a choice between Uber and Uber. And that is good for all of us, because a virtual monopoly in any city means lower waiting times for customers, and higher utilization for drivers. All this helps to explain why Uber is so determined to expand so fast and in so many places, at very high capital cost – there is space in heaven for only one Uber-like firm.

Despite lots of adverse publicity, the venture capital market has placed a higher valuation on Uber, which only started in 2009, than on General Motors, which started 101 years earlier. Uber, of course, makes no cars, and owns no cars, so its potential future profits are thought to be astronomical.

Why is the web so concentrated, with very few mega-winners and most players insignificant? Eric Schmidt, chairman of Google's parent Alphabet, explains:

> *I would like to tell you that the Internet has created such a level playing field that the long tail is absolutely the place to be. Unfortunately, that's not the case.*
>
> *What really happens is something called a power law. A small number of things are very highly concentrated and most other things have relatively little volume. Virtually all the new network markets follow this law. So, while the tail is very interesting, the vast majority of revenue remains in the head.*
>
> *And in fact, it's probable that the Internet will lead to larger blockbusters and more concentration of brands. Which, again, doesn't make sense to most people, because it's a larger distribution medium. But when you get everybody together they still like to have one superstar. It's no longer a US superstar, it's a global superstar.*[4]

The most connected sites in cyberspace are like a hugely fashionable bar, which is popular simply because it's popular. You know you're going to meet lots of people there. What happens is that everyone wants to be where everyone else is – at least within their own category. Liquidity and depth of market attract more members, more liquidity, and greater depth of market. Networks are attractive proportional – nay, super-proportional – to their size. At least for a season, the winner takes all. Nice work. The bar-owner won't become a billionaire. But his counterparts on the web may well do, with astounding rapidity.

Let's look at a second instance of how winning networks become ever-more powerful. This time I've selected an important social trend that is *not* an online example.

Cities

Ever since humans settled down to living in one place 10,000 years ago, cities have been hugely important networks, increasing the exchange of knowledge, culture, and goods and services, as well as providing the basic infrastructure of government and finance. The 'global strategist' Parag Khanna asserts that 'cities are mankind's most enduring and stable mode of social organization, outlasting all empires and nations'.[5] There have been two massively important trends ever since (to be clear, this is my account, not Khanna's, though his is somewhat similar).

One trend is the slow, but steady and now rapidly accelerating increase in the number of people who are urbanized. In 1500, only 1 per cent of people around the world lived in cities. This proportion tripled by 1800 – 3 per cent. In 1900, one seventh of humanity. Today city-dwellers outnumber the rest.

The advance in wealth in Europe – and later the rest of the world – which began around 1450, and made mankind a biological success, would not have happened without the growth in the number and power of cities. They were centres of ideas, trade, commerce, run by a very small but vital (80/20) new middle class of burghers, neither peasants nor aristocrats. Cities were incubators of wealth, tiny 80/20 islands springing up within the vast sea of aristocratic rural estates. Of course, cities have existed for millennia, but it is only from late-medieval Europe that they started to become engines of economic growth and social change.

In 1500 there were only five European cities with 100,000 people. By 1600 there were fourteen – Amsterdam, Antwerp, Constantinople, Lisbon, Marseilles, Messina, Milan, Moscow, Naples, Palermo, Paris, Rome, Seville, and Venice. You will note that half of these were important ports. Without the expansion of these cities, the modern world would never have developed.

Today the world's twenty richest cities are magnets for talent with high concentrations of knowledge and money. More than three-quarters of the world's big companies are based in these twenty cities. Increasingly, it is the big cities that get bigger and wealthier – a continuation and acceleration of the trend started in Europe in 1500. The expansion of cities exhibits classic network effects:

- As the network – the city – gets bigger and denser, the advantages of living in the city multiply. The opportunity to meet other people with complementary knowledge increases exponentially – notwithstanding the very real disadvantages of congestion, expense and stress from living in a teeming city. The positive network effects usually outweigh the negative ones; the evidence for this is that most big cities expand.
- Yet not all cities do. Many municipalities in the US and other developed countries are basket cases. Low rents in New Orleans or Detroit do not make the cities attractive – they are a symptom of decline. As always, network effects display Pareto-like selectivity. The vibrant cities with good networks get even bigger and more vibrant. Other cities decline further.
- Cities are melting pots. They attract ambitious and talented people from less successful cities and countries around the world. The degree of variety and differences between people in the city increases, innovation becomes more prolific, and opportunities mushroom.

These network effects explain the fallacy behind the frequent predictions from the 1970s that information technology would encourage more people to live in the countryside. The network advantages of urban life in the top cities just keep growing, based on the importance of face-to-face meetings and the serendipity of random connections. Parag Khanna predicts that 'by 2030, more than 70 per cent of the world's people will live in cities, with most of them located within fifty miles of the sea ... the demographic concentration, economic weight, and political power of today's coastal megacities makes them ... the key units of human organization.'[6] I would add that one of the best ways to make money slowly but surely over the last half-millennium has been to buy land in the middle of expanding cities.

The other trend is the distribution of people *within* particular sizes of city. Again, the futurists who asserted that cities in the age of the Internet would become relatively dispersed, with more middle-sized cities, have been confounded. It is telling that the cities that grow the fastest in any time period tend to be the biggest and often oldest cities at the start of the period – for example, Tokyo, Beijing (formerly Peking), and Mumbai (formerly Bombay), and in the Americas, New York, Los Angeles, and Mexico City. The Greater Tokyo Area now has roughly 38 million inhabitants, more than the total population of either Canada or Iraq.

Parag Khanna also claims that cities will increasingly combine in the same way that Tokyo and Yokohama have already done – so we will have Los Angeles–San Francisco and Boston–Washington DC, for example. The latter seems a little far-fetched to me, as the two cities are not very close, but the tendency for cities to sprawl and invade green space is long-running. The London church of St Martin-in-the-Fields –

next to Trafalgar Square – really was once outside the city, surrounded by fields.

Khanna is on surer ground, perhaps, in saying that global cities rely for their zest on attracting global talent – 'As the number of global migrants surges, connected and open cities feature ever-higher percentages of foreign-born residents.'[7] In Dallas 24 per cent of the population is foreign-born, in Sydney 31 per cent, New York City and London each have 37 per cent, Hong Kong has 38 per cent, and Singapore 43 per cent.[8]

Summary

This has been quite a long chapter – many thanks for your patience! But I can now summarize the argument:

1. One increasingly dominant reason why the 80/20 Principle works is the power of networks.

2. Networks also operate in line with the principle. In any given market or category, a very small proportion of networks will hold sway over a large proportion of activity or business in that market or category.

3. Networks and their members *like market share concentration and monopoly*, because this provides the greatest depth and reach of the network. Bigger networks are better networks. The bigger network matches supply and demand more efficiently and quickly,

because it has more permutations of possible member matches, and more data about each member's predilections.

4 Having two or three networks with roughly equal size in the same category is unstable, because it is not in the interests of network members. They are best served by a near-monopoly, until innovation creates a new category – which itself will also inevitably lurch towards a few main networks, or one.

5 The influence of networks has soared since the 1970s, and especially since the invention and proliferation of online transactions. Networks are becoming more prevalent and providing an ever-growing proportion of commercial and social activity. This means that the old 80/20 benchmark is rapidly becoming too conservative as a way of describing the principle. Networks are not just increasing the incidence of the principle and making it pretty much ubiquitous, but also increasing the *extremity* of the principle.

In the next chapter we look at where and how 80/20 is sliding rapidly towards 90/10, 95/5, or even 99/1. We'll then examine the practical implications of this shift.

18 When 80/20 Becomes 90/10

The future is already here – it's just not equally distributed.
William Gibson, science fiction visionary

Not so very long ago, in 2007 actually, the world of mobile phone makers was a rather placid and entirely predictable milieu, typical of the 80/20 world. There was a large number of mobile phone manufacturers, but five of them – Nokia, Samsung, Motorola, Sony Ericsson, and LG – had succeeded in capturing about 90 per cent of total worldwide profits. Nothing at all remarkable about that. Today, however, it is a totally different world – in the size of the prize, in the winning companies, in how profits are split, and in how they are made.

Between 2007 and 2015, a new entrant came into the market, and changed everything. The new entrant, of course, was Apple with its iPhone. Not only did Apple reach the top table; like Jesus in the temple, Apple overturned the merchants' tables and drove them away. By 2015, Apple had grabbed 92 per cent of the profits in a much larger and more remunerative market, leaving the erstwhile leaders to fight over the crumbs. Four of the five former market leaders are now making losses.[9]

Not only the identity of the winner was changed, but also the way profits were made. It's worth describing what happened, because the same thing is developing in many other markets, and it is a sea change that will define the coming years.

The shorthand is that 80/20 became 90/10. The longhand is a bit more descriptive, but equally clear. The pattern of business – the way to make mountains of cash – changed abruptly. The old pattern is fading and a new pattern is taking over. Your route to innovation may be to ditch the old pattern and embrace or create a new one in your industry. The mobile phone market pre-dated the Internet. When the Internet came about, mobile phone makers rubbed their hands with glee because the market exploded. More calls; more money for everyone. Mobile phones were increasingly used to access mobile content and transmit it, but the manufacturers remained stuck in the pre-network world.

Until recently the dominant business model was the 'value chain' – a horrid piece of jargon for a logical way of doing business. The start of a value chain may be research or product design, generating a new product. The next stage in the chain is usually to buy materials and services from suppliers – for example, the electronic components and casing to make mobile phones. The chain proceeds via manufacturing, marketing, selling, and the logistics of getting the finished product – the mobile phone – to customers. A 'value chain' is also called a 'pipeline' business because the activities take place in a linear fashion, moving from the supplier to the customer.

Note that the pipeline business is typical of the 80/20 world. Most of the profits go to relatively few producers – maybe a fifth of the total number of suppliers – but it is perfectly consistent with the principle that there may be three, four, five, or even more winners. Profits are concentrated within a few players, but usually more than one or two.

So how exactly is a network business different from a pipeline business? This is where it can get confusing, until you realize that a network venture also needs a pipeline. Apple, for example, still has to design its iPhone, buy raw materials, and have the product made and sold, and so on. But network businesses are different – and almost always superior – because they conceive their role and what they provide in a completely different way. The essence of a network is that it connects two or more different sets of players in a market, and then orchestrates the market for the benefit of both sides – and for its own benefit.

Steve Jobs didn't just want to sell phones to customers, the way Nokia and the other Old Guard pipeline suppliers had done. Jobs wanted to *connect* app developers with app users. Just as the Betfair network has connected gamblers who wanted to take one side of a bet, with other gamblers who took the opposite view. The app developers don't need to know who the customers are or recruit them, because Apple already had potential app customers – all the people using the iPhone.

Apple has a 'platform': the phone itself and all its associated intellectual property. A platform can generate huge profits for the platform owner, as well as offering a great means of setting the rules for how the platform is run. Apple decides who (which app developers) are allowed onto the platform and how app developers and app users interact. For example, Steve Jobs would not allow porn onto his platform.

In both these examples, Betfair's betting exchange and Apple's iPhone platform, network effects – specifically everyone involved having a bigger market with more smartphones, more app suppliers, and more app users – drove phenomenal growth in the market and in profits for the platform owner.

This was the second time that Jobs had hit the jackpot with a platform business. The first time was with iTunes. Recall the parlous position of the music industry in 2003. Sales of CDs and other recordings were plummeting as a result of shadowy Internet sites such as Napster and Kazaa, offering songs for very little or for free. Scared stiff, the record company executives tried and failed to formulate a unified response. Into this scene of chaos and devastation stepped Jobs, a genuine music lover. It was all very well, Jobs said, to take free downloads, but they were unreliable and 'a lot of these songs are encoded by seven-year-olds, and they don't do a great job'. Downloads came with no album art or previews. 'Worst of all,' he concluded, 'it's stealing. It's best not to mess with karma.'[10]

By persuading enough record companies and artists to participate, the iTunes store was able to open with 200,000 tracks, all available for ownership for just 99 cents. A download took just a minute, compared with fifteen for the piracy sites. The iTunes boss, Eddy Cue, made the bold prediction that he would sell a million songs in six months. In fact, it took just six days to hit that target. And Apple made 30 per cent of all sales revenues just for owning the platform.[11]

What has the trend from pipelines to networks to do with the 80/20 Principle?

Everything! The move from 80/20 to 99/1 – via 90/10 and 95/5 – is in large part the move from pipelines to platforms. The pipelines – value chain supplier, for example, Nokia and its rival traditional phone makers – lose out to the new platform providers. When the market leader changes from a pipeline-only business to one that adds a platform, 80/20 gravitates remorselessly to 90/10 and then on towards 99/1. Besides platforms being so much more profitable than pipelines, platforms are also natural monopolies, because of network effects. Everyone – producers and customers alike – want to be on the largest network.

The shift from pipelines to platforms is a profound, epoch-making change, for two reasons:

1 Network markets usually become monopolies or duopolies – and unless prevented by regulations, duopolies will sooner or later become monopolies, if only by merging the two winning networks. This is a winner-take-all world in which market share is hugely more concentrated.

2 In the 90/10, 95/5, or 99/1 world – as opposed to the 80/20 one – the difference between the number one player and numbers three onwards becomes multiplied enormously. The gap becomes a gulf. The profit potential of numbers three and down trends towards zero or less. The hope of overthrowing the

number one player is nearly always forlorn. The *only* hope for an also-ran or a new entrant is to invent a *new segment* it can dominate.

Look at the arithmetic. If 20 out of 100 suppliers in a market make 80 per cent of the profits – and say the profit in the market is $100 – then that means the 20 winners make on average $80 divided by 20, which is $4 per winner. Similarly, the 80 losers make $20 divided by 80, which comes to $0.25 each. So the winners make $4 each, which is 16 times what the losers make each, 25 cents. That's the logic of 80/20 and it explains why it is SO much better to be in the top 20 per cent than the bottom 80 per cent.

But when the market shifts to 90/10, the difference between the winners and losers becomes a chasm. Look at the numbers again. The winners make 90 per cent of the total profit of $100, so they each make $90 divided by 10 which equals $9 each. Meanwhile, the 90 losers share the dregs of the profits, now down to $10 in total. So the losers on average each make $10 divided by 90, which is 11.1 cents each. Thus the multiple of individual winner-take to loser-take is $9 divided by $0.11 – that is, 81 times. So instead of being 16 times more profitable, the winners are now 81 times more so.

And as 90/10 becomes 95/5 and so on to 99/1, the gap between the few winners and the many losers gets closer and closer to being, in all practical terms, infinite. In those markets there is literally *no* place for the losers. The winners end up with bigger and bigger piles of cash, which can be used to increase the gulf between them and everyone else.

Because of the increased incidence and value of networks, the 80/20 world is sliding faster and faster into the 90/10 world. And as a result, the impact on profits, cash flow, the value of companies, and the gap between the winners and the losers, becomes nuclear.

The 80/20 world is lopsided and the 90/10 world is so warped that it belongs on the Starship *Enterprise*. In case you think this is theoretical, let's look at a couple more examples.

➤ *Amazon*, as you know, started as an online book retailer, but has since moved into selling a vast number of products. The company simplified the buying process for customers and became a platform for other suppliers eager to tap into Amazon's large customer base. By selling more items – not just books but almost anything else – to each customer, Amazon has been able to lower its costs of acquiring more sales, as well as reinforcing its skill base and increasing yet further its bargaining power with its suppliers, and thus its ability to sell at very low prices.

Moreover, it has been able to market new products without facing the launch costs that would have been high for any other new entrant. Each new market reinforces Amazon's competitive advantage and makes it harder and harder – and perhaps just plain impossible – for a similar widely based rival to catch up. Over time, Amazon will be able to edge up its prices a tad and still be super-competitive, and all that lovely dosh will drop straight to the bottom line.

➤ *Facebook* displays different specifics but the same general trend – reaping the geometrically increasing returns from increasing dominance. As online marketing guru Perry Marshall explains:

> *Only about 10 per cent of your Facebook fans see your posts if you don't pony up the dough and pay Big Blue to promote them. That's what you get for free. 10 per cent. Do you think that number is going up?*
>
> *Nope. It's going to be 8 per cent, then it's going to be 7 per cent, then it's going to be 5 per cent. It will never be zero, but I'm telling you,* paid social media is the future.[12]

Imagine what that could do to the profits of Facebook, and the costs of its users!

Is e-commerce synonymous with network businesses?

No. Be very clear about a distinction that is often muddied: networks and the online world are not the same thing. There can be networks that are not online; and there can be online businesses which are not really networks.

Network businesses long pre-dated the Internet. For example, classified advertising in newspapers and magazines matches buyers and sellers – because the product and service characteristics get better when there are more users. The secret to all networks is that they are about liquidity – the more buyers and sellers, and the more various and deep their ability to do business with each other, the better it is for everyone. Some observers seem to imagine that network or platform businesses are a recent invention, but that is not so. A newspaper or magazine devoted to classified advertising is a platform. Perhaps the best example is *Auto Trader*, the magazine that for decades dominated the buying and selling of used cars – a fantastically valuable franchise where money went to the owners simply because it was a dominant network.

Shopping centres are another example of an extremely successful network business. A shopping centre is nothing more than a platform connecting buyers and sellers, and the more buyers and sellers there are in a local area, the better it works.

You may ask, if you can have a network business without the Internet, can you have an Internet business without it being a network?

The short answer is yes, you can. Consider an online casino, such as www.888.com. This is a successful business, but it does not demonstrate any network effects, nor does it help to move the world much from 80/20 to 90/10. The casino game is like a pipeline; the casino is not multi-player, there is no community, and no data contributed by customers. From the users' viewpoint, it matters not a fig whether 888 has 10,000 customers or 1 million; if 888 doubled its size, the customer proposition would not improve.

The long answer is, well, a little longer than the short one. It is convenient to divide the world, as we have, into pipeline and network businesses, but this oversimplifies an important characteristic of network businesses – which is this – *network businesses comprise a spectrum of the extent to which they display network effects*. This spectrum ranges from the almost-but-not-quite non-existent network effects, to extremely strong ones.

Examples of strong network-effect businesses have already been given – Betfair, Google Search, Facebook, Twitter, eBay, iTunes, and the iPhone App Store. Here the benefits from having the biggest network is overwhelming, and the product and service characteristics just get better and better the larger the network gets. The result is that the business is not just extremely profitable; it is also largely immune to competitive pressure (unless someone invents a better platform). Businesses with strong network effects move effortlessly from 80/20 to 90/10, and often all the way to 99/1.

By contrast, an online peer-to-peer lender such as Lending Club in the United States displays only weak network effects. At first sight, one might imagine that the more lenders there are, the better it is for borrowers, and vice versa. But the lending side of the market could easily be replaced – and perhaps increasingly *will* be replaced – by one or more institutional lenders. As long as the interest rate charged is not higher than currently for a borrower of any given creditworthiness, the size of the network does not really matter to the borrower.

Or consider TransferWise, a peer-to-peer money transfer service developed in Estonia and based in the UK. This is a simple-to-use way to transfer money to someone in a country with a different currency. The peer-to-peer element is somewhat illusory, because all that TransferWise does is aggregate flows of currencies – for example the pound to the euro and the euro to the pound – in a highly efficient way for people transferring small sums of money. The key to its success is the simplified interface, not the peer-to-peer element, with one exception, which is that the latter drives viral growth. If I send you money via TransferWise, I have introduced you to the system, and you may decide to initiate a transfer yourself later.

Strictly speaking, viral effects are *not* network effects. Viral effects are often bedfellows of network effects, but they are not the same thing. A viral effect enables a company to grow fast, but it does not improve the product or service itself, which does not get better simply because the network is bigger.

On the other hand, a viral effect can help to shift a market some of the way from 80/20 to 90/10 concentration. The largest player will probably benefit most from viral effects, and this will flow through to economies of scale, and hence may increase the competitive advantage of the player. The lead over smaller players may therefore grow, enabling the leader to price lower, or to add better features, or to market the service more heavily. This is good, but it also applies in the pipeline world of 80/20.

A viral effect cannot compare to strong *network* effects, where the product or service *automatically gets better the larger the network.* With network effects, the leader gets all the benefits of larger scale but gets them without having to do anything itself; and more importantly, the advantage of the network leader's product or service increases with greater size, making it harder for rivals.

The key change driving business concentration, therefore, is not the web, but network businesses, especially the trend towards *a few exceptionally profitable and fast-expanding* network ventures. Having said this, most new network businesses today are online; and the web encourages and multiplies network firms faster than before the advent of the Internet.

Conclusion

The world of 90/10 has three interrelated and compounding trends toward greater and greater business concentration, and especially concentration of profits, within fewer and fewer hands:

1 The trend towards a higher proportion of activity – especially highly remunerative activity – within networks.

2 The trend within network markets from 80/20 to 90/10 and even more warped degrees of concentration.

3 Within any particular network or network-based firm there will be a trend over time for the terms of trade to slide in favour of the network monopolist or near-monopolist. Over time, customers – both consumers and other businesses – will pay more, and those that dominate the network will make even larger fortunes.

Practical advice for thriving in the new world

There's a big potential advantage for everyone who works to identify network businesses before they get big. If they are growing fast and the leaders in their niche – ho they are today – such ventures may well become big. If you can engineer it somehow, it makes sense to work for them, getting in on the ground floor, and then growing with them. There is SO much more opportunity in fast-growing firms because they are making it up as they go along. In a low-growth economy, there is typically more talent than openings for it. In a fast-growth enterprise, it is the other way around. The first twenty people into Microsoft, Amazon, and Google, for instance, are nearly all multi-millionaires and some are billionaires. Do you think this was because they happened to be sixty of the most able people on the planet, an extraordinary concentration of talent suddenly arriving at the same place at the same time? More likely, they were talented but also extremely fortunate.

Therefore:

➤ Spend time searching for new networks and platforms that have just got going. Make it a hobby and devote a few hours a week to it; *and*

➤ Once you have joined a new network business, think like an owner. You could well become a fractional owner, through stock options and possible direct investment even of a small sum. A very small fraction of the firm could make you rich. Ensure that you do something that speeds up the firm's growth. Aim to be a winner in the new company, someone who is listened to and respected.

➤ If you are an investor, consider focusing on incipient network businesses. Get in early before the value of the platform is obvious, before people realize how valuable it could become.

If I had known when I started my career how wonderful small, fast-growth network ventures could be, I would never have worked in any other kind of firm. Now you know, do you want to make that resolution?

19 Your Place in the 80/20 Future

If you understand it correctly, the 80/20 future is wonderful. If you don't understand what is happening, the 80/20 future is bewildering. For most people, the 80/20 future will not be a comfy place, nor will it be familiar territory. For those of us brought up in a world of big organizations, a world we believed to be mainly fair and predictable, the new 80/20 world of networks is more than a little scary.

The new world is one where effort is rewarded and increasingly sundered, a world of fewer successful 'command and control' Goliaths, where informal networks are increasingly prevalent, where educational qualifications do not guarantee good jobs, where the only route to security is to relish the flux of insecurity, where the way to wealth or a good life is open to everyone, but closed to anyone who does not hack their own individualized path through the forest of endeavour and the slough of mediocrity.

The 80/20 future is ill-defined, paradoxical, elusive, and subtle; it is not only what you make it, but also how you define it. The 80/20 future does not proclaim itself. It is hidden, gnomic, and requires you to decipher and describe it. It requires you to *make* it – the raw materials are all there, but the finished product is not assembled. You have to do that. The product you and your team will make will not be the one that I and my team will make. That is all to the good. There are infinite routes to success and joy, but they need to be discovered and made manifest. Most of us, especially those who are older or set in our ways, will find it difficult to understand.

Your 80/20 future is completely uncharted territory; it is challenging, thrilling, and exhilarating. It is uncharted because it exists in your own mind, and the minds of your closest friends and colleagues – and nowhere else. The 80/20 future is mysterious, fuzzy, foggy. It is magical and requires the spark of fancy and vision to catch fire and gain momentum. It requires belief in the invisible; the 80/20 future becomes visible through a great idea, unreasonably and fanatically believed in, executed through the fusion of passion and reason, insanity and insight joined together and not to be denied by existing drab reality.

No one can prosper in the 80/20 or 99/1 future with solutions that worked in the 60/40 or 65/35 past. Yet 80/20 diagnostics are available – guidelines that work very well in the new world, given imagination and determination. In keeping with the selective nature of the principle, this short chapter gives you the five most potent hints that I have discovered in four decades of searching.

Hint 1: Only work in networks

Chapter 18 said that the future belongs to networks. Therefore only work in network businesses. This is the most vital hint – for you to enjoy the 80/20 future it is *essential* to heed it. Networks feed on positive feedback – the famous get more famous, the rich get richer, leading companies often become virtual monopolies, and the skilled specialist goes further and further ahead of her less experienced rivals.

Networks exhibit galloping 80/20. Network businesses still comprise a small proportion of total businesses; yet they generate most of the money to be had in business. If you only work in network businesses, you will have a head start, a lead lengthened each year by the march of the 80/20 future.

Head start or albatross. Your choice.

Hint 2: Small size, very high growth

Within the universe of network businesses, you could choose to join one of the established winners – Amazon or Google or Facebook or Uber (not as a driver, but at head office). But that would not be smart. You will arrive at the party far too late to have much fun.

The best type of network business to join is one that has just started but is growing. That way you and your abilities can blossom in parallel – another little positive feedback mechanism. You start off in pole position and learn as you go along. Nobody knows what they are doing and it is exhilarating to test what works best and to learn ahead of anyone else.

It is not just about money. The most fun I have had has been in companies where I was a founder or employee or investor when they were very small but growing extremely fast – Bain & Company, LEK Consulting, Belgo, Betfair, and now Auto1. There is something about growth of 40 to 300 per cent per annum that makes you feel on top of the world. These companies know something that other firms do not, and the personal growth and gratification from being part of a wildly expanding team has to be experienced to be understood. It is a kind of drug, but with only pleasant side effects. I am always looking for the next tiny company that can double its sales or more each year.

Join a company with fewer than a hundred employees increasing revenues by at least 30 per cent a year – ideally fewer than twenty employees and at least doubling each year.

Hint 3: Only work for an 80/20 boss

What is an 80/20 boss? Someone who consciously or unconsciously follows the principle. By their works you shall know them:

- They focus on very few things – the ones that make a BIG difference to their customers, and, if they still have them, their bosses (hopefully a temporary arrangement – the best 80/20 bosses are not themselves constrained by a boss).
- They are going places fast.

- They are rarely short of time, and never flustered. They are usually relaxed and happy, not workaholics.
- They look to their people for a few valuable *outputs*. They pay no attention to *inputs* such as time and sweat.
- They take the time to explain to you what they are doing, and why.
- They encourage you to focus on what delivers the greatest results with the least effort.
- They praise you when you deliver great results, but are constructively critical when you don't – and suggest that you either stop doing something unimportant, or do something important in a more effective way.
- When they trust you, they leave you alone, and encourage you to come to them when you need guidance.

Why is it vital to have an 80/20 boss?

He or she is a role model for you. If you perform well for them they will give you unusual responsibility, so you take on more and more of their job. They will teach you to do the same for the people who report to you. Also, the chances are that when the 80/20 boss gets promoted, you will be too. If they move to another firm, they are likely to take you with them. Anyone who is really successful has had a boss of this type at some stage – whatever the field, whether in business, sport, entertainment, academia, whatever.

To gain momentum in any field is hard, but to use momentum is easy. So you use your boss's momentum before you generate your own.

It is far easier to rise in the slipstream of someone going places fast, than it is to create your own head of steam. So who you work for is more important initially than who you are or what you do. It's not all about you. It's very largely about the boss.

Do you have an 80/20 boss now? If not, find one pronto, and your career will take wings.

Hint 4: Find your 80/20 idea

Behind every business that survives, there is a distinctive idea – a way of serving customers that is at least a little different from that of any other firm. A *great* company is *totally* different, and so is the idea behind it. The idea offers customers an unbeatable price, or else an unbeatable product or service. In either case, the idea delivers more for less. The idea is an 80/20 idea.

80/20 ideas are not confined to business. Behind every great cause, every social movement, every successful organization or institution, there lurks a great 80/20 idea – something that explodes because it delivers a fantastic result for a modest outlay of energy. In 1807 both the United States and the British Empire abolished the slave trade – the penalty for ship's captains in the latter was set at £120 per slave (a fantastic sum then) and the Royal Navy set up a special unit to patrol off the African coast to catch traders. In 1834 all slaves in the British Empire were freed. Slavery was an appalling institution, terrible for slaves but also a cancer to owners who were debased by it, and a ridiculously inefficient economic system to boot. The benefit divided by the cost of abolishing slavery was infinite.

In my lifetime the US Civil Rights movement and the

liberation of all South Africans from the evil of apartheid also led to incalculable good with almost none of the terrible downsides forecast by segregationists. Joining any cause for truth and beauty is one of the best things any of us can do. Such causes are quintessentially 80/20, giving immense advantages not only to the oppressed but also to the liberators and truth-tellers. Nothing can make you feel better than a struggle for justice with real identifiable beneficiaries.

If you want to be happy and a force for good, then, at every stage of your career and life, be part of a group advancing an 80/20 idea – one giving customers or citizens a richer life with relatively little squandering of life energy and finite resources.

Hint 5: Become joyfully, usefully unique

The 80/20 future has no place for people who are pegs, whether round pegs in square holes or round pegs in round holes. There are no holes, there are no roles, that do not feature you at the centre, with a network radiating out from you. For those of us who used to look to organizations for something to do with our lives, this is quite a shift in landscape.

Outside the army and a few other sad essentials, there is no template the individual should fit – goodbye, industrial psychologists! In the 80/20 future, individuals serve themselves and others best by inventing their own template. What they do and what they become are the same; and what they are and what they do is different from what anybody else is or does.

There is no other way to get more for less, than to devise your own formula that plays to your Olympic strengths.

Have you got that? Have you done that? Are you doing that?

Most of us – most even of you all out there, reading this book, which preaches the uniqueness of individuality – have still not really got the idea straight. I am not sure that even I have. The idea is liberating yet so contrary to our culture and work habits.

Make no mistake. The 80/20 future requires and rewards individuality. The 80/20 future does not reward hard work, conformity, diplomacy, compromise, and all the other desiderata that good employees have been trained to show. Instead, the 80/20 future rewards the unique innovator.

However, even individuality is not enough. If it were, we would just cultivate eccentricity and not worry about our value to other people. In some professions, such as the artist, the writer, or the entertainer, this may suffice, at least posthumously – Vincent van Gogh sold one painting in his lifetime, and almost nobody showed up at the funeral of Karl Marx in Highgate, London. But, overwhelmingly, it behoves us to create great results for modest energy.

It is easier to know what 'modest energy' means. Here I need to qualify things a bit. We have all had the experience of working long hours in a job or on a project we don't enjoy much. That sucks out our life energy like nothing else. It drains us of creativity; it can even drain us of our normal resilience and optimism. I had a job like that at the Boston Consulting Group, and I stayed at the coalface for four long, painful years in my late twenties. It nearly destroyed me.

Against this, we all know the joy of working on a project – and the lucky ones of us in a well-paid job – where we would gladly do it for free if we could afford to. We may work very long hours, but it is, as they say, a labour of love. It does not drain our life energy; it feeds it. So time is not the real thing we lack, as we must always remember, despite being told that it is. The thing in short supply for nearly everyone is something completely different – it is *joy*.

So when I say 'modest energy', what I really mean is 'for not doing anything that depletes joy'. If it adds joy, then it uses negative amounts of life energy, which of course is marvellous. What we must do is find tasks we love doing, which other people really appreciate and are willing to pay for, either in money, or in admiration, or in love. Really we need a combination of these things, because we cannot live by money alone, or by love alone – unless we are like an adorable puppy or similar.

To find what we can do that gives pleasure to other people, but which generates joy for us and does not deplete valuable finite resources, may be a lifetime's quest. On the other hand, having read the paragraphs above, maybe that is enough for you. Perhaps you really know what the answer is. Or perhaps you can ask your subconscious mind and get the answer in a few hours or days.

At any time, we may stumble across a breathtaking 80/20 formula for our lives that allows us to spend them doing what we enjoy. We are more likely to do this if we think the right way and keep searching for our unique solution. Keep this motto in front of you – BECOME UNIQUE USEFULLY AND JOYFULLY. We make the world better when we cultivate our individuality to attain results that are fantastic for our customers and those around us.

So what, then, do we make of the 80/20 future? Though it can be challenging, it is unequivocally a good thing. The

80/20 future is the very opposite of a slave society and qualitatively different from, and better than, the ordered industrial society it is replacing.

There is huge delight in creating a great deal with very little, and doing it through our unique mind-power. The job description of every 80/20 individual is to beget more with less, and to do it joyously and through unique knowledge and insight. This wonderful future is quintessentially personal, yet also supremely sociable. May we all experience it to the utmost.

Part Five

The Principle Revisited

20 The Two Dimensions of the Principle

Over the years I've been delighted to receive many hundreds of emails from readers of the first edition of this book. Equally important, and in many ways even more stimulating, have been many reviews posted on the Amazon sites; there are currently over 200 reviews on the amazon.com site alone. These emails and reviews have led to fresh insights into the way the principle works, particularly its relationship to its two dimensions of efficiency and life enhancement.

Some of these reviews are highly critical of the book and the principle, and for me these are the most challenging and useful. The two main critical questions that have been raised are "Does the 80/20 Principle really apply to our personal lives at all?" and "Isn't the 80 per cent really essential too?" I shall come back to these later in the chapter.

The stories that inspired me most were not where readers

had used the 80/20 Principle to enjoy work more, or make more money, or both. The most moving accounts were ones where the principle had focused readers on what was truly important in their lives.

My favourite story comes from a 50-year-old Canadian, 'happily married with three wonderful kids'. Darrel, as I will call him, needs to remain anonymous, but I have not changed anything apart from his name. He's had a successful career as an educator, and is currently the CEO of a large school district. Three years ago he was diagnosed as having a non-verbal learning disability (NLD). He told me:

> *It was a hard pill to swallow, but I know my diagnosis is accurate... when I spend minutes searching for my car in the parking lot, or going through my desk looking for that piece of paper that is right in front of me or maybe even in my hand, I realize just how true the diagnosis is. Here I am, trying to find ways to support children with special needs, which is a big part of my work, and, wouldn't you know it, I have special needs myself...*
>
> *I publish a lot... advocating that teachers become leaders. It was because, when I was a principal, there were so many things that the teachers could do much better than me, I delegated to them the 80 percent of tasks that I wasn't good at. It ended up in them nominating me for a leadership award which I received in 1999. Little did they know that my empowering them and cheer-leading them, while authentic, were also done out of necessity...*
>
> *I realize how the 80/20 principle has really been my reason for success... I also want to use your 80/20 philosophy in helping others with learning difficulties focus on the top 20 percent of what they do well... In the not too distant future, I*

hope to remove the veil that prevents me from showing others the person that I truly am.

Darrel has written a moving article called 'Finding power in weakness', which applies the 80/20 Principle in a novel way. Essentially he says that when our weaknesses are apparent to us, we can rely on our strong suits more potently: partly because we have to, and partly because we realize the gap between our weaknesses and other people's strengths. We appreciate how dependent we are on other people and in return strive to help them with the signature strengths that we happen to have. Denying our weaknesses, or even reducing them, can cut us off from our strengths, and from those of the people around us.

Readers' insights

I'd like to pass along a few of the best or most amusing reader insights into the principle. First, a comment from Sean F. O'Neill:

In the US in the 1920s, there was an accomplished writer named Edmund Wilson. He championed Marcel Proust to the Americans. His 20 percent was his writing and research. Here is how he dispensed with the 80 percent of low-priority stuff. He used to answer requests with a postcard that read: 'Edmund Wilson regrets that it is impossible for him to: Read manuscripts, Write articles or books to order, Do any kind of editorial work, Judge literary contests, Give interviews, Conduct educational ourses, Deliver lectures, Gives talks or make speeches, Take part in writers' congresses, Answer questionnaires, Contribute or take part on symposiums or panels of any kind, Contribute manuscripts for sale, Donate copies of his books to Libraries, Autograph books for strangers, Allow his name to be used on letterheads, Supply personal information about himself, Supply photographs of himself, Supply opinions on literary or other subjects.'

Michael Cloud focused on his professional life:

I did an 80/20 analysis of my income-generating activities [as a speechwriter and fundraiser] and found that in the previous year I had earned 89 percent of my income in 15 percent of my work time, from 15 percent of my work. I gave away or discarded the 85 percent of the work that generated only 11 percent of my income, slashed my work time by 70 percent, doubled my time doing my high-leverage projects – and more than doubled my income...

Then I wrote a high-octane email urging friends and clients to buy and read The 80/20 Principle *with my promise that, if they didn't get extraordinary value from your book, I would refund double their $25 hardcover purchase price. I sent my message to 107 people. Thirty-eight of them bought and read the book. All said they had profited from it... A vice-president of marketing bought a case of your books for his team.*

Michael offers four new insights:

1 *I benefit from urging people to read, reflect on, and apply the 80/20 principle... imagine the benefits from having 20 percent of my community, businesses, country, and 20 percent of the individuals on earth thinking and living*

80/20. Wouldn't you like to live in a world of da Vincis and Mozarts and Einsteins – where everyone offered their highest and best?

2 *Some people succeed by reinventing the wheel. Most fail by reinventing the flat tire. Perhaps you should pen a brief book on the Toxic 20% – the twenty percent that are most costly and damaging.*
3 *Good poker players fold a lot. As Larry W Philips writes in* Zen and the Art of Poker, *'Play only the best 15 to 20 percent of your hands and throw in the rest.'*
4 Good to Great *by Jim Collins has one chapter – chapter 4, The Hedgehog Concept – that's a shimmering application of the 80/20 principle.*

Terry Lee writes from Hong Kong to pick up the connection with chaos theory:

> *Yes, the universe is unbalanced, otherwise, perhaps, there would have been no Big Bang. I see Eliyahu M Goldratt's Theory of Constraints, which focuses on improving or exploiting bottlenecks, as a special version of the 80/20 principle. The idea is to concentrate on the few causes – and usually only one cause – of the bottleneck. That releases enormous power.*

It strikes me that this theory of constraints, like the principle, applies both to our work and personal lives:

➤ At work, what is the one constraint that, if it were removed, would make us five, ten or twenty times as productive? For you, is it your boss, your fear of failure, your lack of qualifications, your inability to choose what you work on, your lack of the right collaborator, or something else altogether? What is the constraint, what stops you from enormous improvement? If you identify the constraint, you can then work on a campaign to remove it.

➤ In your private life, what is the one thing that stops you making the best of your life and bringing happiness to the people you care about? There may be one overriding constraint. What is it?

Does the 80/20 Principle really apply to our personal lives?

Quite remarkably, *nobody* has disputed that the 80/20 Principle works in business. Some readers, indeed, gave examples of very different 'businesses' that have benefited. Dr Mark Shook is pastor of a church in Texas who has increased his congregation 300 times by using the principle. He writes:

> *Your books on 80/20 thinking have transformed my life. I am the pastor of Community of Faith in Cypress, Texas. Following 80/20 principles we have grown from 5 people meeting in my living room to over 1,500 in average attendance in two-and-a-half years. We call ourselves the 80/20 church. I bet you didn't know that you were a church growth guru!*

Since then, however, I've discovered that there's another much larger '80/20 church'. Veronica Abney, the church administrator for the largest mega-church in Chicago, wrote to me that 'our church currently has 25,000 members, with the arena facility next to the United Center, where the Chicago Bulls play and home to Michael Jordan. I would like to grow our ministry from 25,000 to 50,000 using the 80/20 methodology.'

And some readers did value the application of Pareto's concept to the whole of life, starting with business but going well beyond it, which was my biggest innovation in reinterpreting the principle. Kevin Garty, director of relocation for a firm of realtors in San Francisco, told me:

> *I've applied the 80/20 rule to pretty much every aspect of my life with amazing results. I can confirm I'm getting up later in the morning and leaving work earlier in the afternoon, and still making a very healthy six figure income. I had applied facets of 80/20 since I was a kid in New Zealand so when I read your book it was a great validation of the direction I was starting to head in. I felt more confident in my laziness, if that makes sense.*

Yes, perfect sense, Kevin.

A reviewer from Indonesia says that 80/20 can be applied to work and life in the same way because 'the basic concept is *focus*. Choice is important; we only have to do the most important things in life… This is the most easy explanation of how we can achieve more by doing less.' A Japanese reviewer says:

> *I read this book almost two years ago. Applied its theories to the four companies I was working for. Managed to cut my*

> *working hours by 25 percent and still maintained my original salary. Opened my own business in the meantime. With all the extra time I've created I get to think of new ways to make my life more fun and easier on the bank balance. A simple approach to calculating where you are wasting time, money, and effort and where to move the effort to create more time and money. I'm about to… apply the formula to my Japanese language studies, exercise regime and anything else I can think of.*

'Teach this [80/20] to your children,' adds a reader, 'and you will increase the likelihood they will move out when they are grown, because they will be able to afford to.'

Nevertheless, some reviewers question whether the principle should be applied to our private lives. 'Whilst I am sure that the author meant well,' writes one Amazon reviewer, 'in attempting to apply the 80/20 Principle to non-business areas (more specifically, to personal relationships), it has no place within this book, and should have been left well alone.' The reviewer was kind enough to say that there was a pearl hidden within the oyster of the book – the business applications of the principle – that was 'well worth diving for'. But ignore the personal stuff!

A second reviewer says the book:

> *provides an astute evaluation of the economic and social realities of business. Koch goes further, though, and tries to extrapolate the 80/20 theory to success, happiness and life in general. While some of what he suggests makes sense, his examples seem to get progressively weaker as he moves from the world of business.*

Isn't the 80 per cent essential too?

The second and major criticism concerns whether it is realistic, or even desirable, to get rid of the 80 per cent of activity that yields few results. Here is the case against, courtesy of Chow Ching 'Cornholio', probably my most eloquent critic, whose comments have appeared on Amazon. It is worth quoting his review in full:

> *An excellent idea, but 20 percent of the 5 stars is taken out, because [*The 80/20 Principle*] is also packed with other BS, like lecturing you on how to use your life and other areas where the author has no authority. He pointed out some of the voices of opposition, and beat them one after one. However, there is one very important one that he left out. I'm a Hong Kong Chinese. In our 5,000 years' culture, Yin and Yang has come into play from the very beginning; the author seems to ignore this.*
>
> *For example, he tells you to analyse your life and see which 20 percent of your life gives 80 percent of your happiness and concentrate on that 20 percent only. I did just that years ago, but I only got worse. Life is a balance between work and play – you enjoyed that 20 percent of yang activity because you are released from that 80 percent of yin activity.*
>
> *Eighty percent of the tastefulness of a hamburger is from 20 percent of it, the meat inside, but if you drop the bread on the top and bottom, its taste will become too strong – it'll lose its flavour.*
>
> *Similarly, perhaps your honeymoon or a graduation trip to Europe was the most wonderful experience, yet, if you re-do that over and over, by principle of marginal return, it'll be boring.*

> *20/80 can be applied perfectly to work, but to play, not so. I also wonder if the author will think 80 percent of sex pleasures derives from 20 percent of the time between (yang) climax, so probably we should drop the (yin) foreplay altogether?*

A similar concern was raised to me by Lord Carr, formerly a top UK cabinet minister. He cited the case of the then British ambassador to the US, who told him:

> *You might think that much of my time is spent on trivial matters, such as having endless dinners and spending time socially with American leaders. But that time is not wasted. When it comes to the crunch, I know whose judgment can be relied on and who is really flaky. That is invaluable in a crisis, so the 'wasted' time isn't wasted at all.*

Several people have taken me to task along similar lines, because they are rightly concerned that the pursuit of efficiency – cutting out the low-value majority of activity – is self-defeating in the long run. If we become obsessed with efficiency and only doing the important things, we might cut out activities that are necessary for renewing ourselves, our businesses, and even our society.

'What about parks?' demands one of my friends. 'Parks are a relic of feudalism and might be part of the 80 per cent that you would cut out. They have no right to exist if we cost out everything. Parks have no return on capital. They would be invaluable as houses or retail developments. But if you cut out the parks, you'd end up with a really unattractive city.' He might have cited Johannesburg, which has pleasant suburbs but almost no parks or open spaces, and which, not coincidentally, is one of the most dangerous cities on the planet.

A related concern is that, by cutting out the inefficient elements in our work and lives, we may become mindless and soulless, favouring the short-term economic solution and harming our long-term heritage. As Andrew Price writes in his forthcoming book *The Power of the Unessential*:

> *by far the greatest fish harvest come from coastal areas; these make up only a tiny fraction of the oceans' total area. The 80/20 principle tells that coasts are where fishing action should be. And fishing along coasts is precisely what has happened.*
>
> *But exploitation has removed too much stock; not only that, these rich coastal waters coincide with major breeding grounds. So hammering cod and fish stocks around coasts has affected reproduction, leaving insufficient fish available for capture and reproduction in future.*
>
> *For followers of the 80/20 principle, the message is clear. Our efforts to target the disproportionately valuable twenty percent should be not just for use; there should be some non-use too. Otherwise, it can easily disappear, just as fisheries demonstrate. There is another important message. The best-performing stock (fisheries or financial) this year, or most valuable species in an ecosystem over the last decade, is no guarantee for future success. The truth is that the world and its resources do not remain constant for long.*

Criticism of my application of the 80/20 Principle can be summarized under three main concerns:

➤ *The corner-cutting concern.* If 80/20 is viewed as an efficiency device, we may end up being very inefficient but not very effective. Cutting corners is all very well, but unless we go into something fully and deeply, we won't achieve anything worthwhile or enjoy it. We may get 80 per cent of a book's message by reading 20 per cent of it, but if the book is important enough to us, we should want to read all of it, and even remain disappointed that we've finished the book. Getting 80 per cent of results through 20 per cent of effort can appear to represent a simplistic, materialistic and not authentic way of approaching both work and life.

➤ *The sustainability concern.* If the 80/20 Principle leads to a huge focus on what works today, isn't there a danger that it won't work tomorrow? This concern is equally applicable in business and in our broader lives.

➤ *The balance concern.* As Chow Ching says, the concern is that we can't focus just on the 'best' parts of life, because without the rest of life the best would no longer be the best. Balance doesn't matter in business, because the way the economy advances is through the battle of highly specialized – and therefore unbalanced – firms. But balance may be essential for human happiness.

Two different dimensions of the principle

What I have realized from your feedback is that there are really two quite distinct – in some ways even opposite – dimensions or uses of the 80/20 Principle.

On the one hand, there is the *efficiency* dimension. This is where we want to achieve things in the fastest possible way with the least possible effort. Typically this domain involves things that are not hugely significant to us, except as a means to an end. For example, if we look on our work as mainly a means to earn money, because we want to do other things with other people outside of work – and it is these latter things that really matter to us – then work falls squarely into the box marked 'efficiency'. We want to use the 80/20 Principle to get our work done as productively and quickly as possible, and get on with our real life. So the 20 per cent approach is the way we should use the principle. We focus on the most productive 20 per cent, perhaps doubling our time on those matters, and, as far as possible cut out everything that is not in the high-efficiency 20 per cent box. In terms of the illustration I gave in Chapter 10 on 'Time Revolution', we should perhaps spend two days on the high-efficiency 20 per cent, and then devote the rest of the week to what we really care about. Simplistically, we can expect to increase the value of our work to 160 per cent of what it was before (we get two lots of 80 per cent, each derived from one day of work, the 20 per cent). Where possible, we also reduce our working week to two days.

The efficiency dimension can also be applied to matters outside work that are not really important to us, those that are chores. Into this 20 per cent box fall, for example, all the people we have to meet socially but don't really want to, all the obligations we don't want but can't get rid of, doing our taxes, cleaning the garage, doing the gardening if we don't enjoy it and can't slough it off onto someone who does, and so forth. The objective is to find the 20 per cent that is most important and that gives us 80 per cent of the results, and get it out of the way as rapidly and painlessly as we can.

On the other hand, there is the *life-enhancing* dimension of the 80/20 Principle. What belongs in this box is anything that is truly important to our lives, whether it is work, our personal relationships, what we wish to achieve, the hobby that gives us immense pleasure, or anything else that fulfils us and will give us consolation on our deathbed. When we look back on our life to date, and look forward to our life to come, and enjoy our life as it is in the current moment, anything that gives us a warm glow and makes us feel glad to be alive – all of that falls into the life-enhancing box. What the great American industrial psychologist Abraham Maslow labelled 'hygiene factors' – food, shelter, material needs – are important when they are not met, but relatively unimportant once they have been satisfied. The hygiene factors, in my terms, fall into the efficiency box and require a 20 per cent solution, the most productive solution with the least expenditure of life energy.

The 80/20 Principle is an essential part of realizing and enhancing what we could call the poetry of life, for two reasons. First, the principle can help us confront what is really important in our lives. Who are the few people, what are the few things, which really make our life worthwhile? Unless we are really poor or sad, these are not the instrumental aspects of life, the means to an end, like money, acclaim, important jobs or status of any kind. These come and they go. They are outward forms, they do not touch our hearts or souls, they do not define who we are. Provided we have food and shelter, what really matters is loving and being loved, self-expression, personal achievement *and* relaxation, the ability to think and create, the chance to connect with nature and other people – above all, enhancing the lives of the friends and family we truly care about.

Second, the principle clears away space for these fantastic

facets of life. By doing the non-essential things more briskly and economically, with as little absorption of our life energy as we can contrive, we capture time, territory and tranquillity for the essential parts of life. Instead of having what matters crammed into the margins and corners of our life, we can put what's essential where it belongs, centre stage, at the heart of our being.

When it comes to the essential parts of life, the 20 per cent or less that defines our uniqueness and individual destiny, we should devote our energy and our very soul to such matters, without stinting on time, money or any other means to that end. Efficiency requires the 20 per cent approach. But what is life-enhancing deserves a 200, 2,000 or 2,000,000 per cent approach. There is no limit to the amount of effort or time that is appropriate for what enhances – or even defines – our lives.

So to answer the three concerns:

- *Corner cutting.* It's only within the efficiency segment of our lives that we should aim to cut corners and do things lazily and fast. For anything life enhancing, we take the longest, deepest or highest possible route.
- *Sustainability.* A sensible use of the principle requires a long-term view, and an awareness of potential unintended consequences if we assume that the current position with regard to effort and reward will not change. For example, 10 per cent of customers may currently give us (say) 80 per cent of profits. But maybe, if a new competitor focuses on our super-profitable customers, our profits won't last. Moreover, hidden away within the 90 per cent of marginal or unprofitable customers may be a fast-growth company that could, if

carefully cultivated, end up being a new winning account. In the fishing example, too great a focus on the super-abundant waters, without building in some restraints to allow the fish to reproduce, leads to disaster.

In the broader areas of life, too, our focus on what enhances our life needs to be long-term and intelligent. Skills and relationships require investment. We should be selective about which abilities and friends really matter, and then take time and extraordinarily patient effort to build the foundations of a lifetime commitment. No corner cutting here, and equally no instant gratification! It's a mistake to work for the sake of work or to amass riches by doing something we hate. But it's very wise to make a huge commitment to developing skills and relationships that make our lives different, enjoyable and worthwhile.

➤ *Balance.* Should we be balanced or unbalanced? Both. We should be unbalanced on the efficiency stuff, on everything that is not critical to our place in the world. And in a way, we should be unbalanced on the life-enhancing matters too, carefully targeting the few activities and relationships that have the greatest value and potential value for us. But within the life-enhancing domain we need a balance of work and leisure, of self-directed and shared projects, of time for ourselves and time for others, of enjoyment of current enthusiasms and investment to build the future. We can find our yin and yang within the life-enhancing sector. Were it otherwise, we would never find people who enjoy their work and their play, who are happy because wherever they are, they love what they do and they do what they love.

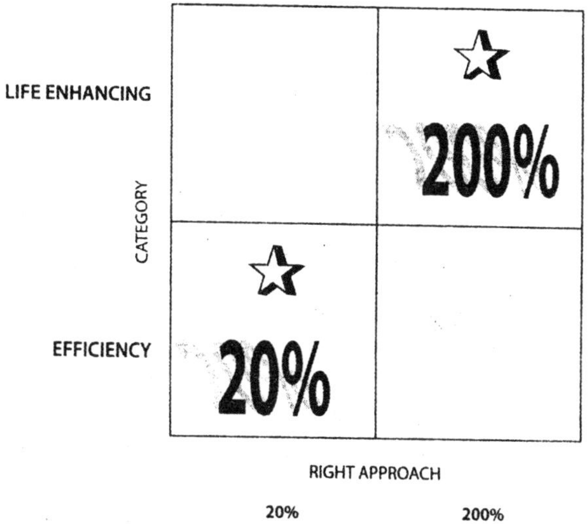

Figure 46 Allocation of our time and energy relative to today

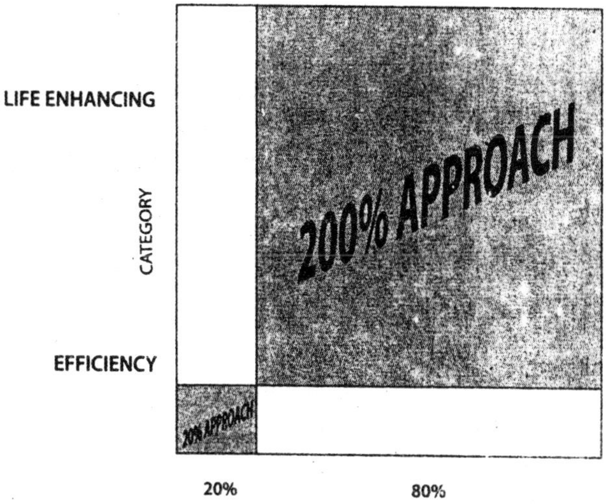

Figure 47 New allocation of time and energy (as percentage of new total)

Figure 46 shows the two dimensions of the principle and the right approach for each.

Once we have made the right decision for parts of our life that fall into each box, we can draw the matrix in a way that reflects the relative proportions. In Figure 47, the efficiency elements have been squashed up so that they only consume 20 per cent of our time and energy. The 20 per cent of life-enhancing areas of life are freed up to take 80 per cent of our life.

Work can fall into either the efficient or the life-enhancing category. Almost certainly, you have some work that falls into each. The trick is to do progressively less of the former and more of the latter, until you reach the happy state where work really is more fun than fun.

Life outside work, too, almost certainly falls into both categories. The answer is the same. Spend less and less time and vitality on the efficiency box, and more and more on the life-enhancing box.

It's worth asking yourself, if you could spend your time and vigour on what counts most for you, what would be the division of work and play? And how would the two relate? Most people who've answered this question for me say they'd spend roughly equal time on 'work' and 'non-work', although 'work' is self-defined and not necessarily paid work. Those who have embraced the principle find that the line between work and non-work becomes increasingly blurred.

In this sense, the yin and yang of life are re-established. Although there are two apparently opposite dimensions to the 80/20 Principle – efficiency and life enhancement – the dimensions are entirely complementary and interwoven. The efficiency dimension allows us room for the life-enhancing dimension. The common thread is knowing what give results we want, and knowing what matters. Always, both for efficiency and life enhancement, the answer is a small part of the total. Always, we progress through subtraction and focus. Equally, however, 80/20 is a sterile philosophy if it just leads to efficiency. There is no point in becoming more efficient or wealthier unless there is some other goal in our mind, the goal of the soul. Those who would put 80/20 firmly back into its traditional work box are missing the point.

Let me give an example from my own life. Every day, when I am living in London or in southern Spain, I take an hour or two to cycle. This is definitely a life-enhancing activity for me: it is wonderful exercise, I travel through great scenery (Richmond Park with its deer, or mountain views in Spain) and I let my thoughts hang out as I ride and often come up with fresh ideas as a result. But it is not effortless. I reckon that 10 per cent of the route in Richmond Park and 15 per cent in Spain is seriously uphill; no doubt taking my heart rate up to the highest levels on the route and constituting more than 80 per cent of the exercise benefit! I'm not a fanatical cyclist and I don't really like hills – I'm glad when I can sail down the other side. But I wouldn't choose a flat route instead. The hills, though in some ways unpleasant, add to the grandeur of the setting and provide me with 'yin' activity to leaven the 'yang' of riding flat or downhill.

I can tell you from personal experience and the testimony of hundreds of readers that it is possible to reverse the proportions of life, from mainly meaningless or stressful activity (yin) to mainly life enhancing (yang). Of course, we don't want to repeat the same honeymoon or the same holiday over and over. We find fresh ways to relax. Nor do most of us want to relax most of the time. We want to exercise, to deploy and develop our skills, to think, to test ourselves, to help other people, to explore relationships of all kinds. We don't want to be obsessed with efficiency, but we do want to dispose of the non-life-enhancing activities as easily and swiftly as possible.

Take responsibility for progress

Put away your scepticism and your pessimism. These vices, like their opposites, are self-fulfilling. Recover your faith in progress. Realize that the future is already here: in those few shining examples, in agribusiness, in industry, in services, in education, in artificial intelligence, in medical science, in physics and indeed all the sciences, and even in social and political experiments, where previously unimaginable targets have been surpassed and new targets continue to fall like skittles. Remember the 80/20 Principle. Progress always comes from a small minority of people and organized resources who demonstrate that previously accepted ceilings of performance can become floors for everyone. Progress requires élites, but élites who live for glory and service to society, who are willing to place their gifts at the disposal of us all. Progress depends on information about exceptional achievement and the diffusion of successful experiments, on breaking down the structures erected by the mass of vested interests, on demanding that the standards enjoyed by a privileged minority should be available to all. Above all progress, as George Bernard Shaw told us, requires us to be unreasonable in our demands. We must search out the 20 per cent of everything that produces the 80 per cent and use the facts we uncover to demand a multiplication of whatever it is that we value. If our reach must always exceed our grasp, progress requires that we grasp whatever a minority has reached and ensure that it becomes the minimum standard for all.

The greatest thing about the 80/20 Principle is that you do not need to wait for everyone else. You can start to practise it in your professional and personal life. You can take your own small fragments of greatest achievement, happiness and service to others and make them a much larger part of your life. You can multiply your highs and cut out most of your lows. You can identify the mass of irrelevant and low-value activity and begin to shed this worthless skin. You can isolate the parts of your character, workstyle, lifestyle and relationships that, measured against the time or energy involved, give you value many times greater than the daily grind; and having isolated them, you can, with no little courage and determination, multiply them. You can become a better, more useful and happier human being. And you can help others to do the same.

Notes and References

Chapter 1

1 Josef Steindl (1965) *Random Processes and the Growth of Firms: A Study of the Pareto Law*, London: Charles Griffin, p 18.

2 Extensive research has revealed a very large number of short articles referring to the 80/20 Principle (usually called the 80/20 Rule), but failed to identify any books on the subject. If a book on the 80/20 Principle does exist, even if as an unpublished academic treatise, would a reader please let me know. One book, although not really about the 80/20 Principle, does draw attention to its significance: John J Cotter's *The 20% Solution* (Chichester: John Wiley, 1995) provides in its introduction the right answer: 'Figure out the 20% of what you do that will contribute the most to your success in he future, then concentrate your time and energy on that 20%' (p xix). Cotter refers in passing to Pareto (p xxi), but neither

Pareto nor the 80/20 Principle (under any name) is mentioned outside the introduction, and Pareto does not even appear in the index. Like many writers, Cotter is anachronistic in attributing the 80/20 formulation itself to Pareto: 'Vilfredo Pareto was a French-born economist who observed 100 years ago that 20% of the factors in most situations account for 80% of what happens (that is, 20% of a company's customers generate 80% of its profits). He called it Pareto's Law' (p xxi). In fact, Pareto never used the expression '80/20' or anything like it. What he called his 'law' was in fact a mathematical formula (given in note 4), which is some way removed from (although the ultimate source of) the 80/20 Principle as we know it today.

3 The Economist (1996) Living with the car, *The Economist*, 22 June, p 8.

4 Vilfredo Pareto (1896/7) *Cours d'Economique Politique*, Lausanne University. Despite the conventional mythology, Pareto did not use the '80/20' phrase in his discussion of income inequality or anywhere else. He did not even make the simple observation that 80 per cent of income was earned by 20 per cent of the working population, although this conclusion could have been distilled from his far more complex calculations. What Pareto did discover, and what greatly excited him and his followers, was a constant relationship between the top earners and the percentage of total incomes they enjoyed, a relationship that followed a regular logarithmic pattern and could be charted in a similar shape whatever time period or country was taken.

The fomula is as follows. Call N the number of income

earners who receive incomes higher than x, with A and m being the constants. Pareto found that:

$$\log N = \log A + m \log x$$

5 It should be stressed that this simplification was not made by Pareto himself nor, sadly, by any of his followers for more than a generation. It is, however, a legitimate deduction from his method, and one that is much more accessible than any explanation Pareto himself gave.

6 Harvard University, in particular, appears to have been a hotbed of Pareto appreciation. Aside from Zipf's influence in philology, the economic faculty demonstrated a hearty appreciation of the 'Pareto law'. For what is still the best explanation of this, see the article by Vilfredo Pareto in *Quarterly Journal of Economics*, Vol LXIII, No 2, May 1949 (President and Fellows of Harvard College).

7 For an excellent explanation of Zipf's law, see Paul Krugman (1996) *The Self-Organizing Economy*, Cambridge, Mass: Blackwell, p 39.

8 Joseph Moses Juran (1951) *Quality Control Handbook*, New York: McGraw-Hill, pp 38–9. This is the first edition, with a mere 750 pages compared to more than 2000 in the current edition. Note that although Juran clearly refers to the 'Pareto principle' and accurately distils its significance, the first edition does not use the term 80/20 at all.

9 Paul Krugman, op cit., note 7.

10 Malcolm Gladwell (1996) The tipping point, *New Yorker*, 3 June.

11 Malcolm Gladwell, ibid.

12 James Gleik (1987) *Chaos: Making a New Science*, New York, Little, Brown.

13 See W Brian Arthur (1989) Competing technologies, increasing returns, and lock-in by historical events, *Economic Journal*, Vol 99, March, pp 116–31.

14 'Chaos theory explodes Hollywood hype', *Independent on Sunday*, 30 March 1997.

15 George Bernard Shaw, quoted in John Adair (1996) *Effective Innovation*, Pan Books, London, p 169.

16 Quoted in James Gleik, op cit., note 12.

Chapter 2

1 Author's calculation based on Donella H Meadows, Dennis L Meadows and Jorgen Randers (1992) *Beyond the Limits*, London: Earthscan, pp 66f.

2 Author's calculation based on Lester R Brown, Christopher Flavin and Hal Kane (1992) *State of the World*, London: Earthscan, p 111, itself based on Ronald V A Sprout and James H Weaver (1991) *International Distribution of Income: 1960–1987*, Working Paper No 159, Department of Economics, American University, Washington DC, May.

3 Health Care Strategic Management (1995) Strategic planning futurists need to be capitation-specific and epidemiological, *Health Care Strategic Management*, 1 September.

4 Malcolm Gladwell (1996) The science of shopping, *New Yorker*, 4 November.

5 Mary Corrigan and Gary Kauppila (1996) *Consumer Book Industry Overview and Analysis of the Two Leading Superstore Operators*, Chicago, Ill: William Blair & Co.

Chapter 3

1 Joseph Moses Juran, op cit. (see Chapter 1 note 8), pp 38–9.

2 Ronald J Recardo (1994) Strategic quality management: turning the spotlight on strategies as well as tactical issues, *National Productivity Review*, 22 March.

3 Niklas Von Daehne (1994) The new turnaround, *Success*, 1 April.

4 David Lowry (1993) Focusing on time and teams to eliminate waste at Singo prize-winning Ford Electronics, *National Productivity Review*, 22 March.

5 Terry Pinnell (1994) Corporate change made easier, *PC User*, 10 August.

6 James R Nagel (1994) TQM and the Pentagon, *Industrial Engineering*, 1 December.

7 Chris Vandersluis (1994) Poor planning can sabotage implementation, *Computing Canada*, 25 May.

8 Steve Wilson (1994) Newton: bringing AI out of the ivory tower, *AI Expert*, 1 February.

9 Jeff Holtzman (1994) And then there were none, *Electronics Now*, 1 July.

10 MacWeek (1994) Software developers create modular

applications that include low prices and core functions, *MacWeek*, 17 January.

11 Barbara Quint (1995) What's your problem?, *Information Today*, 1 January.

12 See Richard Koch and Ian Godden (1996) *Managing Without Management*, London: Nicholas Brealey, especially Chapter 6, pp 96–109.

13 Peter Drucker (1995) *Managing in a Time of Great Change*, London, Butterworth-Heinemann, pp 96f.

14 Richard Koch and Ian Godden, op cit. (see note 12); see Chapter 6 and p159.

Chapter 5

1 Henry Ford (1991) *Ford on Management*, intr. Ronnie Lessem, Oxford: Blackwell, pp 10, 141, 148. Reissue of Henry Ford (1922) *My Life and Work* and (1929) *My Philosophy of Industry*.

2 Gunter Rommel (1996) *Simplicity Wins*, Cambridge, Mass: Harvard Business School Press.

3 George Elliott, Ronald G Evans and Bruce Gardiner (1996) Managing cost: transatlantic lessons, *Management Review*, June.

4 Richard Koch and Ian Godden, op cit. (see Chapter 3, note 12).

5 Carol Casper (1994) Wholesale changes, *US Distribution Journal*, 15 March.

6 Ted R Compton (1994) Using activity-based costing in your organization, *Journal of Systems Management*, 1 March.

Chapter 6

1 Vin Manaktala (1994) Marketing: the seven deadly sins, *Journal of Accountancy*, 1 September.

2 It is easy to forget the deliberate and successful transformation of society that arose from the idealism and skill of a few pivotal early-twentieth-century industrialists, who advocated the 'horn of plenty' argument: that poverty, although prevalent, could be abolished. Here, for example, is Henry Ford again: 'The duty to abolish the more disastrous forms of poverty and want is easily fulfilled. The earth is so abundantly fruitful that there can be ample food, clothing, work and leisure.' See Henry Ford (1991) *Ford on Management*, intr. Ronnie Lessem, Oxford: Blackwell, pp 10, 141 and 148. I am grateful to Ivan Alexander for showing me the draft of his book *The Civilized Market* (1997, Oxford: Capstone) whose first chapter makes this and many other points that I have borrowed (see note 3).

3 See Ivan Alexander (1997) *The Civilized Market*, Oxford: Capstone.

4 Quoted by Michael Slezak (1994) Drawing fine lines in lipsticks, *Supermarket News*, 11 March.

5 Mark Stevens (1994) Take a good look at company blind spots, *Star-Tribune* (Twin Cities), 7 November.

6 John S Harrison (1994) Can mid-sized LECs succeed in tomorrow's competitive marketplace?, *Telephony*, 17 January.

7 Ginger Trumfio (1995) Relationship builders: contract management, *Sales & Marketing Management*, 1 February.

8 Jeffrey D Zbar (1994) Credit card campaign highlights restaurants, *Sun-Sentinel* (Fort Lauderdale), 10 October.

9 Donna Petrozzello (1995) A tale of two stations, *Broadcasting & Cable*, 4 September.

10 Insurance agency consultant Dan Sullivan, quoted in Sidney A Friedman (1995) Building a super agency of the future, *National Underwriter Life and Health*, 27 March.

11 A large number of articles about specific businesses and industries attest to this. For example, see Brian T Majeski (1994) The scarcity of quality sales employees, *The Music Trades*, 1 November.

12 Harvey Mackay (1995) We sometimes lose sight of how success is gained, *The Sacramento Bee*, 6 November.

13 The Music Trades (1994) How much do salespeople make?, *The Music Trades*, 1 November.

14 Robert E Sanders (1987) The Pareto Principle, its use and abuse, *Journal of Consumer Marketing*, Vol 4, Issue 1, Winter, pp 47–50.

Chapter 7

1 Peter B Suskind (1995) Warehouse operations: don't leave well alone, *IIE Solutions*, 1 August.

2 Gary Forger (1994) How more data + less handling = smart warehousing, *Modern Materials Handling*, 1 April.

3 Robin Field, Branded consumer products, in James Morton (ed.) (1995) *The Global Guide to Investing*, London: FT/Pitman, pp 471f.

4 Ray Kulwiec (1995) Shelving for parts and packages, *Modern Materials Handling*, 1 July.

5 Michael J Earl and David F Feeny (1994) Is your CIO adding value?, *Sloan Management Review*, 22 March.

6 Derek L Dean, Robert E Dvorak and Endre Holen (1994) Breaking through the barriers to new systems development, *McKinsey Quarterly*, 22 June.

7 Roger Dawson (1995) Secrets of power negotiating, *Success*, 1 September.

8 Orten C Skinner (1991) Get what you want through the fine art of negotiation, *Medical Laboratory Observer*, 1 November.

Chapter 9

1 This phrase comes from Ivan Alexander (op cit., Chapter 2), whose thinking on progress I have shamelessly plundered.

2 Ivan Alexander remarks nicely that 'though we are now aware that the riches of the earth are finite, we have discovered other dimensions of opportunity, a new compacted yet fertile space in which business can flourish and expand.

Trade, commerce, automation, robotisation and informatics, though almost landless and spaceless, are unbounded domains of opportunity. Computers are the least dimensional machines mankind has yet devised.'

Chapter 10

1 Quoted in *Oxford Book of Verse* (1961) Oxford: Oxford University Press, p 216.

2. The best and most progressive guide to time management precepts is Hiram B Smith (1995) *The Ten Natural Laws of Time and Life Management*, London: Nicholas Brealey. Smith refers extensively to the Franklin Corporation and rather less extensively to its Mormon roots.

3 Charles Handy (1969) *The Age of Unreason*, London: Random House, Chapter 9. See also Charles Handy (1994) *The Empty Raincoat*, London: Hutchinson.

4 See William Bridges (1995) *JobShift: How to Prosper in a Workplace without Jobs*, Reading, Mass: Addison-Wesley/London: Nicholas Brealey. Bridges argues, almost persuasively, that full-time employment by large organizations will become more the exception than the rule, and that the word 'job' will revert to its original meaning of 'task'.

5 Roy Jenkins (1995) *Gladstone*, London: Macmillan.

Chapter 12

1 Donald O Clifton and Paula Nelson (1992) *Play to Your Strengths*, London: Piatkus.

2 Interview with J G Ballard (1989) in *Re/Search* magazine (San Francisco), October, pp 21–2.

3 St Paul was probably of even greater importance to the success of Christianity than was the historical Jesus. Paul made Christianity Rome-friendly. Without this move, fiercely resisted by St Peter and most of the other original disciples, Christianity would have remained an obscure sect.

4 See Vilfredo Pareto (1968) *The Rise and Fall of Elites*, intr. Hans L Zetterberg, New York: Arno Press. Originally published in 1901 in Italian, this is a shorter and better description of Pareto's sociology than is his later work. The description of Pareto as the 'bourgeois Karl Marx' came as a backhanded compliment in his 1923 obituary in the socialist newspaper *Avanti*. It is an apt description, because Pareto, like Marx, stressed the importance of classes and of ideology in determining behaviour.

5 Except possibly music and the visual arts. Even here, however, collaborators may be more important than is generally acknowledged.

Chapter 13

1 See Robert Frank and Philip Cook (1995) *The Winner-Take-All Society*, New York: Free Press. Although they do

not use the phrase 80/20, the authors are clearly talking about the operation of 80/20-like laws. They deplore the waste implied by such unbalanced rewards. See also the comment on the book in a perceptive essay in *The Economist* (25 November 1995, p 134), on which I have drawn extensively in this section. *The Economist* article notes that in the early 1980s Sherwin Rose, an economist at the University of Chicago, wrote a couple of papers on the economics of superstars.

2 See Richard Koch (1995) *The Financial Times Guide to Strategy*, London: Pitman, pp 17–30.

3 G W F Hegel, trans. T M Knox (1953) *Hegel's Philosophy of Right*, Oxford: Oxford University Press.

4 See Louis S Richman (1994) The new worker elite, *Fortune*, 22 August, pp 44–50.

5 This trend is part of the 'death of management', whereby managers are rendered redundant and only the 'doers' have a place in effective corporations. See Richard Koch and Ian Godden, op cit. (see Chapter 3 note 12).

Chapter 14

1 What follows is a highly simplified account. Those who want to take private investment seriously are referred to Richard Koch (1994, 1997) *Selecting Shares that Perform*, London: Pitman.

2 Based on the *BZW Equity and Gilt Study* (1993) London: BZW. See Koch, ibid., p 3.

3 Vilfredo Pareto, op cit.

4 See Janet Lowe (1995) *Benjamin Graham, The Dean of Wall Street*, London: Pitman.

5 Besides the historic P/E, which is based on the last year's published earnings, there is also the prospective P/E, which is based on future earnings as estimated by stock market analysts. If earnings are expected to rise, the prospective P/E will be lower than the historic P/E, thus making the shares appear cheaper. The prospective P/E should be taken into account by experienced investors, but is also potentially dangerous because the forecast earnings may not (and, as a matter of fact, often do not) materialize. See Richard Koch, op cit. (see note 1), pp 108–12, for a detailed discussion of P/Es.

Chapter 15

1 A telling chapter heading from Daniel Goleman (1995) *Emotional Intelligence*, London: Bloomsbury, p 179.

2 See Dr Dorothy Rowe (1996) The escape from depression, *Independent on Sunday* (London), 31 March, p 14, quoting *In the Blood: God, Genes and Destiny* by Professor Steve Jones (1996, London: HarperCollins).

3 Dr Peter Fenwick (1996) The dynamics of change, *Independent on Sunday* (London), 17 March, p 9.

4 Ivan Alexander op cit. (see Chapter 6 note 2), Chapter 4.

5 Daniel Goleman, op cit. (see note 1), p 34.

6 Ibid., p 36.

7 Ibid., p 246.

8 Ibid., pp 6–7.

9 Dr Peter Fenwick, op cit. (see note 1), p 10.

10 Quoted by Daniel Goleman, op cit. (see note 1), p 87.

11 Ibid., p 179.

12 I am indebted to my friend Patrice Trequisser for pointing out this very important manifestation of the 80/20 Principle: you can fall in love in seconds and it can exert a dominant influence on the rest of your life. Patrice would not accept my caveat, since he fell in love at first sight more than a quarter of a century ago and is still very happily married. But of course, he is French.

Chapter 16

1 Quoted in Joseph Murphy (1963, 2007) *The Power of Your Subconscious Mind*, Radford, Virginia: Wilder Publications, p 29.

2 Quoted in Leonard Trilling (1972) *Sincerity and Authenticity*, Cambridge Mass: University of Harvard Press, p 5.

3 Henri F Ellenberger (1970, 1981) *The Discovery of the Unconscious: The History and Evolution of Dynamic Psychiatry*, New York: Basic Books.

4 Sigmund Freud (1927, 1990) *The Question of Lay Analysis*, New York: W W Norton & Co.

5 Carl Jung (1964, 1997) *Man and His Symbols*, Brooklyn, New York; Laurel Press, p 37.

6 Marshall McLuhan (1964, 1993) *Understanding Media: The Extensions of Man*, London: Routledge.

7 Joseph E LeDoux (1996) *The Emotional Brain: The Mysterious Underpinnings of Emotional Life*, New York: Simon & Schuster, p 302.

8 H A Williams (1965, 1968) *The True Wilderness*, Harmondsworth (England): Pelican/Penguin, p 67.

9 Emile Coué (1922) *Self-Mastery Through Conscious Autosuggestion*, New York: American Library Service; also available via www.openlibrary.org.

10 Harry W Carpenter (2011) *The Genie Within – Your Subconscious Mind: How It Works and How to Use It*, Fallbrook (California): Harry Carpenter Publishing, p 74.

11 Nancy C Andreasen (2006) *The Creative Brain: The Science of Genius*, New York: Plum, p 44.

12 Alan J Rocke (2010) *Image and Reality: Kekulé, Kopp, and the Scientific Investigation*, Chicago: University of Chicago Press.

13 John Reed (1957, 2013) *From Alchemy to Chemistry*, Mineola, New York: Dover Publications, pp 179–80.

14 For all of these except Watt, see Joseph Murphy, op. cit., pp 80–82. For Watt and other examples see Harry Carpenter, op. cit., pp 120–22. One suspects that some of these stories are apocryphal, embellished, or invented by the scientists themselves – but many of them are probably

true, and one way or another the scientists must have been using their subconscious minds.

15 Thomas S Kuhn (1962, 2012) *The Structure of Scientific Revolutions*, Chicago: University of Chicago Press, p 90 (emphases added).

16 David Brooks (2011) *The Social Animal*, New York: Random House, pp 244–5.

17 Quoted in Charles Taylor (1989) *Sources of the Self: The Making of the Modern Identity*, Cambridge (England): Cambridge University Press, p 301.

18 Letter to Philemon, 4:8.

Chapter 17

1 For the mathematically inclined: 1,000! / (2! × 998) = 499,500 and 2,000! (2! × 1,998!) = 1,999,000.

2 *Silicon Valley Insider*, 31 March 2011, plus author's own calculations.

3 Shaomei Wu, Jake M Hoffman, Winter A Mason, and Duncan J Watts (2011), 'Who Says What to Whom on Twitter', Yahoo Research, http://research.yahoo.com/node/3386, retrieved 28 September 2012.

4 *McKinsey Quarterly* interview with Eric Schmidt, September 2008.

5 Parag Khanna (2016) *Connectography: Mapping the Global Network Revolution*, London: Weidenfeld & Nicolson, p 49.

6 Ibid, p xxii.

7 Ibid, text at the bottom of Illustration 37, pp 246–7.

8 Ibid.

Chapter 18

1 Marshall W Van Alstyree et al, 'How Platforms Change Strategy', *Harvard Business Review*, April 2016, pp 54–60.

2 Walter Isaacson (2011) *Steve Jobs*, London: Little, Brown, pp 402–3.

3 Ibid, p 403.

4 The Perry Marshall Marketing Letter (2015), Vol 15, Issue 4, p 11, quoted by kind permission of www.perrymarshall.com.

Index

Also in the 80/20 series by Richard Koch

THE 80/20 PRINCIPLE and 92 Other Powerful Laws of Nature

The Science of Success

There is a new paradigm in business: a paradigm in which work is about insight, not input of hours; ideas and product trump strategy; and influence is superior to control. In this essential companion to his bestselling *The 80/20 Principle* – the radical power law that helped thousands of people achieve more by doing less – Richard Koch reveals 92 other universal principles and laws to promote the science of success in this challenging environment.

From natural selection to genes and memes, from Newtonian physics to chaos and co-opetition, Koch demonstrates, in both theory and practice, what science can teach business:

- Why growth is easy to find, but so difficult to sustain
- Why co-operating is better than competing
- How there are infinite ways to fail, but also multiple ways to succeed

'Richard Koch delivers some sharp cross-disciplinary comparisons and knows his onions on both sides of the business/science fence... Koch's feet are firmly on the ground.'

—*Sunday Times*, Business Book of the Week

Paperback ISBN 978 1 47365 686 4
336PP B format
www.nicholasbrealey.com

Also in the 80/20 series by Richard Koch

LIVING THE 80/20 WAY

Work Less, Worry Less, Succeed More, Enjoy More

Acclaimed entrepreneur and author Richard Koch changed the face of the business world with *The 80/20 Principle*. In *Living the 80/20 Way*, a self-help bestseller, he returns to show how working and worrying less can transform our personal lives.

Koch takes the widely renowned 80/20 Principle and shows how in today's cluttered and stressful world, working out the few things that are really important, and the few methods that will give us those things, leads to increased happiness and greater success. *Living the 80/20 Way* explains why 'less is more' isn't just a saying, but a sure-fire method to achieve your goals and live your best life.

'The trick is to apply "less is more" and "more with less" to ourselves, our work and our relationships. This volume does not urge the reader to do more – measuring, managing, talking or whatever – but to do less in total by doing things differently.'

—*Independent on Sunday*

Paperback ISBN 978 1 47365 688 8
192PP B format
www.nicholasbrealey.com